DATE DUE

Activity Experiences and Programming Within Long-Term Care

by

Ted Tedrick, Ph.D.

&

Elaine R. Green, Ed.D., C.T.R.S.

Activity Experiences and Programming Within Long-Term Care

by

Ted Tedrick, Ph.D.

&

Elaine R. Green, Ed.D., C.T.R.S.

VENTURE PUBLISHING, INC.

Copyright © 1995

Venture Publishing, Inc.
1999 Cato Avenue
State College, PA 16801
(814) 234-4561 FAX (814) 234-1651

Production Manager: Richard Yocum
Design, Layout, and Graphics: Naomi Q. Gallagher
Editing: Katherine Young
Cover Design and Illustration: Sandra Sikorski, Sikorski Design
Printing and Binding: Jostens, Inc.

Library of Congress Catalogue Card Number 95-60643
ISBN 0-910251-74-6

*Dedicated to the honorable specialists
who attempt to improve the quality of resident
life within long-term care
through meaningful activity experiences.*

About the Authors

Ted Tedrick, Ph.D., is a full professor in the Department of Sport Management and Leisure Studies at Temple University. His interest in leisure and aging is evident in his work as a practitioner, and scholarly writings and research. Tedrick has written approximately 20 articles for peer-reviewed and practitioner-oriented journals, seven chapters for edited volumes, and acted as both an editor and contributing author for *Aging: Issues and Policies for the Eighties*. He is also the editor of the *Leisure and Aging Bibliography* published through *Activities, Adaptation & Aging*.

Tedrick is a member of the Aging and Leisure Society within the National Recreation and Park Society, reviews books and articles for professional journals, and holds workshops involving leisure and aging at state, regional and national levels.

Elaine R. Green, Ed.D., C.T.R.S., is an assistant professor in the Health, Physical Education Recreation Department at Lincoln University. She has more than twenty years of experience working with the elderly in long-term care facilities and retirement communities. She offers her more than twenty years of experience working with the elderly in long-term care facilities and retirement communities as an independent consultant and lecturer.

Contents

Chapter 3
Institutional Living

Chapter 4
The Activities Program: Organization and Structure

Chapter 5
Documentation and Program Evaluation

Chapter 6
Programming

Chapter 7
The Activity Room: Establishing the Proper Psychosocial Environment In the Long-Term Care Setting

Chapter 8
Personal and Personnel Relationships

Chapter 9
Therapeutic Recreation Research and Older, Geriatric Clients

Chapter 10
Professional Issues

Appendices

Foreword

By Phyllis M. Foster, ACC
Editor of *Activities, Adaptation & Aging,*
former President of the National Association of Activity Professionals

I was both pleased and honored when asked to write a foreword for this book. That request has been a good experience—it caused me to reflect on how far activities programming has advanced, and provided me the opportunity of sharing the birth of a profession.

In 1963 I was hired as activity director of a hundred-bed nursing home by an administer/owner who wanted more for his 'patients' than sitting around waiting for death. He saw the valuable time of human life squandered and decided to do something about it. I was to find out that he was not alone.

The title "activity director" was bestowed upon me with directions to "have at it!" The biggest problem was that neither one of us knew what "it" was! There were no guidelines, no job descriptions, no books like this, no place to turn to help—or so I thought. One day a phone call informed me that there were a few other activity directors in Colorado and they were meeting at one of the nursing homes that week. The purpose of those meetings was to share ideas and attempt to define "it." Administrators supported and encouraged these meetings because of what they say happened upon the activity directors' return.

Programming in the early days was extremely limited and designed for the patient who was up and about, based on that which the activity director was most comfortable and primarily on fun and games. It was a Monday through Friday offering at best, and was not to interfere with meeting the physical needs of the resident in any way. A good friend coined the phrase "BBC" to describe the program—Bible, bingo and crafts. The activity program was considered a frill or luxury, and easily expendable when funds became scarce. Activities were not a requirement and there was no paperwork involved, it was simply a matter of the activity directors "doing their own thing." The fact remained though—activities clearly gave patients reason to get up in the morning.

In spite of this limited scope, observation showed many benefits being derived from these programs. Those patients involved in activities became more active, more interested in life around them, required less medication and posed fewer problems for the medical staff. The true worth of activity programs was realized as patients became residents—individuals to be reckoned with— and feelings of belonging, identity, and self-worth emerged. Nursing homes became long-term care facilities, resident councils were introduced (long before they were ever a requirement), and a sense of community was born.

It may have been enough 30 or more years ago, for an activity program to consist of passive entertainment and making purposeless articles from egg cartons to help patients pass the day or to "keep their little hands busy." Today, thanks to the informed consumer, an industry that listened, and a profession that responded, that attitude is buried.

Activity directors committed themselves to the belief that activities programming plays a major role in the provision of quality care thorough its attention to the social health of residents. We sought education from each other, and from any workshop, class or discipline that might relate to aging and what we were attempting to accomplish. From those early and continuing efforts, a body of knowledge emerged that addresses more stringent regulations related to the qualifications of activities providers and the programs that are now required within long-term care facilities.

This book addresses that body of knowledge in a logical and factual manner. It also responds to the need for a text book that focuses on activities programming in long-term care settings. One can see from the onset that this text was written for both the practicing activity director who is seeking to expand his or her knowledge and the university student with an interest in geriatrics and/or leisure studies who plans to enter the field. The learning exercises at the end of each chapter lend themselves to both self-study and organized classes.

While the focus is primarily on long-term care/nursing homes, the authors provide a good overview of other geriatric settings in which activities can and do occur. Quality of life and environmental issues are vital components to multidimensional activity program that impacts the residents' daily lives; they have been thoroughly addressed in this book.

Phyllis M. Foster, ACC
6549 South Lincoln Street
Littleton, CO 80121-2325
(303) 794-7676

Introduction

The phrase "striving toward professionalism" is found in the chapter dealing with current and professional issues. The material contained within these pages is intended to contribute toward that goal. At the foundation of this effort is the belief that those who design and implement activity experiences in nursing homes and other long-term care settings are engaged in significant, honorable work. We cannot conceive of a meaningful quality of life within a nursing home without a thriving, caring and involved activity department. With a spirit of optimism and a desire to assist those who seek the continued advancement of activities programming, we assembled the following units. In addition to activity specialists, we envision the book as appropriate for undergraduate students enrolled in a course on aging and leisure or, more specifically, one dealing with frail residents of long-term care facilities.

One of the cardinal principles of any type of programming is "begin with the needs of participants." Frequently we are cautioned to "program with, not for" those who partake of leisure offerings. It is this same resident-centered view or perspective which permeates the writing herein. Thus, topics such as relocation and daily life are introduced, as is the variety of human interactions affecting those within a nursing home. The views of residents must be valued and efforts made by staff to secure these perspectives.

At the beginning (or perhaps more accurately) at the close of a project such as this, authors struggle with appropriate descriptions which fit within the limited confines of a title. Envisioned during the inception phase and, as writing progressed, was a book about programming; but more than a how-to-do text, one which placed programming and activity within a broader context. Hence, the interest in where activities take place (the psychosocial environment as discussed in Chapter 7) and the many issues/challenges facing activity specialists who bring about "activity experiences and programming" are descriptive of our intent.

The initial chapter exposes the reader to historical perspectives leading to current quality of life concerns in long-term care as impacted by OBRA regulations. How these elements affect activity programming is the focus of discussion. Chapter 2 presents the continuum of services and settings allied with long-term care. These settings include: life care, senior centers, adult daycare, in-home services or assisted living residences, hospices, and nursing homes. The varieties of care are outlined giving a brief history and description of the services, clientele, and funding. The unit concludes with the role of therapeutic recreation for elders in long-stay environments.

Institutional life brings many changes, particularly for those newly admitted. Chapter 3 describes life in a long-term care setting. From the issues surrounding the initial decision to enter a home to the special concerns of those long-tenured, quality of life is reviewed with attention to the contribution made by the activity department.

Chapters 4 and 5 shift the focus from the resident to the administrator responsible for delivering activity experiences. Organizational structure, purpose, and philosophy are reviewed as are resources necessary to be effective: staff, budget, and equipment. Documentation and evaluation are essential as quality assurance is considered. Steps are give to insure successful documentation along with assessment and evaluation forms in the appendix.

The why and how of activities programming is discussed in Chapter 6. Guidance is provided by way of activity analysis, leisure education, and understanding the aging process and appropriate theories as related to activity involvement. Reality orientation and other specialized programs such as horticulture therapy are reviewed.

Considered together, Chapters 7 and 8 offer insight on how the environment—physical and social—affect the variety of players (i.e., residents, staff, and visitors) in long-term care settings. The physical environment is discussed with particular attention to the activity room or area. How sensory loss may be retarded by a proper environment follows. Relationships—resident to resident, family/friend and resident, and resident to staff—are noted in Chapter 8. These relationships in part are shaped by the physical space and become the social fabric of institutional life.

If "striving toward professionalism" captures the spirit and direction of those managing activities, then units on research (Chapter 9) and professionalism (Chapter 10) are essential considerations. Research and its appropriate application through those who practice are hallmarks of a profession. Particular concerns for researchers working with older, frail participants are the ethical considerations of selection and informed consent. Readers will note the efficacy studies focusing on numerous activity interventions. A question is posed in Chapter 10 regarding the movement toward professionalism—"Who benefits?" Analysis here centers upon professional status from the perspectives of those who practice and those who are served. Improved administration to time management are explored. The unique role of activity staff in assisting those who are dying is the final topic area.

The authors trust that the readers will find the appendix material useful and the practical exercise at the conclusion of each chapter useful. Exercises are designed for those actively employed and for students considering employment in a long-term care setting.

In closing, the authors echo their hope that—if this text aids those engaged in improving the quality of life for residents within long-term care settings, then their efforts have been worthwhile.

Ted Tedrick
and
Elaine R. Green

History, Changes and Developments in Long-Term Care

History of the Care of the Aged and Infirm

The history of the role of the aged in different cultures parallels the history of mankind. Care of the aged and infirm can be traced to the Hebrew, Babylonian, Egyptian, Greek, Roman, Persian, and Chinese cultures. Aged parents were honored and given positions of authority in legal, social, and religious structures. With the scarcity of written materials, the ancient Hebrew acquired, with age, a wealth of knowledge and became a source of information concerning traditions and customs. Because of this wisdom, many sought the counsel of the "Elder," and the older person was treated with reverence and respect. The Hebrew and Chinese cultures followed another important practice; children were responsible for providing care for their aging parents. This practice was formalized by the Hebrew nation. Caring for aging parents became a religious tradition, a law, and the society was structured around this practice (Rogers, 1980).

The medieval period is characterized by the decline of the Greek and Roman cultures and the subsequent breakdown of civilization. Aged members of society were abused, cast aside, and generally neglected during this period of time (Rogers, 1980).

Religious orders intervened and established refuges, known as almshouses, for the indigent elderly. The term "alms" means gift and became synonymous with a gift for a beggar. The almshouse became a dwelling for the indigent who lived on charity.

The almshouse concept was an indirect forerunner of modern practices of providing care for the elderly (Rogers, 1980). Monasteries were another type of care center that offered shelter and some health services. In the twelfth century, missionaries traveled to England to establish care institutions, much like the almshouse. These facilities were attached to religious houses (Rogers, 1980).

The European almshouse, established during the Renaissance period, was an institution that housed a variety of unfortunates and undesirables: orphans, diseased prostitutes, epileptics, the blind, and the aged infirm. As a result, the residents of the almshouse represented an assortment of different ages, health and mental capacities. Living conditions were deplorable, and there was a slim chance of their survival over an extended period of time. The almshouse was a product of the moral thinking of the time. It was believed that poverty was directly related to one's moral shortcomings (Schneeweiss and Davis, 1974).

In 1601, the Elizabethan Poor Laws imposed the first legal responsibility on society to care for the aged and infirm. Almshouses were created to provide custodial care for the aged, poor, and children without financial resources. These laws were harsh and repressive and were intended to instill fear of the consequences of not taking responsibility for managing one's own affairs. Although life in the almshouse was not especially pleasant, it did offer relatively cheap and safe refuge for the aged and infirm (Schneeweiss and Davis, 1974).

In colonial America, settlers established publicly sponsored almshouses that were based on the English poorhouse model. These were residential facilities that provided the basic essentials for those individuals who could not care for themselves, who did not have families, and who would be a burden for their neighbors (Teague and MacNeil, 1992).

Schneeweiss and Davis (1974) note that those who suffered economic losses caused by Indian raids were treated differently. These unfortunates were given financial help from the community.

Although the almshouse was available and had been legally authorized, it was considered to be a last resort. Providing public financial support within the community, known as outdoor relief, was a preferred option for dealing with the aged and infirm until the nineteenth century (Teague and MacNeil, 1992).

However, this view changed, and institutionalization soon became the more popular approach for providing care to the aged and infirm. Public financial support was withheld from those not residing in an almshouse, and institutionalization became a prerequisite for financial assistance. This approach became known as indoor relief and resulted in an increase of almshouses in most cities and towns (Teague and MacNeil, 1992).

In general, several factors contributed to this shift in approaches. Independent investigations on the problems of poverty and alternative solutions all reported similar conclusions. Outdoor relief programs were costly, and recipients were not being adequately educated or supervised. In addition, Americans began to view poverty as a personal problem. Many felt that public financial support removed the incentive to work and that the poor were actually draining the nation's resources (Teague and MacNeil, 1992).

The almshouse concept offered some advantages. First, it satisfied the community's sense of responsibility toward the less fortunate while reducing any uneasiness about them by placing them in an isolated environment. Teague and MacNeil (1978) explained this as the "out-of-sight, out-of-mind syndrome." Second, large numbers of employees were needed to staff the institutions, thereby creating employment opportunities for the host communities (MacNeil, 1982).

However, as an increased number of people were placed in institutions, social reformers questioned the living conditions and the quality of care in the almshouse. By the mid-1800s, specialized institutions were being established to care for various segments of the almshouse population. Facilities were created for orphans, the mentally ill, the mentally retarded, criminals, and the blind. These groups found improved living conditions and a better understanding of their particular problems. The almshouse remained as the accepted institution for the aged (Schneeweiss and Davis, 1974).

In some communities responsibility of the poor was arranged by a bidding process. Often this occurred in rural settings and the term "poor farm" became popular (Rogers, 1980).

By the 1920s, public attention focused again on the issue of the elderly. The aging population was growing, the family was less intact, and urbanization was a reality. All of these factors contributed to how the almshouse or poor farm was viewed. Abuses were publicized, and the almshouse became the target of social reform movements (MacNeil, 1982).

As a result of reform activities, indoor relief policies were modified. Legislation was passed in many states to provide aid to poor people residing in their own homes. Congress also faced pressure to address the problem and to provide some form of income security to the growing number of older people (Teague and MacNeil, 1992).

The enactment of the Social Security Act of 1935 offered a solution to the problem. This act lessened the financial burden placed on local government to care for the aged. The main purpose of the act was to provide federal old-age assistance to the elderly who lived at home or with others. It also withheld aid to older persons who resided in public institutions. At the time the act was passed, many people had large amounts of capital frozen in their homes because of the depression. Some chose to subdivide their homes and make accommodations for the elderly rather than risk losing their properties. Although the system established compensation for the homeowners, it did not offer incentives to develop high standards of care (Schneeweiss and Davis, 1974).

With the trend toward urbanization, other indigent aged began to collect in hotels and

apartments which became known as flophouses (Rogers, 1980).

Reformers soon realized that after the enactment of the Social Security Act that many older people living at home or with others were not receiving the specialized care that they required. Private-for-profit boarding homes were established so that older people could receive the care that they needed without sacrificing their financial assistance. Eventually nurses and other staff were added, and these boarding homes were transformed into nursing homes. Consequently, older people were discharged from public institutions and placed into private facilities (MacNeil, 1982).

Rehabilitation efforts used during World War I to get wounded men back to battle as soon as possible, and the realization that an enriched environment could impact improvement contributed to the evolution of extended care facilities (ECF). Extended care facilities provide more intensive professional nursing and support services to older persons transferred from the hospital (Schneeweiss and Davis, 1974) (see Chapter 2).

Still most nursing homes in the 1930s were rooming houses that also served meals. No regulations were available to guide owners who frequently were the sole employees. Many of these people were merely motivated by the desire to "cash in" on a lucrative situation. As infirmity, senility, and other ailments increased, residents were confined to bed because it was much easier to care for them there. One known case reported that the cook-proprietor had one relief assistant to help care for more than twenty bed-ridden patients (Smigel, Smigel, and Reitner, 1962).

The number of nursing homes continued to grow. This was largely due to federal assistance, an increased life expectancy, and an increased number of older persons. However, conditions remained the same even as late as the 1950s. As various state, local, and voluntary groups increased the efforts for regulation, change slowly began and improvement was steady. This was accomplished by statute, agreement, instruction, threats, and even appeals to the owner's conscience. For example, in some states supplemental financial aid was given only if a code of standards was agreed to by written contract (Smigel, Smigel, and Reitner, 1962).

Problems arose due to overlapping or conflicting requirements as different groups tried to gain control. Fire prevention laws brought one inspection; hospital laws another; and health department orders still another. Many substandard nursing homes were eliminated and others found that they had to adapt to progress or revert back to boarding home status (Smigel, Smigel, and Reitner, 1962).

Since 1960 the nursing home industry has experienced significant growth. One factor attributed to this remarkable growth is the increased number of older persons. In 1900, older persons represented only 4 percent of the total U.S. population or about four million people (Teague and MacNeil, 1992).

In 1987 12 percent of the U.S. population or about 30 million people were in the 65 or older age-group, and 1.3 million of these people were living in nursing homes (Aging America, 1989).

A second factor that affected the growth of the nursing home industry was deinstitutionalization. In 1963 the U.S. government attempted to improve the treatment and care of the mentally ill and mentally retarded. The guiding principle behind the movement was that the mentally disabled are entitled to live as normal lives as possible in the least restrictive environment. Community mental health services were established, and residents in public mental hospitals were discharged. Many of these residents were older people who were transferred to nursing homes instead of being discharged into the community (Teague and MacNeil, 1992).

A third factor that contributed to the growth of nursing homes was the enactment of Medicare and Medical Assistance (Medicaid) legislation in 1965 (Teague and MacNeil, 1992). Medicare is a health insurance program that is administered by the Social Security Administra-

tion. It consists of two parts: Part A, hospital insurance, and Part B, supplemental medical insurance. Part A benefits are financed through payroll deductions and employer contributions to a health insurance trust fund. Part B is a voluntary program administered under Medicare that requires the older person to pay a monthly premium. The federal government matches the premium out of general tax revenues (Atchley, 1987).

Unfortunately, Medicare has created a false sense of security for many older persons. Coverage for long-term care is limited. According to Aging America (1989), in 1987 Medicare dollars paid less than 1 percent of the total expenditure for nursing home care.

As opposed to Medicare, Medicaid is a comprehensive welfare program designed to provide healthcare to the poor, regardless of age. It receives federal and state funds which are administered by local welfare departments. Medicaid is the primary source of payment for nursing home care (Atchley, 1987). Aging of America (1989) reported that Medicaid reimbursement covered 63 percent of nursing home costs in 1987.

Social Security benefits supplement Medicaid reimbursement. In addition, many older persons carry private health insurance to fill the gaps. However, older persons can still expect some out-of-pocket expenses for healthcare since none of the private policies provide complete coverage (Atchley, 1987). In 1987 private funds accounted for 19 percent of nursing home expenses (Aging America, 1989).

The Current Situation

According to Schneeweiss and Davis (1974), the nursing home industry must deal with two major problems:

1. *Adverse Publicity*—Public nursing home scandals impact all facilities, even those who maintain the highest standards of care. Television, magazines, and newspapers often thrive on reporting the latest scandal. Rarely are nursing homes portrayed as

therapeutic environments staffed by caring professionals with older persons receiving support and assistance in maintaining their well-being and independence. All too often one hears of a nursing home incident involving horrendous conditions with the potential for abuse. As a result, older persons and their families dread the idea that nursing home placement may become a reality. And those living in nursing homes worry about what might happen to them. Fear of retaliation forces many to remain quiet about concerns.

2. *Providing Quality Care at a Reasonable Cost*—As the number of older persons increases and budget restrictions continue, healthcare professionals are challenged with providing the highest quality of services in the most cost-effective ways.

In 1983 Medicare implemented the Diagnostic Related Groups (DRGs) in an attempt to control healthcare costs. The DRGs make up a payment system that links Medicare hospital reimbursement with average length of stay, principle diagnosis, and types of procedures performed. Although the system is medically sound in grouping illnesses and procedures, it does not take into consideration individual differences in terms of severity of illness, available resources, and the number of hospital days required. As a result, if the payment system is not covering the cost of care, hospitals are inclined to reduce the length of stay and limit procedures. Critics of the DRGs argue that patients are being released from hospitals "quicker and sicker" (Atchley, 1987). The DRG system may be one explanation why residents who are now admitted to nursing homes require more skilled care. In addition, an increase in home care options such as home-delivered meals, homemaker services, home healthcare, and transportation assistance has delayed nursing home placement for many older persons.

The availability of family support and community services are two determinants of delaying nursing home placement. Although 5 percent of the elderly population reside in nursing homes, another 12 percent to 40 percent living in the community require some kind of supportive services (Brody, 1981). Families are the primary source of informal support for most older persons. However, many family members are old themselves with physical and financial limitations (Atchley, 1987).

In addition, older persons often are not aware of available community services, and many cannot see the connection between their needs and what is available (Ferraro, 1990).

Nursing home placement shifts many of the responsibilities for providing care from the family to the institution. Some researchers suggest that continued family involvement following placement is related to the quality of nursing home care (Shuttlesworth, Rubin, and Duffy, 1982).

Nursing home placement represents one of the greatest fears of older persons. Atchley (1987) reported that negative views of nursing homes result not only from a desire to live in familiar surroundings and to be near friends and family but also because of the "poorhouse" connotation that nursing homes have. Other factors cited were loss of independence, loss of personal possessions, the perception of nearing death, and fear of rejection by children.

In addition, nursing homes often foster these feelings with inadequate facilities and programs, restrictive institutional rules, and lack of respect for residents' privacy and dignity (Atchley, 1987).

Based on in-depth studies of long-term care facilities, which reflected that more than one-third of nursing homes provided substandard care, the Healthcare Financing Administration (HCFA) recommended revisions to federal requirements for long-term care. In 1987 Congress enacted the first law to mandate criteria for quality care in nursing homes. These mandates for nursing home reform are found in the Omnibus Budget Reconciliation Act of 1987 (OBRA). The goal of OBRA was for nursing homes to provide an environment in which each resident could achieve and maintain the highest practical level of physical, mental, and psychosocial well-being (Friedlob, Steinfort, Santaro, and Luten, 1990).

By October 1990, each state was required to follow OBRA regulations or their funding would be at risk. OBRA was implemented by HCFA through its regional offices and the states' survey and certification agencies. The focus of OBRA is to evaluate resident care outcomes and to de-emphasize review of structural measures of quality of care, such as policies and procedures (Freidlob, Steinfort, Santoro, and Luten, 1990).

Quality of Life Requirements

The OBRA regulations address specific considerations with regard to quality of life.

483.15 Level A requirement: Quality of life. A facility must care for its residents in a manner and in an environment that promotes maintenance or enhancement of each resident's quality of life.

a. Level B requirement: Dignity.
The facility must promote care for residents in a manner and in an environment that maintains or enhances each resident's dignity and respect in full recognition of his or her individuality.

b. Level B requirement: Self-determination and participation.
The resident has the right to:
1. choose activities, schedules, and healthcare consistent with his or her interests, assessments, and plans of care;
2. interact with members of the community both inside and outside the facility; and
3. make choices about aspects of his or her life in the facility that are significant to the resident.

c. Level B requirement: Participation in resident and family groups and in other activities.
1. A resident has the right to organize and participate in resident groups in the facility.
2. A resident's family has the right to meet in the facility with the families of other residents in the facility.
3. The facility must provide a resident or family group, if one exists, with private space.
4. Staff or visitors may attend meetings at the group's invitation.
5. The facility must provide a designated staff person responsible for providing assistance and responding to written requests that result from group meetings.
6. When a resident or family group exists, the facility must listen to the views and act upon grievances and recommendations of residents and families concerning proposed policy and operational decisions affecting resident care and life in the facility.
7. Level B requirement: Participation in other activities. A resident has the right to participate in social, religious, and community activities that do not interfere with the rights of other residents in the facility.

e. Level B requirement: Accommodation of needs.
A resident has the right to:
1. reside and receive services in the facility with reasonable accommodations of individual differences and preferences, except when the health or safety of the individual or other residents would be endangered; and
2. receive notice before the resident's room or roommate in the facility is changed (Federal Register, 1989).

IMPLICATIONS FOR ACTIVITIES

Activities must be adapted to the functioning level of each individual resident, and adaptive equipment must be made available. The dignity of the resident is maintained by using an adult-oriented approach and by making sure that residents are dressed appropriately when attending activities. Residents are given choices when a variety of individual and group programs are offered on a daily basis as well as in the evenings and on weekends.

RECENT DEVELOPMENTS

New research based on the "use it or lose it" theory applied to both the body and mind combined with the OBRA regulations has radically changed nursing home standards. Custodial care is no longer acceptable. Nursing homes now are expected at least to maintain the residents' present level of functioning, possibly restoring or improving it, taking into consideration new problems or progressive conditions (Brink, 1993).

OBRA has already had an impact. The most significant change is the reduction in the use of physical and chemical restraints. Not only are fewer residents restrained (a drop from 40 percent to about 22 percent) but also nursing home staff now are using innovative techniques and strategies to secure residents for safety and comfort. Pillows, pads, buckled seatbelts and alarm systems now replace chest restraints and other methods (Brink, 1993).

Another change in nursing home care is the reduction in the use of urinary catheters. Research indicates that catheterized residents have more urinary tract infections than noncatheterized residents in similar health. These residents also are hospitalized more frequently, and their death rate is significantly higher. Again, innovative strategies such as scheduled toileting and the use of diapers reduce the number of catheterized residents (Brink, 1993).

In addition, Brink (1993) cites other examples that support the "use it or lose it"

theory. Exercise and strength training programs for nursing home residents are minimizing falls, increasing mobility, and decreasing dependence. Computers are being used to enhance memory and recall and to aid residents with speech problems (see Chapter 10). Many nursing homes are using various environmental modifications to minimize the sensory and cognitive deficits associated with the aging process.

All of these approaches impact on the dignity of the nursing home resident. As a result of these efforts, nursing home residents are beginning to take a more active role in assuring that they receive quality care. Each resident must receive a copy of the Resident Rights. A copy of the Resident Rights should be posted in the facility and be periodically reviewed and explained for the residents. Residents' Council meetings are excellent opportunities for this. Staff members, volunteers, and families should be provided with in-service training on the Resident Rights so that everyone understands the rights and knows how to comply with them. Residents and their families should be invited and encouraged to participate in the care planning conferences. In this way, residents are made aware of the goals and specific treatment plans that have been outlined for them.

Resident concerns and complaints are also addressed in the Residents' Council meetings and administrative action is required. Family support groups allow residents and families to discuss issues related to living in a nursing home. If a concern is not handled properly, residents and families do have access to the state ombudsman, the advocate for nursing home residents.

The Older Americans Act of 1965 created local agencies on aging which are responsible for appointing the ombudsmen. If the nursing home resident or his/her family member is still not satisfied or the problem has not been resolved, a complaint can be filed with the state nursing home certification or licensing agency. OBRA requires each nursing home to post the phone number of the ombudsman and the state agency (Brink, 1993).

Nursing home residents have been further empowered by other advocacy and support groups that have been established, or are being formed, in different areas to improve the quality of life in nursing homes (Brink, 1993).

CHALLENGES AND OPPORTUNITIES

A key term in defining the need for long-term care is functional ability. Limitations in functioning are related to the ability to perform activities of daily living (ADLs) which include eating, dressing, bathing, toileting, walking, getting in and out of bed or a chair, and going outdoors. In addition, data reported from a 1984 Supplement on Aging (SOA) to the National Health Interview Survey (NHIS) identified functional dependency as an individual's need for assistance with instrumental activities of daily living (IADLs) which included preparing meals, shopping, managing money, using the telephone, and doing housework. By emphasizing functioning ability, the behavioral consequences of the illness or disease become the focus of care and not the illness or disease itself (Ferraro, 1980).

Today the fastest growing segment of the older population is the 85 or older group. This increase is one of the achievements of improved healthcare in this country. However, it also has implications for an increased need for health and social services in the future (*Aging America*, 1989).

The National Health Interview Survey concluded that people 85 and over needed more help with ADLs and IADLs than people in the 65-74 age group (Ferraro, 1990). Also, the likelihood of nursing home placement increases with age. In 1985, 22 percent of people 85 and over resided in nursing homes (*Aging America*, 1989).

Another challenge is the fact that more than 50 percent of all nursing home residents have some type of mental impairment (Teague and MacNeil, 1992). Most nursing homes operate under a medical model and make the assumption that cognitive impairments are the result of organic or biological causes and are irreversible and untreatable (Johnson, 1989). However, in their discussion of functional disorders Teague and MacNeil (1992) indicate that cognitive decline may be a result of loss of meaningful roles and lack of social interaction. In addition, Hellebrandt (1978) reported findings that suggest confusion and dependency may be the result of sensory deficits, social isolation, and physical immobility. Therefore, nursing home professionals must address the social dimension of providing care. Quality recreation programs are a key component in meeting the physical, mental, and psychosocial needs of the nursing home resident.

Atchley (1987) offered other suggestions to deal with the healthcare needs of the older person. He cites the need for public education in the areas of health promotion and wellness: rehabilitation services that are not solely linked with gainful employment; education for caregivers on the rehabilitation process; and the establishment of an improved continuum of services including home care, outpatient services, residential care, and long-term care. In addition, the issue of financing healthcare needs to be addressed to ensure proper healthcare services for older persons and others as well.

Some programs have already been initiated to assist with paying for long-term care. Reverse home mortgages and private long-term care insurance are two approaches that have been explored. Other alternatives being investigated include: revising Medicare and Medicaid requirements and covered services; offering financial incentives for caregivers; and coordinating case management to reduce institutionalization (Ferraro, 1990).

Finally, the older population of the future will view recreation in a different way from today's elderly. These individuals have valued recreation and leisure throughout their lives and will come to expect programs comparable to their lifestyle habits. Self-expression and creativity, lifelong learning, physical fitness, social bonding, sensory pleasure, and political expression will be among the program ingredients of successful recreational pursuits of the older person.

Summary

This chapter traced the history and evolution of long-term care and discussed how the issue of caring for the elderly has been dealt with over time. It was noted how the social circumstances of a particular era dictated the type of care that was provided.

Legislative changes that have impacted long-term care policies in this country were also presented. These changes have significantly affected quality of life in nursing homes. A discussion of recent developments and present challenges emphasizes the importance of recreation programs in long-term care facilities.

LEARNING EXERCISES

1. Based on the history and recent development in long-term care, can you make any projections for the future?
2. Obtain a copy of the Resident Rights (see Appendix B). Carefully read each section. Do you understand the meaning of Resident Rights? What are the implications of the Resident Rights for recreation programming? How can you modify the existing program to enhance quality of life in your facility?

References

Atchley, R. C. (1987). *Aging: Continuity and change* (2nd ed.). Belmont, CA: Wadsworth Publishing Co., Inc.

Brink, S. (1993, April 26). Elderly empowerment. *U.S. News and World Report,* pp. 65-70.

Brody, E. (1981). "Women in the middle" and family help to older people. *The Gerontologist. 21,* 471-480.

Department of Health and Human Services: Health Care Financing Administration. (1989, February 2) *Federal Register / Rules and Regulations, 54*(21). Washington, DC: U.S. Government Printing Office.

Ferraro, K. F. (Ed.) (1990). *Gerontology: Perspectives and issues.* New York, NY: Springer Publishing Company, Inc.

Friedlob, A., Steinfort, C., Santoro, V., and Luten, E. (1990, April). Moving ahead with the challenge: Meeting the OBRA mandate. *Provider,* pp. 14-19.

Hellebrandt, F. (1978). A comment: The senile dementia in our midst. *The Gerontologist, 18*(1), 67-70.

Johnson, C. J. (1989). Sociological intervention through developing low stimulus Alzheimer's wings in nursing homes. *American Journal of Alzheimer's Care and Related Disorders and Research, 4*(2), 33-41.

MacNeil, R. D. (1982). The out-of-sight, out-of-mind syndrome: A three act play on the development of the nursing home in America. In M. L. Teague, R. D. MacNeil, and G. L. Hitzhusen (Eds.), *Perspectives on leisure and aging in a changing society,* (pp. 24-49). Columbia, MO: University Printing Services.

Rogers, W. W. (1980). *General administration in the nursing home* (3rd ed.). New York, NY: Van Nostrand Reinhold Company.

Schneeweiss, S. M. and Davis, S. W. (Eds.) (1974). *Nursing home administration.* Baltimore, MD: University Park Press.

Shuttlesworth, G. E., Rubin, A., and Duffy, M. (1982). Families vs. institutions: Incongruent role expectations in the nursing home. *The Gerontologist, 22,* 200-208.

Smigel, J. O., Smigel, E. O., and Reitner, W. H. (1962). *Nursing home administration.* Springfield, IL: Charles C. Thomas, Publisher.

Teague, M. and MacNeil, R. D. (1978, October). "The institutionalized age: Out-of-sight, out-of-mind syndrome." Paper presented at the 1978 National Recreation and Park Association Congress, Miami, FL.

Teague, M. L. and MacNeil, R. D. (1992). *Aging and leisure: Vitality in later life.* Englewood Cliffs, NJ: Prentice-Hall, Inc.

U.S. Senate, Special Commission on Aging. (1989). *Aging America: Trends and projections.* Washington, DC: U.S. Government Printing Office.

Long-Term Care as a Continuum of Service Delivery

BY B. J. MCNEILLIE

ED.M., TEMPLE UNIVERSITY

Introduction

As Americans approach the year 2000, most have been made aware in some form or fashion of the coming explosion of the country's elderly population. Increased life expectancy has combined with other factors to create a demographic shift toward the elderly comprising a larger percentage of the total population than at any other time in this century.

In 1900, only 2.9 percent of the population of the United States was over age 65. By 1977 fully 12 percent of the nation's citizens were over age 65 (Fowles, 1978). And by the year 2030 the over-65 crowd may comprise over 21 percent of the total population (Fowles, 1988).

Unfortunately, elderly Americans are still the subjects of many myths and stereotypes. Stories and jokes about "that helpless old woman" or "that dirty old man" are all too commonplace. It is important to remember that the elderly are not a homogenous group despite similarities of age (Teaff, 1985).

A brief sample of some enlightening statistics may help shatter some common stereotypes of the elderly.

At any given time, only 4.2 percent of elderly men and 5.3 percent of elderly women are living in an institution (U.S. Bureau of the Census, 1976). Most older persons, 70 percent, live independently in homes they own rather than rent (Carp, 1976). States with the highest percentage of older residents are Arkansas, Florida, Iowa, Missouri, Nebraska, Pennsylvania, Rhode Island, South Dakota, and West Virginia, all with at least 13.8 percent of their populations age 65 or more (U.S. Bureau of the Census, 1987). America's elderly have not all moved to the desert or the tropics, and they are not all rocking their remaining days away in a nursing home.

But America's elderly do have many needs. The increased mobility of the society has left many older individuals alone and isolated from their families. Even when children are nearby, the prevalence of the two-income household often makes it very difficult to care for elderly loved ones. The service needs of America's elderly population and their caregivers are indeed diverse.

In response to the great variety of needs presented by today's elderly, a continuum of services has been developed by the public and private sectors of society. The often dreaded nursing home is not the only option available. In the United States today, life and continuing care retirement communities, multipurpose senior centers, adult daycare, respite care services, shared housing, foster care, congregate housing, home healthcare, personal care, hospice, and various long-term care residences are all available to help older adults and their families with their unique needs. Many of these services are relatively new and therefore not well understood. This unit examines many of the care options available for today's older Americans.

Residential Settings: Life Care or Continuing Care Retirement Communities

DEFINITION AND HISTORY

The concept of life care or continuing care can be traced back over 100 years to the sectarian convent tradition in which a person turned over all worldly possessions to support a community of believers. In turn, the community agreed to provide care to that person for a lifetime (Townsend, 1971). Until recently, most continuing

care retirement communities were run by non-profit organizations, many with religious affiliations. However, in today's booming market, for-profit companies are jumping on the bandwagon in record numbers. These developers are no longer solely from the healthcare industry, and include such large corporations as Marriott and Avon Products (Netting and Wilson, 1987). Terms such as continuing care, life care, perpetual care, residence and care, and life lease are often used interchangeably, although there are differences.

A continuing care retirement community (CCRC) is an organization established to provide housing and services, including healthcare, to people of retirement age (Netting and Wilson, 1987). At a minimum, the community must meet the following criteria:

1. campus consists, at least, of independent living units; it may also contain healthcare facilities such as congregate living, personal care, and intermediate or skilled nursing care;
2. community offers a contract that lasts for more than one year and guarantees shelter and various healthcare services; and
3. fees for healthcare services are less than the full cost of such services and have been partly prepaid by the residents.

This third criterion is where some make the distinction between life care and continuing care. A life care community imposes no additional charge for healthcare services. A continuing care community, on the other hand, requires the resident to pay some or all healthcare expenses. This distinction, however, is not clear. Even state regulations governing the provision of these services jumble the terminology, creating confusion. The resident contract will spell out exactly what type of services will be provided at what cost.

Whether discussing life care or continuing care, it is important to remember that the resident is investing in a contract, not buying real estate (Topolnicki, 1985). If financial insolvency should strike a community, the residents may lose the entire entrance fee, a substantial sum.

Perhaps the term life lease is slightly more accurate and less confusing.

TYPICAL RESIDENTS

Tell, Cohen, Larson and Batten (1987) identify five broad categories of what makes life care or a CCRC attractive to older adults. These are health reasons, security and support reasons, family reasons, social reasons, and financial considerations.

Looking at demographics, the median age of CCRC residents is approximately 81 years (Coopers and Lybrand, 1985). A resident typically joins the community between the ages of 70 and 75 and lives there 12 to 15 years.

TYPICAL FACILITIES, PROGRAMS, AND CARE PROVIDED

The independent living units at life care and CCRCs can range from small studios to spacious three-bedroom apartments with balconies and verandas. Of course, the fees vary accordingly. Most CCRCs have some type of community center that serves as the social and recreational hub for residents (Newsfront, 1986). Other facilities may include restaurant-quality dining rooms, a library, gift shop, coffee shop, barber and beauty shop, arts and crafts and woodworking shops, auditoriums, and swimming pools. Many CCRCs are located in suburban areas, and most are conveniently located near grocery stores and shopping centers. Communities themselves vary greatly, and CCRCs must be viewed as innovative, offering diverse options, and not necessarily conforming to a specific model (Netting and Wilson, 1987).

A nationwide survey by Coopers and Lybrand, (1985) found that over 70 percent of the responding communities included the following services in their monthly fee:
- apartment cleaning,
- bed and bath linen,
- emergency call systems,
- kitchen appliances,

- parking,
- personal laundry facilities,
- transportation,
- recreation therapy,
- replacement of apartment equipment,
- social services,
- special diet,
- storage, and
- utilities.

Perhaps most important, healthcare is guaranteed. At most communities, several levels of care are available. These may include congregate living, personal care, and intermediate or skilled nursing care. Although healthcare facilities might be located on campus, the community may also contract with existing healthcare agencies to provide necessary services for residents. Either way, a continuum of accessible healthcare services is guaranteed.

FUNDING AND FEES

Life care and continuing care retirement communities are expensive. Only a very small proportion of older persons can afford a CCRC, and probably less than 1 percent of the elderly population currently lives in this type of community (Tell et al., 1987). Most CCRCs charge an entrance or endowment fee. This can range from less than $50,000 to well over $200,000. One veteran developer of retirement communities, Adult Communities Total Services Inc. (ACTS) based in Spring House, Pennsylvania, uses a unique payment plan to stabilize cash flow. ACTS requires the people who contract with them to pay a $1000 deposit, one-third down as construction begins, one-third down halfway through the construction, and one-third as they move into the facility (Rogers, 1987). This system prevents the developer from having to take out huge construction loans to build the facility and, ACTS claims, increases financial stability from the start. Moreover, ACTS does not begin construction on any phase of a project until it is at least 70 percent presold.

At some CCRCs, 90 percent of the entrance fee is refunded when the contract is terminated due to the resident's death or relocation

(Branch, 1987). Specifics regarding entrance fee refunds will be spelled out in the resident's contract. Communities that offer this refund are depending on reendowment to maintain financial stability. The pool of entrance fees from all residents acts as a voluntary group self-insurance policy. This money will pay for healthcare services needed by residents in the near and distant future.

In addition to the entrance fee, life care and CCRCs charge a monthly service fee which may range from about $500 to well over $1500. This monthly fee covers operation costs and is likely to include the list of services discussed earlier. As mentioned before, residents of life care communities do not pay increased fees for required healthcare services. In CCRCs the resident often pays some additional cost when healthcare is needed.

A 1986 Wall Street Journal article (Lublin, 1986) reported that life care communities geared toward affluent seniors over 75 years old were suddenly becoming the nation's hottest real estate market. Lublin also reported that 850 life and continuing care type communities were serving 150,000 households. Lublin estimated that another 4400 communities may spring up by 1995, creating a $46 billion industry.

However, there are critics who predict that life care will not survive. Many of the earlier communities went bankrupt when residents outlived mortality projections and remained in the project (Seip, 1986). Seip's main concerns are financial, but also include the possibility of market saturation in urban areas. Critics of life care and CCRCs, however, seem to be in the minority.

The new and related concept of Life Care At Home (LCAH) has recently been introduced (Tell et al., 1987). LCAH is very similar to a CCRC, except that the members of the community remain in their own homes, thus greatly reducing cost. LCAH combines the financial security and health services of a CCRC with the freedom and independence of living in the broader community. This is an area to be monitored for future expansion.

LEGISLATION

In 1987 only 20 states had statutes regulating life and continuing care communities (Netting and Wilson, 1987). The first of these was California in 1939. The other states enacted their original statutes between 1975 and 1986. State statutes vary widely in purpose, coverage, implementation agencies, certification or registry requirements, disclosure provisions, and contract contents.

According to Netting and Wilson (1987), most states require some type of certification whereby communities can be screened by the responsible agency. However, there is some question as to whether or not these responsible agencies have sufficient information and knowledge to do their jobs effectively. Many existing regulations lack enforcement systems, appropriations, and evaluation mechanisms.

In summary, current legislation regarding life care and CCRCs is as varied as the communities themselves. Although the public must be protected from unqualified care providers, the lack of specific standards may not be all bad. Life Care Services Corporation (LCS), the nation's largest developer of life care retirement communities, believes it is critical to tailor the product to meet the needs and desires of the elderly population in a community (Mitchell, 1987). The lack of stringent standards in current legislation gives LCS the freedom to match its product to the specific marketplace. CCRCs, as all elderly care programs, should focus on the person in need, not a menu of approved services.

Alternatives in the Community: Multipurpose Senior Centers

DEFINITION AND HISTORY

The National Council on the Aging (1978) defines a multipurpose senior center as "a community focal point on aging where older persons as individuals or in groups come together for services and activities which enhance their dignity, support their independence and encourage their involvement in and with the community." The center also serves as an information resource for many aging-related issues, including training professional and lay leadership and developing new approaches to aging programs. At a senior center individuals maintain their independence while reaching out to others and to the community in a variety of activities (Gelfand, 1988).

Although organized clubs specifically for older adults can be traced back to the 1870s, people have been coming together with other members of their own age to exchange common experiences, wonder at the other generations, and solve the problems of the world from their vantage point since time began (NCOA, 1972).

The first recognized senior center was the William Hodson Community Center, established in 1943 by New York City's welfare department (Lowry, 1985). The idea originated with a group of social workers who wanted to help their lonely and isolated older clients. At first, the organizers of the project simply secured a meeting place, contributed games, suggested the serving of refreshments, and figured the old people could manage by themselves. A more structured program developed under the leadership of Harry Levine and Gertrude Landau, and another center opened on Second Avenue to serve the older population in that New York neighborhood (Maxwell, 1962).

The senior center idea spread quickly, and the next centers were established in California. The San Francisco Senior Center, which opened its doors in 1947, was created through efforts of the United Community Fund, the American Woman's Volunteer Services, the city's Recreation Department, and individual local citizens (Kent, 1978). In 1949 suburban Menlo Park became the home of "Little House," which was designed to meet the needs of that community's middle class elderly. The distinguishing feature of Little House was that most of its program was designed and directed by the seniors themselves.

The centers in New York and Menlo Park became the prototypes for the two conceptual models of the senior center that are dominant in the United States today (Gelfand, 1988). The social agency model postulates that the poor and disengaged are the likely candidates for senior center participation, while the voluntary organization model hypothesizes that those elderly who are active and manifest strong attachments to the community are the ones who will most likely make use of senior centers.

TYPICAL SENIOR CENTER USERS

Many research studies attest to the variety of needs of the elderly and the many reasons older adults choose to participate in senior center programs. Studies have shown that senior center attendance is closely related to loss of the work role and increase in leisure time among the young old (Anderson, 1969; NCOA, 1972; NISC, 1974).

Kent (1978) found that about 18 percent of all older Americans had recently attended a senior center. The National Institute of Senior Centers (1974) gives the following demographic information:

- Only about 25 percent of clients are between 75 and 84 years of age (participants tend to be the young old);

• Eighty-five percent of participants are white, and 75 percent are women;
• Forty-seven percent of members come from blue-collar backgrounds, 16 percent from white-collar clerical backgrounds, and 16 percent from professional or managerial backgrounds;
• Thirty-three percent of participants would have difficulty paying fees if required; and,
• Of senior center members, 59 percent live alone.

Other studies examining the differences (if any) among users and nonusers of senior centers have yielded conflicting results regarding health, social orientation, and life satisfaction (Leanse and Wagner, 1975; Toseland and Sykes, 1977; Hanssen, Meima, Buckspan, Henderson, Helbig, and Zarit, 1978). It is safe to say that senior center participants, while they do tend to be the young old, are a diverse and heterogeneous group.

TYPICAL FACILITIES, PROGRAMS, AND CARE PROVIDED

Senior centers may be housed in a number of different types of facilities (Jordon, 1978). Some centers use space such as vacant schools, post offices, libraries, storefronts, church halls, or municipal buildings. Other centers may share space in an intergenerational facility such as a church or synagogue, YMCA, YWCA, YMHA, YWHA, school building, recreation center, fraternal organization meeting hall, or other community building. Senior centers may operate from facilities renovated to provide for the special needs of participants, or from newly-built facilities especially designed for older persons. Jordan also suggests that the location of a senior center be selected with the consideration of community, neighborhood, and site characteristics.

The programs and services offered by multipurpose senior centers are almost limitless. Programs are designed to respond to an individual's social, intellectual, cultural, economic, emotional, and physical needs (NCOA, 1978). Programs and services may also be offered within the center itself, at other appropriate locations, and through linkages with other agencies. A review of Lowry (1985), Teaff (1985), and Gelfand (1988) reveals the following list of services that multipurpose senior centers may offer:

• leisure services such as arts and crafts, music, drama, dance, movies, physical fitness, sports, table games, camping, tours, outings, trips, parties, celebrations, and hobby and special interest groups;
• education services such as lectures, forums, and round tables on nutrition, home safety, health, consumerism, law, creative writing, defensive driving, Bible study, and leadership development;
• information, counseling and referral services which may include general information, intake, registration, use of resource files, and personal counseling in topics such as housing, health, nutrition, transportation, finances, family, religion, retirement, law, and more;
• health services such as screening for high blood pressure, glaucoma, hearing loss, and other health concerns, as well as dentistry, podiatry, pharmacy, speech therapy, and health education;
• housing services such as information and trips to apartments, rooms, or houses with appropriate cost, location, and safety;
• employment services such as job referral, employment counseling, job aptitude testing, job training, and job placement. This may be for full-time or part-time, paid or voluntary positions;
• financial aid and counseling services such as information on Supplemental Security Income (SSI), budgeting and spending of limited resources, and avoidance of dishonest salespersons;
• legal aid services such as advice on will preparation, guardianship or commitment proceedings brought by family or friends, personal abuse, protective services, and fraud;

- nutrition services such as food stamp information, group meals at the center, or home-delivered meals;
- transportation services to and from the center by way of center-owned vans or buses, or through the coordination of volunteer drivers;
- homebound services such as telephone reassurance and friendly visiting;
- homemaker services such as housecleaning, occasional cooking, yard work, and minor home repairs;
- daycare services and other respite services which provide relief for families that want to keep an elderly loved one at home but cannot be with them due to work or other responsibilities;
- services for special populations such as the visually impaired, hearing impaired, or nursing home residents; and
- community action and advocacy programs such as planning for community projects, making facilities accessible to older people, and representing the interests of older people through legislative information services.

All these services contribute to the development of new knowledge and skills, a more useful and less dependent feeling on the part of the older person, meaningful relationships, and overall health and well-being. They also help communities become aware of not only the needs, but also the value, of their older citizens.

FUNDING, FEES, AND LEGISLATION

Early multipurpose senior centers were funded by a wide variety of community organizations. In the 1970s, however, federal legislation made more funds available for the development of senior centers. A critical piece of legislation was *Title V of the Older Americans Act* (OAA). Initially passed by Congress in 1965, the 1973 amendments, Section 501, inserted into the Act the new "Multipurpose Senior Centers" title. Title V, although not funded until 1975, pro-

vided funds for "acquisition, alteration, or renovation" of centers, but not for construction of new centers or the costs of operating a center. Title III made it possible to fund senior centers for the development and delivery of a variety of specific services (Gelfand, 1988).

The 1978 amendments to the OAA consolidated the Title V program into Title III, repealing Title V. This consolidation provided a greater opportunity to organize senior centers under the direction of the Area Agencies on Aging (AAAs), since the AAAs were now authorized to fund senior centers from the beginning to the fully operational stages. This basic structure did not change in the reauthorizations of the OAA passed by Congress in 1981 and 1984 (Gelfand, 1988). Senior centers have continued to be supported in the older Americans Act Amendments of 1987 and 1992.

Specifically, Title III of the OAA authorizes each state to receive four allocations: administration, social services, congregate meal programs, and home-delivered meal programs (Coombs, Lambert and Quirk, 1982). Under Title IV-C of the 1978 amendments, a variety of research/demonstration projects were also authorized. These were specified as:

1. special projects in long-term care;
2. special demonstrations in legal services;
3. national impact demonstrations; and
4. energy assistance demonstrations.

The OAA also specifies three categories of priority services:

1. access services (transportation, outreach, information and referral);
2. in-home services (homemaker, home health aid, visiting, telephone reassurance, chore maintenance); and
3. legal services (Gelfand, 1988).

The existence of the OAA does not, however, guarantee adequate appropriations for senior centers. Only during 1977 and 1978 were separate funds for senior centers appropriated (Lowry, 1985). Since then, senior centers have had to compete for funds via budgets of Title III and other federal programs besides the OAA. The need for communities to finance basic services such as schools, fire departments, and police protection makes it increasingly difficult for senior centers to get their share of the shrinking dollar base. Funds from nongovernmental sources and creative fund-raising activities are the basis of fiscal survival for today's senior centers.

A number of other pieces of legislation have also had an impact on senior centers. The local Public Works Development and Investment Act of 1965 authorized funds that may cover 100 percent of construction, renovation or repair costs for senior center facilities. Title XX of the Social Security Act, authorized in 1974, provided funds for group services for low-income persons in senior centers. The Housing and Community Development Act, also passed in 1974, provided funds for the expansion of community services (Gelfand, 1988).

When Ronald Reagan signed the OAA amendments in 1984, he created a new Title VII, "Personal Health Education and Training Programs for Older Individuals," for discretionary grants and contracts with institutions of higher education to design health education and training programs for replication in multipurpose senior centers (Lowry, 1985).

Although obtaining adequate funding may be a constant struggle for those who operate senior centers, participants undoubtedly get one of the best deals in town. Members can count on a free hot meal at the center, as well as a great variety of services, for little or no charge.

Alternatives in the Community: Adult Daycare

DEFINITION AND HISTORY

The National Institute on Adult Daycare (1979) developed the following definition of adult daycare: "Adult daycare is a generic term for a variety of programs, each providing a gamut of services. These services range from social and health related to the provision of active rehabilitation and physical and mental healthcare. Various terminology is applied: daycare, day treatment, day health services, psychiatric day treatment, therapeutic center, day hospital. It is coordinated with, and related to, other agencies and services such as senior centers, in-home services and institutional and hospital care. It is an innovative way to organize and blend the more traditional health and social services for disabled older persons."

Since this initial definition was written, the number of agencies providing various types of day services to the elderly has steadily increased. In 1984 the NIAD released a more specific definition of adult daycare which reflects its unique identity within the expanding elderly care system:

Adult daycare is a community-based group program designed to meet the needs of functionally impaired adults through an individual plan of care. It is a structured, comprehensive program that provides a variety of health, social, and related support services in a protective setting during any part of a day but less than 24 hour care.

Individuals who participate in adult daycare attend on a planned basis during specified hours. Adult daycare assists its participants to remain in the community, enabling families and other caregivers to continue caring for an impaired member at home (NIAD, 1984).

Although there may be some similarities between adult daycare programs and daycare programs for children, it is critical to point out from the start that the elderly should not be viewed as childlike. Unlike preschoolers, adult daycare clients "are adults who may be limited for shorter or longer periods of time in their capacities for total self-care—but they are participants in their own care programs with everything that the term implies" (Trager, 1976). Dependency in the elderly is usually a result of some physical or cognitive impairment, not a lack of knowledge and skill as with children.

Adult daycare exists not only to provide services to its elderly clients, but also to provide respite for family members and other caregivers. Adult daycare has its roots in England, where outpatient centers in psychiatric hospitals were established during the 1940s. In the 1950s, these centers were expanded to include geriatric patients (Gelfand, 1988). Crowley Road Hospital in Oxford, England, came to serve as the model adult daycare program for elderly patients with illnesses and physical disabilities (Lorenze, Hamill and Oliver, 1974).

The first geriatric adult daycare program in the United States opened in 1947 under the auspices of the Menninger Clinic, Topeka, Kansas. In 1949 a similar program began at Yale University (McCuan, 1973). The 1970s brought increased interest and funding for aging programs, and most states developed their own adult daycare programs. A recent study released in Pennsylvania claims that the number of Area Agencies on Aging providing adult daycare services to older persons in the Commonwealth has increased dramatically during the 1980s (Kaye, Kirwin and Schulke, 1989). Estimates of the prevalence of adult daycare have ranged from more than 600 programs serving approximately 13,500 clients (Robins, 1981) to more than 800 programs serving approximately 20,000 elders (NIAD, 1982). It is a safe bet that these numbers have greatly increased as we approach the year 2000.

TYPICAL CLIENTS

Most clients come to adult daycare centers because their families cannot provide the care and supervision they need at home during the day, but at the same time, caregivers do not want to institutionalize their elderly loved ones. Caregivers appreciate adult daycare for respite, while clients appreciate it most for socialization.

Using the previously-cited Bryn Mawr College study (Kaye et al., 1989) as a reference, the following are the characteristics of adult daycare clients:

- The typical client is a 77-year-old white female, living with a daughter or spouse in a single family dwelling.
- The typical client needs assistance with three or more activities of daily living.
- Clients with Alzheimer's disease and cardiovascular problems are typically the most physically impaired.
- Median monthly income is approximately $481, which typically comes from the single source of Social Security.
- The typical client has been a consumer of adult daycare services for two years and feels they are participating for reasons of socialization.
- Adult daycare clients and their caregivers express high levels of satisfaction with program performance.

Different agencies providing adult daycare services may have different criteria for program eligibility. Factors such as ambulation, continence, and living distance from the facility may play a part in an individual's acceptance into a particular program.

TYPICAL FACILITIES, SERVICES, AND CARE PROVIDED

A national survey of adult daycare in America (Von Behren, 1986) indicates the great variety of adult daycare settings. While many centers are housed in buildings used primarily for adult daycare, it is more common to find centers that share facilities with other organizations. Facilities are most frequently shared with nursing homes (22 percent) and churches (17 percent). Adult daycare centers may also be located in senior centers, community centers, hospitals, school buildings, clinics, board and care residences, or home health agency offices.

The NIAD (1984) specifies standards for daycare facilities. Buildings must be accessible according to Section 504 of the Rehabilitation Act of 1973; lighting shall be adequate and avoid glare; sound transmission shall be controlled; heating, cooling, and ventilation systems shall keep the environment comfortable; the design shall facilitate the participants' movement throughout the center; the facility shall be sufficiently equipped with safe, comfortable furniture; and a telephone shall be available for participant use.

There has been some disagreement among daycare advocates regarding the relative emphasis on particular services (Gelfand, 1988). Many programs, as they should be, are tailored to meet the unique needs of their particular clientele. Perhaps the most valuable services provided are companionship and emotional support. In any case, the following is a list of services that may be included in a very comprehensive adult daycare program (Rathbone-McCuan and Coward, 1985):

- counseling for individuals and families;
- education;
- exercise;
- group and individual activities;
- healthcare (including psychiatry, podiatry, dentistry);
- health screening;
- information and referral;
- meals;
- medical and social evaluation;
- occupational therapy;
- physical therapy;
- reality orientation;
- recreation therapy;
- remotivation therapy;
- speech therapy;
- socialization;
- supervision; and
- transportation.

Other commonly-provided services include social services, diet counseling, art and music therapy, dressing/grooming/toileting, bathing, and laundry services (Von Behren, 1986). Most centers will conduct at least one enrollment interview with the potential client and family. This provides an excellent opportunity to learn what specific services are provided at a particular center.

FUNDING AND FEES

In the 1986 national survey, two funding sources were revealed to be the primary supporters of adult daycare: Medicaid and participant fees. But adult daycare is kept afloat by funds obtained from a variety of sources. Monies for adult daycare are also received from social services block grants, agency fund-raising efforts, *Title III of the Older Americans Act*, local and state government funds, mental health, private insurance, Medicare, the United Way, and community development block grants. In addition to cash, adult daycare centers receive in-kind contributions such as space, equipment, transportation, food, and even personnel.

The 1986 national survey also revealed that there are adult daycare centers that offer services at no charge or accept donations only. However, most centers do have a participant fee. This may be charged by the hour, day, week, or month, and centers may have fixed rates or sliding fee schedules. For those centers that do charge a participant fee, daily rates may range from about $5 to more than $50. The most typical daily charge seems to be between $20 and $30. Most centers include all services in this basic fee, although some may charge extra for things like special therapies, shopping, or beauty shop.

LEGISLATION

As is true for most services for the aging, two pieces of legislation that have a major effect on adult daycare are the *Older Americans Act* and *the Social Security Act*. These acts are instrumental in authorizing services to be provided and also in appropriating funds to support those services. Research and demonstration projects made possible by these acts have focused on the effectiveness of adult daycare, and therefore brought continuing support.

In addition, some state or local governments license adult daycare centers to show the public that the center has met a defined set of standards. The NIAD State Agency Survey (Von Behren, 1986) found that 15 states had standards for licensure. These included California, Florida, Hawaii, Kentucky, Louisiana, Maryland, Minnesota, Missouri, New Jersey, Pennsylvania, South Carolina, Texas, Utah, Virginia, and West Virginia. The licensing agency is most often the state or local Health Department, or the state or local Social Services/Welfare Department.

Adult daycare centers may also meet certain certification standards to become eligible for particular reimbursement. Certification is most commonly required for Medicare and Medicaid. In addition, states may certify for Title XX Social Services Block Grant or Older Americans Act funds. The 1986 national survey found that only 12 states—Arizona, California, Colorado, Delaware, Kansas, Massachusetts, Michigan, New Jersey, New Mexico, North Carolina, Rhode Island, and Wisconsin—require certification.

Assisted Living: In-Home Services

DEFINITION AND HISTORY

In-home services can be divided into two broad categories: home healthcare and home care. The term home healthcare refers to a variety of services provided at the client's home, usually supervised by a physician or nurse. Medical services may be provided by trained professionals such as registered nurses, licensed practical nurses, nurses' aides, allied health therapists, or even technicians to administer chemotherapy treatments (AICR, 1990). Personal care services, such as help with dressing or grooming, are provided by homemaker-home health aides (AARP, 1986).

Home care, on the other hand, offers only nonmedical services such as minor household repairs, cleaning, yard work, meals, friendly visiting, emergency response systems, and telephone reassurance. Home care services, like home healthcare, may be critical in maintaining an elderly person in his or her own home. Too often, older adults are admitted to more expensive nursing homes when all they may need is limited periods of less expensive home care or home healthcare during the day.

Welfare agencies were the first to provide in-home services. Early in the twentieth century, private agencies provided homemakers to care for children whose mother had taken ill. During the Great Depression of the 1930s, poor, unemployed women were hired as housekeepers for other poor persons who needed the service (Gelfand, 1988). By 1958, approximately 145 agencies offered homemaker or home healthcare services (U.S. Administration on Aging, 1977).

The emphasis of in-home services shifted to caring for the elderly after the introduction of Medicare and Medicaid in the mid-1960s. The type of care provided also shifted from home maintenance to personal care. By 1985, over 5000 agencies were providing in-home services throughout the United States. It is important to note that, in 1986, 76 percent of all hospitals affiliated with the American Hospital Association reported plans to add or expand their in-home services (Gelfand, 1988).

THE NEED FOR IN-HOME SERVICES

An older adult may need in-home services on an acute or chronic, short-term or long-term basis. It may be appropriate for someone recovering from a heart attack, stroke, or accident; or for someone with diabetes, high blood pressure, or even a terminal illness. Remaining at home can help an older adult maintain social ties and involvement as well as a sense of independence and security (AARP, 1988).

Family members still provide the great majority of in-home services to elderly adults. However, the ability and willingness of family members to continue meeting these needs has come into question (Hess and Soldo, 1985; Stoller and Earl, 1983). As the over-75 population grows dramatically, so will the demand for professional in-home services. The elderly adult age 75 or over is six times more likely than the person aged 65 to 74 to utilize hospital facilities or special residential accommodations (Brody, 1974).

Approximately 19 percent of the senior citizens in this country are hampered in at least one major activity of daily living, while 4 percent are severely disabled (U.S. Senate, 1987). A recent study supported by the Administration on Aging and the National Institute of Mental Health (Noelker and Bass, 1989) investigated how the chronically impaired or frail elderly use family and professional service providers to meet their personal and home healthcare needs. The study looked at the level of physical impairment in the older adult as well as the care-related health change in the primary family caregiver. As might be expected, family members were able to provide the needed care in situations with lower levels of physical impairment and health change in the primary caregiver. Conversely, higher levels of physical impairment and care-related health change were more likely to necessitate the use of a professional caregiver for respite.

TYPICAL CARE AND SERVICES PROVIDED

In-home services should be personalized to the individual situation and the unique needs of the older adult being cared for. The U.S. Senate (1972) has grouped in-home services into three broad categories:

1. *Intensive or skilled services.* Ordered by a physician and supervised by a nurse, skilled care is given to individuals with such problems as cardiac difficulties, bone fractures, open wounds, diabetes, and terminal illnesses involving catheters and tube feedings. The services could involve physician, nurse, or allied health therapist visits, as well as nutritional services, delivered drugs and medical supplies, home health equipment, transportation, and other diagnostic and therapeutic services.

2. *Personal care or intermediate services.* Bathing, ambulation, prescribed exercises, and medications for medically stable individuals.

3. *Homemaker-chore or basic services.* Light housekeeping, meal preparation, laundry and other maintenance activities that help sustain the individual at home.

The homemaker-home health aide is the primary service provider for cleaning, planning and preparing meals, grocery shopping, doing laundry, changing bed linens, bathing, shampooing hair, helping people transfer from bed to chair, checking the pulse rate, helping with simple exercises, assisting with medications, teaching new skills, and providing emotional support (Gelfand, 1988). Heavy house cleaning, painting, and minor carpentry repairs may be performed by a person specifically employed for that type of work. Other services such as telephone reassurance and friendly visiting may be available from various sources.

In-home services may be offered through home care units of community hospitals, community health centers, social service departments, private nonprofit community agencies, or sometimes proprietary agencies. The number of agencies providing in-home services has been growing rapidly. In the United States, 32 states require licensing, but there is no uniform requirement for training, certification, and supervision of home health aides nationwide (Leader, 1986).

FUNDING OF IN-HOME SERVICES

Gelfand (1988) discusses five basic methods of payment for in-home services. The most common is client fees. Voluntary agencies are likely to offer services on a sliding fee scale if they receive contributions from individuals, civic organizations, religious groups, disease-related groups, or United Way fundraising organizations.

The second payment method for in-home services is Medicare. To be eligible for Medicare reimbursement, an agency must provide primarily skilled nursing service and at least one additional therapeutic service. Reimbursable services usually focus on acute or short-term needs, not chronic or custodial ones.

Medicaid is the third payment method. Medicaid coverage is available to those who meet strict income requirements, whether or not they are age 65 or over. Medicaid may cover nursing services, home health aide services, medical supplies and equipment, and nonmedical services related to activities of daily living. Individual states, however, decide what services are provided under Medicaid, and the majority of funds are used to pay for institutional care, not in-home services.

A fourth funding source for in-home services was the former *Title XX of the Social Security Act*. State departments of social services received Title XX funds based on the state's population. But the program was limited by client income eligibility and the amount of money available to agencies for personnel to provide services. Only limited funds from Title XX have been used to meet the home health needs of older adults.

Title III of the Older Americans Act is the fifth funding source of in-home services. Title III monies are available through Area Agencies on Aging to provide a variety of services to assist older individuals to continue living independently in a home environment. The recipient must be age 60 or over and there is no income restriction, although efforts are usually made to serve the low-income elderly. The older Americans Act Amendments of 1992 also include provisions for support activities for caretakers who provide in-home services to frail older individuals.

Some say that funding restrictions are still the major factor limiting access to in-home services (Reif, 1988). The current healthcare system in the United States is structured to reimburse the most expensive, most specialized institutional care. If older adults were able to receive various in-home services, they may not need the more expensive institutional care. With the current efforts at national healthcare reform reimbursement structures need to be revised to allow in-home services to play a

larger role in the continuum of care available to older adults.

Assisted Living Residences

DEFINITION AND HISTORY

It is difficult to define this level of care since there are no strong federal regulations governing it. Each state has adopted its own regulations—and its own terminology. The varied labels for assisted living residences include residential care facilities, board and care homes, community care homes, personal care homes, domiciliary homes, sheltered care facilities, adult foster care, group homes, family homes, transitional living facilities, homes for the aged, continuing care facilities, halfway houses, supervisory care homes, and adult congregate living facilities (Benjamin and Newcomer, 1986; Mor, 1986).

Among the various states' legislation, the Colorado regulations may provide the best definition of this type of facility:

> An establishment operated and maintained to provide residential accommodation, personal services, and social care to individuals who are not related to the licensee, and who, because of impaired capacity for self-care, elect or require protected living accommodations but who do not have an illness, injury, or disability for which regular medical care and 24-hour nursing services are required. (Glasscote et al., 1976)

Gelfand (1988) summarizes this level of care as primarily personal and custodial. Usual requirements are that local and fire safety codes are met; a full-time administrator supervises staff, residents, and safety; nursing personnel are on call; and facilities for distribution of medication are available. Residents receive meals, some personal care, and a protected environment without being restricted or organized into a forced pattern of activities.

Many states do not license, inspect, or monitor these residences, and costs and quality of care vary widely (AARP, 1989).

Assisted living residences actually preceded nursing homes as places for frail or poor elderly to receive assistance with housing and food services (Ross, 1988). Early homes for the poor often could not meet basic food and housing needs due to financial hardships. Medicaid was enacted in 1965 to improve services for these individuals, but policymakers targeted funds toward the medically oriented nursing home. Many nursing homes focused on forced dependency needs rather than the social and independency needs of most elderly.

RESIDENTS, FACILITIES, AND CARE PROVIDED

Several societal changes have resulted in a larger number of older adults seeking assisted living arrangements. These include the deinstitutionalization movement in state mental hospitals, the Social Security Act amendments providing SSI payments, increased state licensure and regulation of facilities, and the rising costs of nursing homes (Ross, 1988).

Assisted living facilities accommodate anywhere from one resident to several hundred. Nationwide, the average is approximately 15 residents per home with 65 percent of all licensed board-and-care-home beds occupied by older adults. The range, however, is from less than 5 percent to more than 90 percent elderly resident occupancy (Benjamin and Newcomer, 1986). Mental health residents, including the elderly, utilize approximately 20 percent of licensed board-and-care-home beds, with the remaining 80 percent occupied by a mix of physically, socially, or developmentally disabled adults.

Although many assisted living facilities are designed for low income adults, others can be quite expensive and are designed for the older adult with considerable financial resources. The quality of care and number of services provided is likely to be related to the fees paid by residents.

Recreation services are not required in most assisted living facilities, but many do provide them. Homes for the aged, often church-sponsored, go well beyond standards set by the various states in providing comprehensive activities, social services, and personal care programs (Gelfand, 1988). In many "Mom and Pop" facilities, a surrogate family and natural community situation for residents often emerge (Ross, 1988). And in many of the more expensive facilities, residents have the opportunity to participate in a full range of activities, having the freedom to come and go as they choose. Procedures may or may not be in place to transfer residents to other facilities if they need skilled healthcare in the future.

FUNDING

The funding sources for assisted living facilities are as varied as the facilities and residents themselves. Public and private monies may be involved. Because this level of care is so varied and so often unregulated, a specific facility should be closely scrutinized before a new resident moves in.

An Option Not To Be Overlooked: Hospice Care

DEFINITION AND HISTORY

Hospice care should perhaps be thought of more as a philosophy than a specific service available to the elderly. The term hospice, originally a place of rest for pilgrims and travelers, reflects the idea that a hospice should offer the skills found in a hospital along with the warmth and hospitality found in a home (Teaff, 1985). The hospice concept is concerned with providing comforting care to the dying person as well as understanding and support to the family.

The General Accounting Office (1979) explained the idea of hospice care as follows:

an organized interdisciplinary team systematically provides palliative care (relief of symptoms) and supportive services to patients dying from terminal illness. The team also assists the patient's family in making the necessary adjustments to the patient's illness and death. It is generally agreed that the hospice concept in the United States is a program of care in which the patient's remaining days are made as comfortable and meaningful as possible and to help family members cope with the stress.

Although specific hospice programs vary, many emphasize home care as opposed to hospital care. Home care is predicated on maintaining normality for the patient and family to whatever degree possible (Smith, 1985). The hospice concept has been a controversial one in the medical community because of the focus on palliative care as opposed to curative care. Physicians in the United States are often taught to preserve life at any cost. Palliative care is more attuned to the holistic concerns of the patient to remain pain-free, alert, and to die with dignity.

The recognized origin of hospice care came with the work of Dr. Cicely Saunders, who developed the St. Christopher's Hospice in Syndeham, England, in 1967 (DuBois, 1980). Dr. Saunders was inspired through her work and conversations with David Tasma, a 40-year-old man with inoperable cancer who died some twenty years before St. Christopher's was opened (Smith, 1985). Tasma and Saunders shared many dreams about the kind of place and the quality of care that would best respond to his needs. Before his death, Tasma bequeathed 500 pounds sterling to Dr. Saunders to be a "window in your home."

The first hospice in the United States opened in 1971 in New Haven, Connecticut, under the leadership of Yale University (Lammers, 1983). Along with the popularity of right-to-die and death-with-dignity issues, the hospice concept spread across the country. By the early 1980s, more than 75 hospices were

scheduled to be in operation, and more were being developed (Cohen, 1979). The escalating AIDs epidemic of the 1980s and 1990s has tragically brought increased attention to the hospice philosophy.

THE ELDERLY AS HOSPICE CLIENTS

Although hospice care is a viable option used by many elderly individuals, the number of older adults served by hospice in the United States is proportionately low (Kalish, 1985). Kalish states that there are several reasons why this is the case. First, many hospice programs are not set up to provide lengthy inpatient services, which are often required by the dying elderly patient. Second, many hospices are not equipped to handle persons with cognitive impairments. Third, since hospice emphasizes home care, this means that at least one available caregiver must be in the home. With the elderly, this needed caregiver may not be present. And finally, Kahlish proposes that many older adults may retain a more traditional view of appropriate healthcare and may be less likely to seek newly developed models.

However, physicians have started to write about the need to expand the hospice concept to include treatment of patients with advanced progressive dementia, including Alzheimer's disease (Volicer, 1986). Dr. Volicer discusses recent "mercy killings" involving the elderly and argues that in most cases these tragedies are due to inappropriate use of medical technology and lack of consensus among ethicists and courts concerning both the ethical and the legal acceptability of limited medical care for patients in a vegetative state, as well as for patients with advanced dementia. Although the hospice movement rejects active euthanasia or suicide to terminate suffering, its palliative care is aimed toward maximal comfort, not maximal period of survival, of the patient.

Dr. Volicer also draws a parallel between patients suffering from Alzheimer's disease and those suffering from incurable cancer. Although hospice care is quite common for individuals with cancer, most hospices do not accept patients with progressive neurologic diseases which result in dementia. One of the reasons for this situation is fear of malpractice suits. A demented patient cannot legally give consent to hospice treatment, and therefore the hospice has to rely on the consent of family members.

It is likely, however, that the numbers and types of patients who receive hospice care will continue to grow. Hospice care has proved to be both cost-effective and care-effective, and so it meets the approval of both those who are primarily concerned with the cost containment of healthcare and those who are primarily concerned with patient satisfaction (Kalish, 1985).

TYPICAL FACILITIES, PROGRAMS, AND CARE PROVIDED

As we have seen in other aging service areas, there are numerous variations within the basic parameters for hospice care (Kalish, 1985). Although hospice programs emphasize home care whenever possible, they may be outpatient or a combination of outpatient plus inpatient. They may also work through available resources, such as the Visiting Nurse Association, or develop their own staff. A hospice program may be integrated with one inpatient facility or it may be associated with several. The hospice may be a free-standing agency, or it may be under the control of a hospital or long-term care facility.

Hospice programs use a combination of trained volunteers and professionals to provide healthcare and education to terminally ill patients and their families. The emphasis is on palliative care which attempts to alleviate pain and other symptoms, not cure disease. In the hospice philosophy, quality of life for the dying person and the family is paramount.

Palliative care not only attempts to alleviate pain, but is dedicated to the goal of ensuring that dying persons maintain whatever control is possible during their final days of life

(Garner, 1976). This most often includes the use of analgesics, from aspirin to morphine, depending on the individual situation. The dosage is carefully monitored until the patient is receiving just enough medication to remain pain-free. In some cases, a nerve block may be the best solution to ease the patient's pain. Palliative irradiation may also be used, for example, to reduce a tumor that is causing pain (Saunders and Baines, 1983).

Hospice care will also work toward the easing of other related concerns. Smith (1985) specifies the following:
- breathing difficulties,
- insomnia,
- anorexia,
- body image and self esteem,
- spiritual pain, and
- psychosocial needs.

Hospice services are, in effect, a supplement to the family's primary efforts (Cohen and Wellisch, 1978). Some families are prepared to provide more services than others, but even in an inpatient setting, it is important that the family remain in control.

After the patient dies, hospice continues to provide care for the family. A hospice bereavement program is likely to include initial viewing of the body after death, funeral rites, and follow-up visits and phone calls with surviving family members (Smith, 1985). The value of the entire hospice care process depends on establishing effective communication, and this includes bringing closure to the helping relationship. Hospice workers and family members can benefit from reflections about the meaning and value of their investment in terminal care.

FUNDING

Like other emerging services in the continuum of care, hospice has received funding and support from a variety of sources. Efforts have been made to include hospice care as a Medicare-funded service (Teaff, 1985). Support to date has come from federal grants, Area Agencies on Aging, the United Way, Health Maintenance Organizations, and voluntary contributions.

Funding is needed not only for facilities and programs themselves, but for the recruitment and training of personnel for this demanding but rewarding work. The hospice interdisciplinary team includes physicians, nurses, and volunteers, as well as consultants such as clinical pharmacologists, psychiatrists, radiologists, and physical therapists. The recreation therapist also has an important contribution to make toward the hospice goal of helping the patient and family to enjoy life until death.

Institutional Care: Nursing Homes

DEFINITION AND HISTORY

According to the American Association of Retired Persons (AARP, 1989), nursing home care is for those who are chronically ill or recovering from an acute illness and need extended care but not hospitalization. Although most people think of nursing homes when they hear the phrase long-term care, there are actually three levels of care that may be provided at a nursing home facility. AARP (1989) describes these three levels of care as follows:

- *skilled nursing care*—intensive, 24-hour-a-day care and supervision by a registered nurse, under the direction of a physician who is available in an emergency;
- *intermediate nursing care*—some nursing assistance and supervision, but less than skilled, round-the-clock nursing care; and
- *custodial care*—room and board, as well as assistance with personal care, but not necessarily healthcare services.

These levels of care may be provided at many types of long-term care residences. In addition to private and public nursing homes, these residences include chronic care hospitals, homes for the aged, psychiatric hospitals, and, Veterans Administration facilities (Gelfand, 1988).

While there are many different types of long-term care facilities, the term extended-care facil-ity (ECF) is defined mostly by Medicare reimbursement standards. According to Cohen (1974), an ECF is a short-term convalescent care facility that cares for selected patients coming from hospitals. It involves rehabilitation, social work, medical and nursing care, and supportive services. Since the Medicare definition of extended care is so narrow, there are very few ECF beds actually in use.

The history of long-term care facilities in the United States can be traced back to the poor houses of colonial America. In the almshouses, orphanages, workhouses, hospitals, and prisons, the elderly were mixed together with the disabled, orphaned, widowed, deranged, and victims of disasters who had become the responsibility of the government (Gelfand, 1988).

At the beginning of the twentieth century, the variety of institutional care available increased due to the growth of private foundations and philanthropy (Gelfand, 1988). However, early versions of the Social Security Act, one of many important pieces of legislation enacted in the 1930s, prohibited federal financing of any relief given in any kind of institutional setting. While this legislation was intended to encourage older adults to live at home or with foster families, it actually displaced many people from public facilities. A good number of these displaced older adults were moved to boarding homes. As these boarding homes added nurses to their staffs, the name "nursing home" (Moss and Halmandaris, 1977) came to be used.

Since the 1930s the number of long-term care facilities in the United States has increased tremendously. In 1939 there were 1,200 facilities with 25,000 beds. In 1954 approximately 450,000 beds were available in over 25,000 facilities. By 1982, 27,817 facilities provided over 1,700,000 beds (Sirrocco, 1985). It is likely that this trend will continue in the near future as the elderly population continues to increase.

NURSING HOME RESIDENTS

A survey conducted by the American Healthcare Association (AHCA, 1988), gives a good picture of nursing home residents in the United States. Over 75 percent of nursing home residents are women, and nearly 90 percent are white. Although some residents are less than 65, nearly 20 percent are age 65 to 74, over 42 percent are age 75 to 84, and nearly 40 percent are age 85 or older. Only 13.6 percent are married. In spite of this, approximately two-thirds of residents in the AHCA sample receive visits at least weekly from a family member or other visitor.

The survey also shows that nearly half of all nursing home residents are incontinent of bowel or bladder or both; and nearly 40 percent have some type of diagnosed dementia. One quarter of residents must be spoon fed, less than 10 percent display abusive or aggressive behavior, and less than 6 percent are bedridden.

Statistics make it clear that nursing homes are increasingly being used for the care of individuals who are very old, sick, and often alone. Because of this change, care has become more medical, rather than social and psychological (Gelfand, 1988). But it is important to remember that social needs continue even after self-sufficiency ends. Every effort must be made to provide life-sustaining social as well as physical supports to these most needy elderly (Tobin and Lieberman, 1976).

FACILITIES, PROGRAMS, AND CARE PROVIDED

The average size of a nursing home facility is just over 100 beds (AHCA, 1988). Homes may be either proprietary, nonprofit, or government owned. Each home has its own policies regarding use of personal possessions and furniture, special diets, room assignments and charges, visiting hours, emergency procedures, self-care, phone calls, and access to personal funds (AARP, 1987). These issues should be discussed with the nursing home staff when visiting a particular facility.

Services offered in a nursing home include medical, dietary, pharmacy, recreation, and social services, plus rehabilitation, occupational, physical, and speech therapy (AARP, 1987). Each facility has a professionally trained staff to provide these services.

FUNDING AND FEES

Nursing homes charge a daily rate for a specific package of services. Skilled nursing care can range from $65.00 to more than $140.00 a day; intermediate care from $41.00 to over $70.00 a day; and custodial care from $37.00 to over $55.00 a day (AARP, 1989). Other services not included in the basic package may be available at an additional cost. The escalating costs of nursing home care have not yet been brought under control.

Nursing home care may be financed in a number of ways. Personal resources may determine whether or not a resident will be admitted to a specific facility. Many people believe that Medicare will pay for nursing home care, but this is rarely true. Medicare coverage for nursing home care is available to eligible low-income individuals, and also to nursing home residents who have "spent down" and exhausted their resources paying for nursing home care (AARP, 1987). Private insurance, often referred to as Medigap, may also provide some nursing home coverage. However, more and more companies are now offering special long-term care insurance policies to finance the expensive care offered by nursing homes. The quality of these policies varies, so extensive research should be done before purchasing one. The whole area of financing nursing home care is one that will continue to undergo major changes in the future.

LEGISLATION

The nursing home industry is one of the most regulated industries in the United States. One of the most important regulations is the nursing home residents' bill of rights. The federal government has enacted one bill for skilled nursing facilities and one for intermediate care facilities. Many states have enacted bills of rights which provide additional protection and safeguards. These bills cover issues such as knowledge of services available and their costs, participation in the planning of medical treatment, management of personal financial affairs, freedom from abuse, confidentiality, and more. Each resident should receive a copy of the residents' bill of rights.

Another set of regulations involves meeting Medicare and Medicaid eligibility requirements. These are related to the regulations that the federal-government and state-survey agencies follow when inspecting nursing homes and approving or disapproving them for operation (Morford, 1988). All regulations focus on two central concerns: physical safety and quality of care.

Nursing home regulation is a very complex area where major legislation passed in the early 1990s is making significant changes in the nursing home environment. Most new regulations will be direct statements of expectations for patient care, quality of life, and residents' rights (Morford, 1988). The same fundamental principle underlying all services along the continuum of care also underlies nursing home regulations. This is the principle that individuals should receive care that improves their health and functional status, or at least minimizes and delays further deterioration to the extent possible.

The Role of Therapeutic Recreation in Services to the Aging

THERAPEUTIC RECREATION SERVICES AND THE ELDERLY

The need for therapeutic recreation services to older adults is expanding. In addition to those elderly individuals with some type of impair-

ment, there is a growing number of nonimpaired clients such as retirees who could benefit from therapeutic recreation intervention (Carter, Van Andel, and Robb, 1985). Older adults at any point along the continuum of care for the elderly have much to gain from therapeutic recreation services.

Many researchers have produced data suggesting that leisure satisfaction contributes much more to the life satisfaction of older adults than the simple act of leisure participation (Ragheb and Griffith, 1982; Agostino, Gash, and Martinsen, 1981; Mancini and Orthner, 1980). This work indicates that merely remaining active will not bring maximum benefit to elderly individuals. Therapeutic recreation professionals can help the elderly participate in activities that will offer maximum satisfaction and maximum benefit.

With the impaired elderly, it is important to recognize that barriers to leisure should not impose further limitations on the individual's already restricted lifestyle (Singleton, Makrides, and Kennedy, 1986). Leisure activities should be planned with the help of clients, and clients should be offered choices and some sense of control in their leisure lives. Iso Ahola (1980) proposes that "it is not the recreational activity itself that is crucial, but the extent to which such an activity induces a sense of control over one's behavior, environment and life."

The most effective therapeutic recreation specialists working with the elderly are highly skilled at developing meaningful relationships with their clients. It is through these relationships that therapeutic recreation specialists are able to tune into what is most important to their clients and be facilitators in bringing about desired changes. Oliver and Tureman (1988) write that building personal bonds and ties is the essence of the therapeutic recreation professional's job.

Older adults face many barriers to satisfying recreational lifestyles. The problems of not having facilities available, not having anyone to do things with, and prohibitive costs have been identified as barriers to leisure participation across the life span (Buchanan and Allen, 1985). However, Buchanan and Allen's study found the most significant barriers to participation among older adults to be fear of crime (the study was done in an urban area), inadequate time, and poor health. Older adults with various types of impairments will also present their special needs and challenges. It is the job of the therapeutic recreation professional to look beyond the limitations of the elderly client and instead see the knowledge, skills, and potential for learning that the older adult possesses. The therapeutic recreation professional and the elderly client can work together to improve the quality of life for the client through satisfying recreation participation.

The following quote from Pfeiffer (1977) concisely states the importance of recreation to successful aging, and therefore the great value of therapeutic recreation services to the elderly:

> Studies of successfully aging individuals indicate that such persons characteristically maintain regular and vigorous physical activities, extensive social contacts, and pursue intellectually and emotionally stimulating activities. Decrease of these functions in this age period through disuse can lead to unnecessary physical limitations, social isolation, disorientation, and apathy.

THE SPECIAL NEEDS OF INSTITUTIONALIZED ELDERS

The therapeutic recreation practitioner cannot single-handedly change unhealthy and unsatisfying lifestyle patterns of an older adult living in an institution. The typical American nursing home is not perceived as a stimulating place to live. According to Moss and Halmandaris (1977), the average older adult views a nursing home as "a human junkyard, as a prison, a kind of purgatory halfway between society and the cemetery, or as the first step of an inevitable slide into oblivion. Nursing homes are not synonymous with death, but with the notion of protracted suffering before death."

But it doesn't have to be that way. Therapeutic recreation professionals can help lighten this dark image by working with nursing home residents on these basic goals: (1) restoring independent functioning to as near normal as possible; (2) helping to prevent further mental, physical, and psychological deterioration; and, perhaps most important, immediately following admission, (3) easing the adjustment to an unfamiliar and abnormal environment (MacNeil and Teague, 1983). These goals are best accomplished through cooperative efforts with members of an interdisciplinary team.

The role of the recreation therapist in a nursing home has been defined as "to engender an incentive to live by furnishing purposeful activity" (Goodman, 1983). More specific goals discussed in the literature include: restoring self-care and self-esteem; promoting and maintaining normal, meaningful activities; increasing physical, intellectual, and social functioning; creating or recreating a sense of identity; promoting a happy, home-like environment; relieving loneliness; minimizing boredom; providing psychological escape from pain; and providing the opportunity for socially acceptable self-expression through, for example, art, music, dance, and exercise (de Vries, 1970; Hardie, 1970; Dudish, 1974; Dixon, 1978; Armstrong, 1980; Carroll, 1980; Clements, 1982).

It is perhaps most important for the therapeutic recreation professional always to remember to work **with** elderly clients, not in spite of them. Therapeutic recreation services should be provided according to the needs of the clients, not the needs of the therapist.

References

AARP (1986). *Making wise decisions for long-term care*. Washington, DC: American Association of Retired Persons.

AARP (1987). *Nursing home life: A guide for residents and families*. Washington, DC: American Association of Retired Persons.

AARP (1988). *A handbook about care in the home: Information on home health services*. Washington, DC: American Association of Retired Persons.

AARP (1989). *Making wise decisions for long-term care*. Washington, DC: American Association of Retired Persons.

Agostino, J., Gash, T. and Martinsen, J. (1981). The relationship between recreational activity programs and life satisfaction of residents of Thunder Bay homes for the aged. *Activities, Adaptation & Aging, 1*(4), 5-16.

AHCA (1988, October). American Health Care Association's industry survey. *Provider*, pp. 16-25.

AICR (1990). Finding home healthcare. *American Institute for Cancer Research NEWSLETTER*, Issue 26. Washington, DC.

Anderson, N. (1969). *Senior centers: Information from a nationwide survey*. Minneapolis, MN: American Rehabilitation Foundation.

Armstrong, P. (1980). Some philosophical objectives for an activities program in a long-term care facility. In E. Deichman and C. O'Kane (Eds.), *Working with the elderly: A training manual*. Buffalo, NY: Potential Developments for Health and Aging Services, Inc.

Benjamin, A. and Newcomer, R. (1986). Board and care housing. *Residential Aging, 8*, 388-407.

Branch, L. (1987). Continuing care retirement communities: Self-insuring for long-term care. *The Gerontologist, 27*(1), 4-8.

Brody, S. (1974). Long-term care in the community. In E. Brody (Ed.), *A social work guide for long-term care facilities*. Rockville, MD: National Institute of Mental Health.

Buchanan, T. and Allen, L. (1985). Barriers to recreation participation in later life cycle stages. *Therapeutic Recreation Journal, 19*(3), 39-50.

Carp, F. (1976). Housing and living environments of older people. In Binstock, R. and Shanas, E., (Eds.), *Handbook of aging and the social sciences*. New York, NY: Van Nostrand Reinhold Co.

Carroll, M. (1980). Activities: How to use them, who to involve in their preparation and presentation. In E. Deichman and C. O'Kane (Eds.), *Working with the elderly: A training manual*. Buffalo, NY: Potential Developments for Health and Aging Services, Inc.

Carter, M., Van Andel, G., and Robb, G. (1985). *Therapeutic recreation: A practical approach*. St. Louis, MO: Times Mirror/Mosby College Publishing.

Clements, W. (1982). Therapeutic functions of recreation in reminiscence with aging persons. In M. Teague, R. MacNeil, and G. Hitzhusen (Eds.), *Perspectives on leisure and aging in a changing society*. Columbia, MO: University Printing Service.

Cohen, E. (1974). An overview of long-term care facilities. In E. Brody (Ed.), *A social work guide for long-term care facilities*. Rockville, MD: National Institute of Mental Health.

Cohen, K. (1979). *Hospice: Prescription for terminal care*. Rockville, MD: Aspen Systems Corp.

Cohen, M. and Wellisch, D. (1978). Living in limbo: Psychosocial intervention in families with a cancer patient. *American Journal of Psychotherapy, 32*(4), 561-571.

Coombs, S., Lambert, T., and Quirk, D. (1982). *An orientation to the Older Americans Act*. Washington, DC: National Association of State Units on Aging.

Coopers and Lybrand (1985). *A layman's guide to healthcare V: Continuing care retirement communities*. New York, NY.

de Vries, H. (1970). Exercise training produces psychological effects in older men. In C. Peterson and K. Slivken (Eds.), *Research into action: Applications for therapeutic recreation programming*, (Vol. 1). Urbana, IL: University of Illinois.

Dixon, J. (1978). Leisure activity status, outcome and causal attribution. In C. Peterson and K. Slivken (Eds.), *Research into action: Applications for therapeutic recreation programming*, (Vol. 1). Urbana, IL: University of Illinois.

Du Bois, P. (1980). *The hospice way of death*. Port Washington, NY: Human Sciences Press, Inc.

Dudish, L. (1974). Starting a recreation program with limited funding in nursing homes. *Therapeutic recreation ideas and experiences*. Springfield, IL: Charles C. Thomas Publishing.

Fowles, D. (1978). *Some prospects for the future elderly population*. Washington, DC: Administration on Aging.

Fowles, D. (1988). *A profile of older Americans*. Washington, DC: American Association of Retired Persons and Administration on Aging.

Garner, J. (1976). Palliative care: It's the quality of life remaining that matters. *Canadian Medical Association Journal, 115*(2), 179-180.

Gelfand, D. (1988). *The aging network: Programs and services* (3rd ed.). New York, NY: Springer Publishing Company.

General Accounting Office (1979). *Hospice care: A growing concept in the United States*. Washington, DC: Comptroller General of the United States.

Glasscote, R., Biegel, A., Butterfield, A. Jr., Clark, E., Cox, B., Elper, J., Gudeman, J., Gurel, L., Lewis, R., Miler, D., Raybin, J., Reifler, C., and Vito, E. Jr. (1976). *Old folks at homes*. Washington, DC: American Psychiatric Association and the Mental Health Association.

Goodman, M. (1983). I came here to die: A look at the function of therapeutic recreation in nursing homes. *Therapeutic Recreation Journal, 17*(3), 14-19.

Hanssen, A., Meima, N., Buckspan, L., Henderson, B., Helbig, T., and Zarit, S. (1978). Correlates of senior center participation. *The Gerontologist, 18*, 193-199.

Hardie, E. (1970). Therapeutic recreation for the institutionalized ill aged: A rationale. *Therapeutic Recreation Journal, 4*(3), 9-11, 43.

Hess, B. and Soldo, B. (1985). Husband and wife networks. In W. Saur and R. Coward (Eds.), *Social support networks and the care of the elderly: Theory, research and practice*. New York, NY: Springer Publishing Company, Inc.

Iso Ahola, E. (1980). Perceived control and responsibility as mediators of the effect of therapeutic recreation on institutionalized aged. *Therapeutic Recreation Journal, 14*(1), 36-43.

Jordan, J. (1978). *Senior center design: An architect's discussion of facility planning*. Washington, DC: National Council on the Aging.

Kalish, R. (1985). Services for the dying. In A. Monk (Ed.), *Handbook of gerontological services*. New York, NY: Van Nostrand Reinhold Company.

Kaye, L., Kirwin, P., and Schulke, S. (1989). *An evaluation of adult daycare programs in Pennsylvania: Executive summary*. Bryn Mawr, PA: Bryn Mawr College, The Graduate School of Social Work and Social Research.

Kent, D. (1978, May/June). The how and why of senior centers. *Aging*, pp. 2-6.

Lammers, W. (1983). *Public policy and the elderly*. Washington, DC: CQ Press.

Leader, S. (1986). *Home health benefits under Medicare*. Washington, DC: Public Policy Institute, American Association of Retired Persons.

Leanse, J. and Wagner, R. (1975). Senior citizen center participation and other correlates of life satisfaction. *The Gerontologist, 17*, 235-241.

Lorenze, E., Hamill, C., and Oliver R. (1974). The day hospital: An alternative to institutional care. *Journal of the American Geriatrics Society, 22*, 316-320.

Lowry, L. (1985). Multipurpose senior centers. In A. Monk, (Ed.), *Handbook of gerontological services*. New York, NY: Van Nostrand Reinhold Company.

Lublin, J. (1986, October 22). Costly retirement-home market booms, raising concerns for aged. *The Wall Street Journal*.

MacNeil, R. and Teague, M. (1983). Bingo and beyond: A rationale for recreation services within nursing homes. *Activities, Adaptation & Aging, 3*(3), 39-46.

Mancini, J. and Orthner, D. (1980). Situational influences on leisure satisfaction and morale in old age. *Journal of the American Geriatrics Society, 28*(10), 466-471.

Maxwell, J. (1962). *Centers for older people*. Washington, DC: National Council on the Aging.

McCuan, E. (1973). *An evaluation of a geriatric daycare center as a parallel service to institutional care*. Baltimore, MD: Levindale Geriatric Research Center.

Mitchell, J. (1987). Life Care Services reorganizes for growth. *Contemporary Long Term Care, 10*(6), 35-36.

Mor, V. (1986). A national study of residential care for the aged. *The Gerontologist, 26*, 405-417.

Morford, T. (1988). Nursing home regulation: History and expectations. *Health Care Financing Review*, 1988 Annual Supplement, 129-132.

Moss, F. and Halmandaric, V. (1977). *Too old, too sick, too bad*. Germantown, MD: Aspen Systems Corp.

National Council on the Aging (1972). *The multipurpose senior center: A model community action program*. Washington, DC.

National Council on the Aging (1978). *National Institute of Senior Centers senior center standards: Guidelines for practice*. Washington, DC.

National Institute of Senior Centers (1974). *Directory of senior centers and clubs*. Washington, DC: National Council on the Aging.

National Institute on Adult Daycare (1979). *Operating procedures*. Washington, DC: National Council on Aging.

National Institute on Adult Daycare (1982). *Why adult daycare?* Washington, DC: National Council on Aging.

National Institute on Adult Daycare (1984). *Standards for adult daycare*. Washington, DC: National Council on Aging.

Netting, F. and Wilson, C. (1987). Current legislation concerning life care and continuing care contracts. *The Gerontologist, 27*(5), 645-651.

Newsfront (1986). Marriott to build lifecare community in San Ramon. *Contemporary Long-Term Care, 9*(5), 11-12.

Noelker, L. and Bass, D. (1989). Home care for elderly persons: Linkages between formal and informal caregivers. *Journals of Gerontology, 44*(2), S63-70.

Oliver, D. and Tureman, S. (1988). The human factor in nursing home care. *Activities, Adaptation & Aging, 10*(3-4), 103.

Older Americans Act Amendments of 1992, § 304, 106 U.S.C. § 1219 (1992).

Pfeiffer, E. (1977). Psychopathology and social pathology. In J. Berien and K. Schiac (Eds.), *Handbook of the psychology of aging*. New York, NY: Van Nostrand Reinhold Company.

Ragheb, M. and Griffith, C. (1982). The contribution of leisure participation and leisure satisfaction to life satisfaction of older persons. *Journal of Leisure Research, 14*(4), 295-306.

Rathbone-McCuan, E. and Coward, R. (1985). Respite and adult daycare services. In A. Monk, (Ed.), *Handbook of gerontological services*. New York, NY: Van Nostrand Reinhold Company.

Reif, L. (1988). Funding restrictions are still the major factor limiting access to home care. *Home Health Care Services Quarterly, 8*(4), 1-4.

Robins, E. (1981). Adult daycare: Growing fast but still for lucky few. *Generations, 5*(3), 22-23.

Rogers, S. (1987). Making life care work. *Contemporary Long Term Care, 10*(6), 30-32, 113.

Ross, V. (1988). Protected living for the vulnerable. *Geriatric Nursing, 9*(6), 330-333.

Saunders, C. and Baines, M. (1983). *Living with dying: The management of terminal disease*. Oxford, NY: Oxford University Press.

Seip, D. (1986). Can life care survive? *Contemporary Long Term Care, 9*(10), 28-30.

Singleton, J., Makrides, L., and Kennedy, M. (1986). Role of three professions in long-term care facilities. *Activities, Adaptation & Aging, 9*(1), 57-70.

Sirrocco, A. (1985). Services and activities offered to nursing home residents. *Vital and Health Statistics, 12*(17), 1-42

Smith, W. (1985). *Dying in the human life cycle: Psychological, biomedical, and social perspectives*. New York, NY: Holt, Rinehart and Winston.

Stoller, E. and Earl, L. (1983). Help with activities of everyday living: Sources of support for the noninstitutionalized elderly. *The Gerontologist, 23*, 64-70.

Teaff, J. (1985). *Leisure services with the elderly*. St. Louis, MO: Times Mirror/Mosby College Publishing.

Tell, E., Cohen, M., Larson, M., and Batten, H. (1987). Assessing the elderly's preferences for lifecare retirement options. *The Gerontologist, 27*(4), 503-509.

Tobin, S. and Lieberman, M. (1976). *Last home for the aged.* San Francisco, CA: Jossey-Bass, Inc., Publisher.

Topolnicki, D. (1985). The broken promise: Life care communities. *Money, 14,* 150-157.

Toseland, R. and Sykes, J. (1977). Senior center participation and other correlates of life satisfaction. *The Gerontologist, 17,* 235-241.

Townsend, C. (1971). *Old age: The last segregation.* New York, NY: Grossman Publishers, Inc.

Trager, B. (1976). *Adult day facilities for treatment, healthcare and related services.* Washington, DC: U.S. Government Printing Office.

U.S. Administration on Aging (1977). *Human resources issues in the field of aging: Homemaker-home health aide services.* Washington, DC: U.S. Government Printing Office.

U.S. Bureau of the Census (1976). *Demographic aspects of aging and the older population in the United States.* Current Population Reports. Washington, DC: U.S. Government Printing Office.

U.S. Bureau of the Census (1987). Cited in Fowles, D. (1978). *A profile of older Americans.* Washington, DC: American Association of Retired Persons and Administration on Aging.

U.S. Senate, Special Committee on Aging (1972). *Home health services in the United States.* Washington, DC: U.S. Government Printing Office.

U.S. Senate, Special Committee on Aging (1987). *Developments in aging, 1986: Part I.* Washington, DC: U.S. Government Printing Office.

Volicer, L. (1986). Need for hospice approach to treatment of patients with advanced progressive dementia. *Journal of the American Geriatrics Society, 34*(9), 655-658.

Von Behren, R. (1986). *Adult daycare in America: Summary of a national survey.* Washington, DC: National Council on the Aging.

Institutional Living

On a personal level the decision to enter a nursing home is one of life's most difficult. The term "decision" as used here can connote an orderly, calculated process whereby steps are taken from assisted living to the point where nursing care becomes essential in a skilled nursing facility, or it can mean the abrupt forcing of a weakened elder without relatives into whatever facility the system dictates. The purpose of this chapter is to describe and explore the typical patterns and rhythms of daily life within long-term care facilities for older adults.

The focus will be two-fold. As mentioned previously, the personal impact of recognizing that a new lifestyle will result from placement in a nursing home is often traumatic. Loss of independence, worries about what lies ahead, concerns about the daily routine—these are consuming thoughts on the part of those beginning a residency in a nursing home. These anxieties must be considered by the activity specialist.

Second, discussion of the institutional environment as a part of the administration of long-term care facilities will attempt to summarize characteristics of daily life as represented by what staff and management offer to residents. Rather than just a reporting of staff-to-resident ratios or the percentages of time spent in various categories, this chapter will present the discussion with a philosophy of what might be done to change for the better. In other words, what is known about quality care in long-term facilities, and what characteristics lead to positive perceptions on the part of residents? Activity directors should focus on the positive from the institutional level and transfer that to what they can control at the departmental level.

Relocation: A Difficult Decision

The process of relocation from one's own home or the residence of a family member or from a hospital to a nursing home is one which is often not orderly, progressive, or carefully planned. Those without family resources may reside in nursing homes because no other options exist. For others an external event may set in motion a course of action which transpires quickly and leads to placement in a long-term care setting—the fracture of a hip leading to a hospitalization followed by a rehabilitation stay leading to residency in a nursing home, as an example. This crucial decision-making process frequently involves competing and at-odds factors, e.g., guilt of loved ones versus what is best for mom or dad, the need for immediate bed space versus the availability of a bedroom within a nursing home, and the desire of the elder to remain independent versus the advice of professionals. In the end the combination of personal needs and circumstances must be meshed with a system of regulations and guidelines not always suited to individual needs at a particular time.

Brody (1985) has summarized the issues and problems of relocation for the frail elderly. She characterized the decision of nursing home placement as one laden with guilt on the part of family members. Overtures of death are present; the loss of "what was" is immediate. Often knowledge about admission procedures to long-term care settings has not been adequately researched or has been gathered quickly and, frequently, the elder has not been involved in the decision.

The negative effects of nursing home placement have been grouped under the term of "relocation trauma" (Brody, 1985; Teaff, 1985; Ferraro, 1990). Among the negatives are loss of independence and control, the need to conform to someone else's rules, the worries about a roommate, and potentially, even higher morbidity and mortality rates for new residents of long-term care facilities (Brody, 1985). There are those, however, who feel the concept of relocation trauma has received too much emphasis. Tobin and Lieberman (1976) found many of the negative effects associated with entering a nursing home were already present in persons on waiting lists, and this preadmission period may be the most difficult. Follow-up showed most residents adapted psychologically within the first year. A study of older adults living in residential care homes also analyzed the relocation process. It was found that those who were ill-suited to their environment were less likely to have made the decision themselves (Mor, Sherwood, and Gutkin, 1986). Thus, the decision process used in determining when and where a frail elder is to relocate appears to be a significant factor in the success or failure of that movement.

There are also many positives associated with relocation. For many adults nursing home residency represents the best option available. Brody (1985) stresses a number of factors which ought to be present when the decision to relocate is being considered. Ideally the process should be orderly and involve a variety of players—the potential residents, their family members, medical staff, and other professionals. Options need to be explored and information about admission carefully gathered and reviewed. Orientation, prior to and after admission, may also ease the concerns of residents and smooth the transition. It can also be assumed that activity staff can play an important role in the process. The leisure setting may prove to be an ideal arena to integrate new residents, and social groupings or activities planned by staff may be used to create comfortable situations where friendships can develop. Favored activities, such as art or weaving, may bring new residents to the activity room, and this opportunity to assist with the orientation period should be seen in a positive fashion.

The Characteristics of Nursing Home Residents

In 1992 there were approximately 17,000 nursing homes in the United States with 1.7 million beds and an average occupancy rate of 95 percent (Hardwick, Pack, Donohoe, and Aleska, 1994). The increasing size of nursing homes and the provision of specialized, intensive services to residents are trends likely to continue through the year 2000 (Brody and Foley, 1985). Slightly over 5 percent (57 per 1,000 in 1990) of the 65 and older population reside in a nursing home at any given time (Hardwick, et al., 1994); yet somewhere between one-forth to one-third of the older population can expect to spend some time in a long-term care setting (Brody, 1985; Brody and Foley, 1985).

An important characteristic of nursing home residents is their poor family and social support networks as compared to noninstitutionalized elders. Fewer in nursing homes are married, fewer have at least one living adult child, and fewer have daughters in comparison to older adults not living in nursing homes (Brody, 1985). Indeed this lack of support is a primary reason that frail elders enter nursing homes.

Nursing home residents are primarily the "old-old" with three-fourths over the age of 75 and 40 percent over age 65. The median age is slightly over 80 (Hing, 1989).

Older white females who are widowed predominate in nursing homes. Females outnumber males 3 to 1 in this setting, and they are more than twice as likely as male residents to have suffered the death of their spouse. The rate of nursing home residency (1985) was 46.2 per 1,000 for those 85 and over. Hing (1989) also notes that nursing home residency rates for those 85 and over dropped slightly between 1973 and 1985 with a very tight supply of nursing home beds or alternative forms of care perhaps being reasons for the decline.

As to typical length of stay, the mean (1985) was 2.9 years, while the median was 1.7 years. Two-thirds have been residents for at least one-year, and nearly one-fifth have a tenure of five years or more. Primary reasons for entering nursing homes center on functional problems or family or caregiver situations where full-time care becomes impossible. The inability of family to provide the level of care needed (78 percent), and no person available to provide care (65 percent) were the top-ranked reasons given for being admitted to a nursing home (Hing, 1989).

Difficulties in performing activities of daily living (ADLs) are experienced by a majority of those in nursing homes. Over one-third of residents (36.7 percent) face difficulties with five or six ADLs, while another 35 percent have limitations with three or four ADLs (Hardwick, et al., 1994). Bathing (87 percent) and dressing (75 percent) present the most frequent problems (Hing, 1989).

The physical and mental health of elders living in nursing homes is characterized by chronic conditions. Heart disease (16 percent), cerebrovascular disease (ten percent), and organic brain syndrome (9 percent) occur most frequently as primary diagnoses. Those under 65 in nursing homes are likely to have mental disorders as a primary problem than are those over 65. For those 75 and older, heart disease, cerebrovascular disease, and organic brain syndrome are dominant (Hing, 1989).

Two-thirds of nursing home residents have at least one mental disorder. Most often these disorders are senile dementia or chronic and organic brain syndrome (43 percent), depressive disorders (14 percent), and personality disorders (11 percent). Senile dementia and chronic/organic brain syndromes increase with residents' age, and females are more likely to have these disorders than are males in the nursing home population. Sixty-two percent of residents suffer memory impairments to the degree that performance of ADLs requires assistance nearly every day (Hing, 1989).

In reviewing such demographic data the tendency to generalize based upon medians, means, and rankings must be overcome by the reality that each resident is unique and that strengths, weaknesses, and abilities to overcome persistent problems vary markedly in each individual. As background data the preceding statistics are useful in describing the nursing home population in broad strokes. It must be remembered, however, that each home has its own mix of persons creating a demographic profile that must be segmented into groups of individuals by the activity department. Learning the significant characteristics of each resident is the foundation of effective leisure programming.

Life in the Nursing Home

If one is to become an effective programmer of leisure activities for those in nursing homes, there is a need to know not only the general characteristics of those who reside there and the issues they have found in relocating, but one must also understand how the environment is perceived and how the daily rhythms of life in a long-term care setting impact upon persons. Much has been written about the constraining, administratively oriented processes which often aid staff more than individual residents. Eating schedules, medical treatments, and activity programs must contend with administrative efficiency. Yet, some nursing homes have been better able than others to offer opportunities for individual control (for example, see Lemke and Moos, 1986). The purpose of this section is not to review extensively the literature on the psychosocial environment in institutional settings; this is provided in greater detail in Chapter 7. The intent in the following paragraphs is to highlight some of the daily life issues faced by older residents and how these patterns help to shape behavior.

Williams (1985) has provided an excellent account of what the first few days in a nursing home may be like. Using a case study technique, one is reminded that the first experiences with staff are focused on question and answer sessions. Forms must be signed, diets must be assessed, schedules must be constructed and coordinated. The erosion of independence is triggered by this initial assessment phase.

While the long-term care system does signal a loss of independence (and the degree of loss can vary greatly from site to site), through William's (1985) description we come to understand the role of coping skills as one adapts to a new living situation. One resident described by Williams (1985) moves from a state of depression in which the value of living is questioned to a situation where staff become trusted and the role of the helper to other residents is assumed by the resident. This living, adapting pattern is a process; yet, as time progresses, the coping skills used throughout life return and are used regularly. Difficulties in integrating with new residents and becoming a part of a social network are described. The message for activity personnel is apparent—they will play a role in the development of the social world of new residents. This case study would caution all to let each person evolve at their own pace. Social interaction of a forced nature and begun too soon may have negative consequences. Staff must grasp the readiness level of each resident to enter into specific leisure programs.

Another case study of a long-term care institution and the residents therein is provided by O'Brien (1989). Two years were spent tracking the rhythms and feelings of staff, administrators, and most important, residents and their families at "Bethany Manor" (fictitious name), a 230 resident setting with five levels of care. Qualitative techniques were used and patterns of living for residents were framed under the categories of relationships with others, relationships with caregivers, visitors, activities of daily living, quality of life issues, issues about the future, death, and religion/spirituality. What emerges from these portraits of residents are feelings about daily life in a nursing home, the challenges presented to all, and how one adapts to this situation.

The ability to conform is a common theme in the social histories of residents (O'Brien, 1989). While each person relocates under differing circumstances, most adapt by learning not to "rock the boat." Reasons for entering were mainly of two types: the desire of residents (often with the notion of not wanting to be a burden) or the inability of caregivers to provide the level and degree of attention needed. The nursing home was viewed by residents and their families as a safe, secure place to go.

Friendships were very important to those living in Bethany Manor. Most developed close relationships with a few other residents, and many felt close to selected staff members. Contact with family members was especially valued although the instance of resentment towards family members for placement in the facility was noted as well. This feeling typically dissipated over time. Privacy was an issue, and numerous residents spoke of many activities available even though they, themselves, didn't always feel the need to be an active participant. Reminiscing was a popular activity and externality, or living through the lives of others (often their children) was a theme of many residents interviewed (O'Brien, 1989).

In one section O'Brien (1989) focuses on issues related to those newly admitted to nursing homes. The admission process itself is laden with anxieties; review committees evaluate potential residents with the knowledge that some will be rejected if bed space is not available. Family members always carrying some degree of guilt with them, are told that loved ones should not expect their new residence to be just like "home." Papers must be signed. The physical process of packing belongings (limited by the amount of storage space) and cutting oneself free from the previous living setting creates a whirlpool of mixed feelings.

These case studies (O'Brien, 1989, pp. 79-82) typify the admission experience. Interviews with staff and residents at Bethany Manor re-

sulted in two profiles of the newly admitted: those who didn't want to burden family members and those who felt abandoned. Upon admission, however, most adapted to the nursing home in a short period. Many accepted the regimentation imposed by scheduling in the home as necessary. Food received complaints yet the research noted that half had had poor diets prior to admission, and most residents were receiving nutritional requirements. Difficulties in making new friends were noted. An acclimation period was needed to assimilate the various resident and staff personalities; some turned inward postponing opportunities to meet others.

O'Brien (1989, pp. 86-88) describes the transitional phase encountered by new residents as a time to "distance" oneself from the previous lifestyle. Residents learn to "let go" of both people and things from their prior lifestyle. Those objects brought to the nursing home often take on special importance. Residents generally perceived Bethany Manor as a secure place—one that protected their physical safety and one which offered emotional security through staff and other residents. Conformity and attempting to please staff were also themes brought out in interviews.

At the opposing end of the spectrum from the recently admitted residents are the survivors, those having spent considerable years in a nursing home. O'Brien's (1989, pp. 205-227) research resulted in the creation of four different categories of residents who have adapted to nursing home life. As time passes for individuals in long-term care settings, change is inevitable. Decline, often in both the physical and mental areas, is a characteristic of longevity. These changes bring reactions in living patterns and behaviors of residents with long tenures.

Multiple physical difficulties including foot problems, infections, skin ulcers, and fatigue were noted among those living longest at Bethany Manor (O'Brien, 1989). Senile dementia and Alzheimer's disease were diagnosed in many of the oldest residents, and understandable changes in daily patterns and relationships resulted from these difficulties. It was noted

that family members often felt useless and reduced visits with loved ones who were in the
latter steps of Alzheimer's disease. The early
stages of Alzheimer's disease brought significant change and anxiety for residents; they
were aware that memory was fading and often
began to socialize less, preferring to spend more
time alone.

Other problems experienced by long-stay
residents were mobility problems, falls or the
threat of falling, and fears of hospitalization.
From 13 percent to 17 percent of residents used
walkers, wheelchairs, canes, or had gait problems. Often these devices meant a change in
the degree to which residents toured the entire
home. Comments surfaced in interviews which
indicated that some did not want friends to see
them using such aids and therefore a more restricted living space (near their room or avoiding the main lobby) became the norm. Hospi-
talizations were greatly feared, and at times
symptoms were even disguised. Relocation
within the home (moving to an area offering
greater care) was traumatic for older residents
requiring such a move, which signaled a more
restricted, inward lifestyle. Long residency also
meant changes in support from family members. For some the family/friend network
eroded due to death; others experienced fewer
visits because relatives thought that excellent
care was being provided, or they felt uncomfortable with the deteriorated state of their loved
one (O'Brien, 1989, 212-222).

Culminating the qualitative interviews,
O'Brien (1989) has developed a typology of how
long-term residents adapt to nursing home life.
Presented in Table 3.1, note that the styles are
labeled: "Socialite," "Guardian," "Single-Room
Occupant," and "Free-Lancer." The "Socialite"
would be typically well-integrated into the activity program. Involvement characterizes this
type of adapter. "Guardians" seek to assist others; volunteer activities and planning of special
events or celebrations are good ways of utilizing
their talents through the activity program. The
"Single-Room Occupants" present a different
challenge to activity staff. Secure in their per-

sonal spaces, they are unlikely to seek group
activities. They are frequently self-directed in
their leisure activities and may be content
without individualized activity services. Activity personnel should ascertain the degree to
which they are satisfied with their daily routine
and offer suggestions of individualized activities with the intent of expanding the activity
repertoire. "Free-lancers" will typically avail
themselves of selected activity opportunities
and also seek out quiet, reflective, solitary activities. Choice is an important characteristic
here, and knowledge of what is available or
planned relative to leisure programs is needed
by free-lancers.

The preceding paragraphs have dealt with
the patterns and issues of living in a nursing
home. Issues and needs vary by length of stay
and by individual, yet generalizations can be
made. "Newness" brings certain fears on the
part of these relocated. Also, those residing the
longest in nursing homes present another set of
challenges often highlighted by diminished
physical or mental capacities. There is no substitute for activity professionals being aware of
each person's needs and fitting them into the
scheme of departmental activities. For many
residents the leisure activities offered will become part of the structure of their daily living
patterns.

"Total" Institutions and Their Effects

Many who have studied and written about the
phenomenon of long-term care describe the settings as "total institutions" or "closed environments" (Brody, 1985; Ferraro, 1990; Goffman,
1961; MacNeil and Teague, 1987; Weiner,
Brak, and Snadowaky, 1978). These descriptions refer to the constant and complete interactions of a group of persons with similar characteristics occurring in close proximity within a
confined environment. Rules or guidelines,
both formal and informal, govern much behavior and sleep, leisure, personal maintenance,

Table 3.1: A Typology of Long-Term Adaptation to Nursing Home Care			
TYPE I: The Socialite	TYPE II: The Guardian	TYPE III: The "Single-Room Occupant"	TYPE IV: The "Free-Lancer"
Actively involved in all aspects of nursing home life.	Actively directed toward the support of other residents	Activities carried out in the personal space of the nursing home room	Vacillates between active participation in nursing home life and passivity
Attends organized social activities, interacts with other residents, and participates in committee work or small tasks to assist in the running of the home	Assists other residents by pushing wheelchairs, helping residents get on and off the elevators, and taking residents to meals, church, or social activities.	Spends much time in such activities as reading, writing letters, praying, and watching TV.	Divides time between involvement in social or interactional situations and private activities.
Derives pleasure and satisfaction from social and "work" activities.	Derives pleasure and satisfaction from helping other residents.	Derives comfort from carrying out activities in private.	Derives pleasure from the freedom to choose privacy or social interaction as desired
Desires community or "family" involvement in the home.	Desires community or "family" responsibility in the home.	Desires to withdraw from community or "family" involvement in the home	Desires a modified involvement in the home's community.
Other-oriented and autonomous	Other-oriented and autonomous	Self-oriented, limited autonomy	Self-oriented autonomous

Reprinted with permission: From O'Brien, M. (1989), *Anatomy of a Nursing Home: A New View of Resident Life*. Owings Mill, MD: National Health Publishing, p. 224.

and other activities take place under one roof. As has been discussed previously, when frail, older adults are placed in "closed environments," a frequent reaction is a style of coping which emphasizes conformity (O'Brien, 1989).

As a group, nursing homes have been shown to vary greatly in the degree to which they downplay administrative autocracy and allow self-determined behaviors, and the effect of these differing management styles can be seen in residents' perceptions and actions (Lemke and Moos, 1986; Vallerand, O'Connor, and Blais, 1989). Those nursing homes high on scales of totality and low on measures of self-determined behavior foster negative adaptations on the part of residents.

What are these negative reactions? Brody (1985) identifies depression, negative self-image,

and withdrawal as responses which must be recognized and dealt with. She urges nursing home administrators to allow the residents greater choice thereby fostering independence. Goffman (1961) described mortification of self or multiple losses of roles, property, and identity as a typical reaction to nursing homes. Disidentification "I really don't belong here" frequently occurs (Goffman, 1961). MacNeil and Teague (1987) detailed the characteristics of closed environments and the effects upon residents. Personal defacements exist resulting in loss of belongings, friendships, and ties to the community. Links to the outside world are often cut off, resulting in isolation and restriction of communication channels. O'Brien's (1989) research showed residents of Bethany Manor to take a particular joy in knowing what was going on in the world. The third characteristic of closed environments is the dominance of institutional authority. This brings about attitudes of staff "knowing what's best" for residents and the use of labels which further suppresses individuality. Enforced idleness and dependency on medication to sedate residents are also typical in homes classified as "closed." Here the reactions are further loss of independence and possible addiction to medications. The goal (MacNeil and Teague, 1987) must be to encourage all long-term care settings to move away from "totality" and being "closed" to becoming much more open thereby reducing the negative impacts on residents.

The social breakdown syndrome has been described by Gruenberg (1963) and elaborated upon by MacNeil and Teague (1987). This syndrome is particularly applicable to frail, older adults living in "total" institutions who are susceptible to dependency. It refers to reactions of withdrawal or hostility leading to a breakdown in personal relationships. Deficiencies in self-esteem, the first stage, are often exacerbated in "total" institutions. Losses are many and independence is often not favored by staff. Next, one moves into a dependent role and learns certain cues. The nurse call buzzer overused or any action done for a resident (that he or she is capable of doing) are examples of cues which lead to learned behavior. In the third stage persons are labeled as incompetent or deficient; relocation within the setting itself to a floor or ward signified by greater care typifies this labeling process. The final two stages, learning the chronic role and accepting oneself as sick or incompetent, follow in a natural sequence. Once the resident has accepted total dependency, the cycle is complete. Chances for reversal are unlikely because staff and the environment have encouraged the process in the first place. The key issue, it seems, is to create more settings where "total" and "closed" do not apply and "openness" is encouraged. This leads to notions of quality, the next topic addressed.

Quality in Nursing Homes

The concept of quality is not a simple notion to describe or determine. Phrases such as "quality of life" or "quality assurance" abound in the literature. Certain criteria are usually identified and standards or objective measures applied. Perhaps a more pertinent concern is, "whose quality?" In terms of nursing homes the measure of quality may be perceived quite differently. For corporations it may signify a certain level of profit, for staff it may mean a degree of efficiency centering on numbers served, for residents it represents the totality in their day-to-day experiences. A line of reasoning based upon previous sections links with the concept of quality. If certain negative reactions occur in "total" institutions and if administrators and staff have some degree of control over the environment in nursing homes, then exploring what constitutes "good" nursing homes and how changes for the better can be undertaken should be an area of concern.

Lemke and Moos (1986) concur that "quality" can be interpreted in many ways. In surveying nursing homes, residential care facilities and congregate apartments they sought to measure quality of care for older residents in those settings. The assessment tool used (the Multiphasic Environmental Assessment Procedure, MEAP) gave some indication of how quality can be interpreted. The MEAP consisted of eight indices:

1. comfort , measuring spaciousness and pleasantness of surroundings;
2. security, measuring physical features that support optimal functioning such as visual cues or safety devices;
3. staffing levels, resident to staff ratios;
4. staff Richness, the expertise, training and diversity of personnel;
5. services, types of healthcare and assistance with ADLs and recreation programs;

6. autonomy, opportunities for resident control and privacy;

7. control, if and how residents were involved in decision making; and

8. rapport, relationships among staff and residents, and, among residents themselves.

The research of Lemke and Moos (1986) sought primarily to compare the three different types of residences. As to nursing homes specifically, it was found that they offered greater security, more services, higher staffing levels, and more diverse staff than the other two residential settings. Nursing homes ranked lowest on autonomy and control and lower on rapport, as well. They concluded (p. 294), "Nursing homes provide a protective environment with more security, services, and staffing, but less autonomy."

Comparisons were made among nursing homes based on size and whether or not facilities were profit-oriented. Proprietary homes were noted as efficient and showed less control for residents; nonprofit homes scored highest in comfort, staffing levels, and staff richness. Nonprofit homes also offered more comprehensive services. Size of settings was a factor, as well. Larger facilities had lower staffing levels and were lower in rapport. Lemke and Moos (1986) indicated that the level of care provided was tied to staffing levels, richness of staff, and the types of services provided. They concluded that quality is a multidimensional concept and that the eight measures used are not exhaustive, but can be used by researchers or administrators in the future.

Another recent attempt to measure quality in the nation's nursing homes was undertaken by the Health Care Financing Administration (Findlay, 1988). Thirty-two measures were used to assess quality and critics pointed out some of the difficulties in determining quality. Measurement of the standard was either a pass or fail proposition; degrees of missing the standard were not noted. Nor did the study seek to determine if minor infractions were going to be corrected. Others claimed it was impossible to obtain an accurate reading of a nursing home on a one-day visit by investigative teams. At any rate it was found that only 15 percent of the nation's nursing homes met minimum standards on all 32 criteria. The highest areas of failure (percentages noted) related to care and treatment were: food preparation (43 percent), hygiene and grooming care (30 percent), medication (29 percent), contagion and infection (25 percent), rehabilitation procedures (22 percent), skin care (18 percent), catheter assistance (18 percent), meal assistance (18 percent), privacy and personal needs (17 percent), and incontinence control (16 percent).

There were also strengths noted. The highest ranked categories (percent of homes passing the standard) were: notification when transfer or medical assistance needed (99.7 percent), availability of emergency care (99.5 percent), right to assemble in privacy (99.6 percent), medical care supervised by a doctor (99 percent), lack of physical or mental mistreatment (98 percent), rules specifying residents' rights (98 percent), personal belongings (78 percent), nursing care available at all times (95 percent), accounting of residents' personal funds (95 percent), and availability of appropriate therapies (94 percent).

Improving the Nursing Home Environment — Attention to the Leisure Setting

The question of how the environment in nursing homes might be improved for residents is a pertinent one because the measures of quality include areas over which staff have control. Quality is much more comprehensive than physical spaces and designs of rooms and hallways. All personnel working in long-term environments have the direct ability to affect quality for residents through their procedures and actions.

One positive action on the part of staff would be to allow residents to choose leisure options whenever possible. "Empowerment" has become one of the buzz-words of the 1990s. For long-term care settings to move away from being "total institutions," however, empowerment of residents and self-determination are keys. Research by Vallerand, O'Conner, and Blais (1989) found a direct link between self-determination and life satisfaction. Those nursing homes which allowed little self-determination had residents who were less-satisfied with life, whereas residents in nursing homes with high self-determination were higher on life satisfaction scales, even to the degree of being comparable in life satisfaction to older adults in community residences. Measures of self-determination included areas such as choice at mealtime, personal care, the ability to decorate rooms, and the degree to which staff encouraged personal initiative in residents.

The process by which decisions are made also ties directly to notions of empowerment. Wells and Singer (1988) analyzed quality of life in a nursing home as it related to communication procedures between staff and residents. By way of a case study the authors reported discrepancies between residents and staff in key areas such as privacy, the need for regulations, and the need for sensory satisfaction. Staff essentially were not aware of residents' needs for self-expression, and conformity was the behavior desired by staff. Through a joint resident-staff committee, communication was greatly improved and steps were taken to allow residents more control. Wells and Singer (1988) stress that the process of establishing such joint committees sends a message that residents will be heard. The lack of outlets for self-expression should alert activity personnel. This need could be met through a variety of opportunities: writing, art projects, and planning social activities are methods of encouraging self-expression.

Voelkl (1986) has also addressed life quality of older residents as it pertains to activity staff. Based upon behavioral theories of learned helplessness, instrumental passivity, and perceived control, she offers important guidelines for activity directors. First, the arena of leisure activity is a natural one for allowing independent behavior. Staff must capitalize on this at every opportunity. Staff convenience must play a subordinate role to self-determination by residents. It is essential to take the time to discover how residents experience their world. By so doing an individualized activity plan may be developed, but even more important, reactions of older adults to different stimuli may be understood. Finally, Voelkel (1986) recommends that activities be structured for success. A fine line often exists between too much challenge and frustration and a successful experience guided by the activity therapist which still permits individuality to surface. A goal must always be to encourage independent leisure choices.

A key element of quality of life in nursing homes is the manner in which staff interact with residents. Stein, Linn, and Stein (1986), measured perceptions of residents as to the quality of nursing services. Professional assessments were made of ten nursing homes ranging from excellent to poor. When residents were queried, their judgments of the homes were similar to the professionals. Older residents living in homes judged as "poor" displayed unfavorable perceptions of nursing staff. The authors (1986, p. 151) discuss the ability of residents to make judgments as follows:

> It is likely that patients formed an overall impression of their environment soon after admission, and the global nature of this impression was reflected in high correlations between their responses to questions dealing with their evaluation of the nursing staff, and it is likely that their responses about the staff would also correlate with other aspects of care.

While nursing staff may have more direct contact with residents, the implication for activity staff is clear. Quality of life in a nursing home consists of a variety of elements, one of which is opportunities provided through the activity department. Residents form opinions of these interactions early on, and they are part of the total assessment of the environment in which they live.

Summary

This chapter has explored institutional living from the perspective of those who enter long-term care facilities and with an eye toward what staff (particularly activity staff) can do to assist with life quality. The decision to enter a nursing home is one of life's most difficult, one that causes anxiety on the part of new residents and their loved ones. The decision making process is often less than ideal and is one in which the needs of individuals are frequently at odds with the requirements of institutions and various federal and state regulations.

The characteristics of nursing home residents were reviewed. Being in one's late seventies or eighties, being female and white, and being without a strong support network are characteristic of those in nursing homes. Having chronic ailments which limit the ability to complete activities of daily living unassisted is also a problem faced by most older adults in nursing homes.

Patterns of life were discussed for the newly-admitted and the long-stay residents in nursing homes. Losses are to be expected—leaving a home and personal possessions—and are not easily overcome by many. Personal independence is threatened by a system which must serve many. Some nursing homes encourage independence and self-determination to a higher degree than others. With the passage of time most residents do adapt, and conformity is a behavioral style used by most.

Long-stay residents face other issues. The need for greater levels of care due to worsening disease or mental frailty causes great anxiety. The nature of visitations with family members frequently changes over time. Loved ones may become uncomfortable with the weakened physical or mental state of residents and visits may be reduced.

Quality of life is a critical and, yet, not easily defined concept for nursing homes and the elderly who live there. Measuring quality of life can include different criteria depending upon the viewpoint of administrators, staff, or residents themselves. A recent national survey by the Health Care Financing Administration (Findlay, 1988) found nursing homes to rate highest in areas of notification when medical transfer was required, availability of emergency care, and the right of residents to assemble in privacy. Weakness were noted in food preparation, hygiene care, and medication procedures.

How quality of life might be improved with focus on activity staff was addressed. There is a great deal of agreement which favors movement from "total" institutions to those allowing self-determination, empowerment on the part of residents, and independence whenever possible. Personnel must always remember that they have a direct hand in quality of life for residents. Leisure can often promote independence, and this strength should be utilized by all staff.

LEARNING EXERCISES

1. The importance of personal possessions was discussed in this chapter. If you were moving and could only bring four or five personal possessions (beyond clothing), what would you bring? Discuss the significance of these items to you. Would it be difficult for you to narrow your selection to four or five items? Talk with residents and staff at a nursing home about this issue. Is there a formal policy on the number of possessions allowed? What factors entered into the decisions of residents when they decided what to bring?

2. If *you* were to move into a nursing home, what concerns would you have in terms of becoming adjusted to this environment? What types of friends would you seek? What qualities would be important to you in the way staff would treat you? In what ways would you assert your independence?

3. Obtain a copy of the *1988 Health Care Financing Administration Survey of Nursing Homes* for your state. What

generalizations can be made about the quality of life in nursing homes? What were areas of strength and weakness? What can be said about the provision of leisure opportunities through activity departments in nursing homes?

4. The MEAP (Multiphasic Environmental Assessment Procedure) was reviewed as a tool capable of assessing quality of nursing homes. Eight criteria are used:

   1. comfort —pleasantness of surroundings;
   2. security—use of physical features that support functioning such as visual cues or safety devices;
   3. staffing levels—resident to staff ratios;
   4. staff richness—training and diversity of personnel;
   5. services—healthcare, assistance with ADLs, recreation;
   6. autonomy—resident control and privacy;
   7. control—residents involved in decision making; and,
   8. rapport—staff-resident relationships and resident-resident relationships.

   Which of these indicators do you feel are most important to quality of life in nursing homes? Which criteria do you feel would be most valued by residents? by support staff? by administrators?

5. Empowerment, self-determination, and independence on the part of residents were noted as key concepts or goals which can be directly influenced by staff and the services they provide.

Select an activity program in a nursing home. How do programs promote (or not promote) self-determination and independence? List specific ways these goals are encouraged. What more could be done to promote the empowerment of residents?

References

Brody, E. (1985). The social aspects of nursing home care. In E. Schneider, C. Wendland, A. Zimmer, N List, and M. Ory (Eds.), *The teaching nursing home*. New York, NY: Raven Press.

Brody, E. and Fodey, D. (1985). Epidemiologic considerations. In E. Schneider, et. al. *The teaching nursing home*. New York, NY: Raven Press.

Ferraro, K. (1990). *Gerontology: Perspectives and issues*. New York, NY: Springer Publishing Company, Inc.

Findlay, S. (1988, December). Sorry marks for nursing homes. *U.S. News and World Report*, pp. 92-93.

Goffman, E. (1961). *Asylums*, New York, NY: Anchor Books.

Gruenberg, E. (1964, January). In J. Zusman, "Some explanations of the changing appearance of psychotic patients: Antecedents of the social breakdown syndrome concept," *The Milbank Memorial Fund Quarterly*, pp. 387-390.

Hardwick, S., Pack, P., Donohoe, E. and Aleska, K. (1994). *Accross the states, 1994: Profiles of long-term care systems*. Washington, DC: American Association of Retired Persons.

Hing, E. (1989). Nursing home utilization by current residents: United States, 1985. National Center for Health Statistics. *Vital Health Statistics, 13*(102).

Lemke, S. and Moos, R. (1986). Quality of residential settings for elderly adults. *Journal of Gerontology, 41*(2), 268-276.

MacNeil, R. and Teague, M. (1987). *Aging and leisure: Vitality in later life*. Englewood Cliffs, NJ: Prentice-Hall, Inc.

Mor, V., Sherwood, S. and Gutkin, C. (1986). A national study of residential care for the aged. *The Gerontologist, 26*, 405-417.

O'Brien, M. E. (1989). *Anatomy of a nursing home: A new view of resident life* . Owings Mill, MD: National Health Publishing.

Stein, S., Linn, M., and Stein, E. (1986). The relationship between nursing home residents' perceptions of nursing staff and quality of care. *Activities, Adaptation & Aging, 8*(3/4), 143-156.

Teaff, J. (1985). *Leisure services with the Elderly*. St. Louis, MO: Times Mirror/Mosby College Publishing.

Tobin, S. and Lieberman, M. (1976). *Last home for the aged*. San Francisco, CA: Jossey-Bass, Inc., Publishers.

Vallerand, R., O'Connor, B., and Blais, M. (1989). Life satisfaction of elderly individuals in regular community housing, and high and low self-determination nursing homes. *International Journal of Aging and Human Development, 28*(4), 277-283.

Voelkl, J. (1986). Effects of institutionalization upon residents of extended care facilities. *Activities, Adaptation & Aging, 8*(3/4), 37-46.

Weiner, M., Brak, A., and Snadowaky, A. (1978). *Working with the aged: Practical approaches in the institution and community*. Englewood Cliffs, NJ: Prentice Hall, Inc.

Wells, L. and Singer, C. (1988). Quality of life in institutions for the elderly: Maximizing well-being. *The Gerontologist, 28*(2), 266-269.

Williams, C. (1985). And this is home? In E. Schneider, C. Wendland, A. Zimmer, N. List, and M. Ory (Eds.), *The teaching nursing home*. New York, NY: Raven Press.

The Activities Program: Organization and Structure

Role of the Administrator

The administrator of the nursing home sets the general tone of the facility. Control may be established in a direct way in the form of explicit verbal or written requests or orders. In addition, the administrator exercises a great deal of indirect influence through casual remarks and comments to employees about the operation of the facility and in expressed interest in certain activities. Regardless of the manner of influence, there is a "trickle down effect" existing in all facilities when the administrator sets the priorities. Other employees tend to fall in line with the direct dictates or indirect expectations of the top person (Schneeweiss and Davis, 1974).

The nursing home administrator must be aware of the fact that his/her ideas, attitudes, and biases have a profound impact on every aspect of the nursing home including the activities program. There are several different models that describe how each administrator perceives the nursing home environment:

- *The medical model*: The emphasis is on providing for the health needs of the older person through nursing, physical therapy, and food services. Activities would be geared toward therapeutic intervention.
- *The custodial model*: The emphasis is on protection, safety, and comfort. Activities in this environment would be passive in nature.
- *The social model*: The emphasis of this model is to involve every resident in some type of individual or group activity.

Ideally, the nursing home administrator adopts a balanced viewpoint combining all of these models (Schneeweiss and Davis, 1974).

The nursing home administrator must also deal with his/her own attitudes about aging. Atchley (1987) noted that service providers generally have two basic assumptions that they use in designing programs and services for the elderly. The first approach, "assist the capable," is based on the assumption that older people are generally capable but require assistance in some way. The second approach, "help the helpless," assumes that older persons are incapable of self-determination and lack the resources needed to cope on their own with daily demands. Both of these assumptions can be valid depending upon the situation. Programs and services need to be designed based on the needs of the older person and not on the basis of stereotypes or preconceived ideas.

Staff Relationships

In a nursing home the activities director must cooperate and work with a number of people. The administrator is responsible for all aspects of management including compliance with regulations, staffing, budgets, allocation of space and work areas, and the purchase of supplies and equipment. He/she may also provide assistance in the development of an organization structure of the department including policies and procedures, legal responsibilities, and insurance coverage. The services of an outside consultant may be utilized as a source of information for changes in legislation and standards, staff training, and resource ideas (see Chapter 10). The resident's attending physician must review and approve all plans of care. The activities schedule should not conflict with nursing routine. Nursing personnel should be consulted regarding the resident's health and may be able to provide particular information on specific resident needs and interests. Nursing assistants are especially helpful in offering insights based on resident comments, likes and dislikes, and can

assist in ensuring that residents are ready for activities, transporting them, if necessary, and assisting residents in participation. Activities staff should also report to nursing any changes in the residents' condition so that the residents can be closely monitored. The food service department is a valuable resource for the activities department. They can suggest refreshments for parties and snacks that are nutritionally appropriate and that conform to the special dietary requirements of the residents. They can also assist with ideas for cooking classes. Housekeeping and maintenance helps with setting up rooms, cleaning, and rearranging work areas. Coordination with housekeeping and maintenance is a necessity. In addition, the activities director works closely with other therapists (e.g., physical therapy, occupational therapy, speech pathology and audiology) and support services (e.g., social services and religious leaders). Proper follow-up of specific treatment approaches is then ensured (Teaff, 1990) (see Chapter 8).

Usually, the activities director in a nursing home has the responsibility for recruiting, orienting, training, supervising, and recognizing individual volunteers and community groups who can supplement the regular activities program (Mullen, 1979). Local colleges and universities are an excellent resource for program ideas as well as a source for student interns. The activities director is often the bridge between the nursing home and the community and projects the image of the nursing home to the community. The nursing home is not an isolated entity but an integral part of the community.

Purpose

The OBRA regulations state:

> The facility must provide an ongoing program of activities designed to meet, in accordance with the comprehensive assessment, the interests and the physical, mental, and psychosocial well-being of each resident" (Federal Register, 1989).

The key word in this definition is "the facility" meaning that all staff, regardless of department or position, have a responsibility in insuring resident involvement in appropriate activities. Bachner and Cornelius (1978) introduced another perspective in a long-term care setting. They consider life an activities program and that:

> Everything we do can be considered an activity. Each thing that we do allows us to exercise certain abilities. Therefore, bathing, walking, talking, and singing are all activities. Oftentimes, illness, disability, or nursing home placement prevents us from exercising either our physical, mental, or social abilities. Disuse may result in lost abilities. The primary purpose of an activities program is to create opportunities for a person to exercise his/her abilities and to have continued involvement in previous interests.

This perspective parallels what Atchley, (1977) wrote:

> . . . as individuals grow older, they are predisposed toward maintaining continuity in habits, associations and preferences.

This approach represents the role continuity theory of aging, and suggests that older persons continue to respond to life activities as they had done so previously. An activities program in a nursing home can help the older individual to maintain continuity of lifestyle habits, associations, and preferences (Davis, 1982).

Nursing home residents have many talents and abilities that they no longer are given the opportunity to use. They also may not be given the chance to learn new skills. As a result, one aspect of living, the possibility of continued growth and achievement, has been suppressed. Activity programs can help motivate residents to function in the normal routines of living (Incani, Seward, and Sigler, 1975).

Activities can also be defined as outward expressions of who we are. Some of us express ourselves by maintaining a well-kept home and garden. Others may use exercise and physical pursuits to challenge our capabilities. Crafts and hobbies provide an outlet for creative expression, and games challenge us in intellectual, competitive ways (DeBolt and Kastner, 1989).

Tibbitts (1960) developed a list of specific social needs of older persons that include:

1. to render some socially useful service;
2. to be considered part of the community;
3. to occupy increased leisure time in satisfying ways;
4. to enjoy companionship;
5. to be recognized as an individual;
6. to have opportunities for self-expression;
7. to have health protection and care;
8. to be mentally stimulated;
9. to have suitable living arrangements and maintain family relationships; and
10. to be spiritually satisfied.

After analyzing this list, it is clear that recreation programs have the potential to meet the social needs of older persons in long-term care facilities.

Teague and MacNeil (1992) suggest four specific benefits of recreation programs in long-term care facilities. They are:

1. *Satisfaction and Quality of Life:* Recreation programs provide enjoyment and contribute to the residents' perception of a positive self-image and to their overall feeling of well-being.
2. *Therapeutic Benefits:* Recreation is considered to have therapeutic value because of the various physical, mental, and psychosocial benefits that can be derived from recreation participation. Structured recreation experiences oftentimes compliment and supplement the approaches of the other therapeutic disciplines to enhance rehabilitation and restore functioning.
3. *Preventative Benefits:* Recreation provides nursing home residents with opportunities and the motivation to use

existing capabilities to prevent further decline and possibly to learn new skills.

4. *Adjustment*: A well-designed recreation program that closely matches the interests and skills of the residents can offer opportunities for social interaction and combat feelings of helplessness by providing challenge, control, and choice in their lives.

Activity programs should do more than occupy time. Each type of program serves an important function for the nursing home resident. Large group activities such as parties and socials provide entertainment, social interaction, and create a sense of community. Small group activities such as exercises and sports enhance physical functioning; current events and discussion groups provide intellectual stimulation; pets and volunteer services improve emotional well-being; and religious programs and life review exercises relate to spiritual well-being. Nursing home residents can also be encouraged to continue lifelong interests such as reading, writing letters, and pursuing hobbies and other creative pursuits. Relationships that involve trust, acceptance, and understanding can be established and maintained through one-to-one activities (DeBolt and Kastner, 1989).

Organization

Each facility is unique due to location, size, management practices, staffing and resident population. Teague and MacNeil (1992) identified several factors that are consistently used in program organization.

1. *Knowledge of Activities*: The recreation professional should continually maintain files of activities and their application; maintain records of past activities; seek out new program ideas; and be able to modify programs to meet the interests and needs of the particular resident population.

2. *Knowledge of the Aging Process*: The aging experience is characterized by changes in the physical, sensory, mental,

and social functioning of each individual. This includes being able to distinguish between normal and pathological conditions that might affect resident participation. It is also important for staff to be able to identify their own attitudes about aging and how these attitudes impact on the recreation program.

3. *Ability to Adapt Activities*: Many times, activities do not work because they do not fit the needs and/or interests of the population. In addition, adaptive equipment and supplies may not be available or may be too costly to purchase. Creative thinking can help in program adaptation. Lower functioning residents may become more involved when the activity is broken down into simple tasks (see Chapter 6).

4. *Activity File and Resources*: In addition to maintaining files of program ideas, records should be kept of volunteers, community programs and resources, and available recreation equipment. Information should include:
   - Name of the program (including a brief description of the program/service);
   - Contact person and phone number;
   - Availability of program (dates and times);
   - Materials or equipment needed,
   - Cost; and,
   - Evaluation.

Other program resources that can be used to supplement the activity file include the names, addresses, and phone numbers of the following:
   - Recreation-related organizations such as National Recreation and Parks Association (NRPA), National Therapeutic Recreation Society (NTRS), American Therapeutic Recreation Association (ATRA), and the National Association of Activity Professionals (NAAP);

- Local parks and recreation departments;
- Aging-related organizations such as Gerontological Society of America, National Council on Aging, American Society on Aging, the Office on Aging, the Alzheimer's Disease Association, and the American Association of Retired Persons;
- Volunteer resources such as Retired Senior Volunteer Program, church groups, service organizations (Lions Club, Rotary, and Kiwanis);
- Recreation, gerontology and non-credit and lifelong learning divisions at local colleges and universities;
- Books, newsletters, magazines, and catalogs related to recreation and aging. *Activities, Adaptation & Aging*, a quarterly journal published by the Haworth Press, Inc., New York, NY and *Creative Forecasting*, a monthly newsletter published in Colorado Springs, CO are excellent references for program ideas; and
- Audiovisual resources.

Budgets

A budget is essential in the organization of an activities program. The amount of money available will determine staffing and programming. Generally, the nursing home administrator has the ultimate responsibility for budgetary decisions. Ideally, each department manager has input into the development of the facility budget. In order to participate effectively in this process, the activities director needs to have a basic understanding of budgets and how they work. The activities budget is part of the facility's operations budget which determines the amount of money needed to operate the facility for a period of one year. The activities budget can be divided into four categories:

1. *Personnel*—These expenses include the cost of salaries, fringe benefits, payroll taxes, and staff development.

2. *Equipment*—These expenses may be computed differently from the operations budget. Equipment expenses generally represent capital expenditures which can be depreciated over several years. For example, a new VCR costs $400, and has a usable life of more than one year. This expense would then be spread out over several years.

3. *Supplies*—These expenses include all the materials needed for the daily operation of the activity department. The amount may be a predetermined annual amount, a predetermined monthly amount, a per resident/per month amount or separate budget line items such as arts and crafts, entertainment, parties, etc. The format depends on the accounting practices of the facility.

4. *Miscellaneous*—This category may include items that are difficult to determine ahead of time and various other expenses such as seasonal decorations, film developing, and volunteer certificates. (Bachner and Cornellius, 1978).

In addition, it is important to determine how to allocate the costs of supplies, equipment, or other items that are shared by several departments. For example, if cake and ice cream are served at a party, does the cost get charged to food service and activities? Making these decisions ahead of time eases interdepartmental cooperation (Bachner and Cornelius, 1978).

Budgets are not "wish-lists" and should realistically reflect how much money is needed to operate the department for one year. Maintaining accurate records throughout the year will assist in future budget preparation. Information about possible future purchases may be kept for planning purposes.

In some facilities, the activities department is expected to offset operating expenses with various revenue generating or fund-raising activities such as bake sales, craft fairs, and bazaars. When properly planned, these activities can be a source of meaning and purpose for the residents, can boost community relations, and

can generate funds to enhance the existing program. Monies raised in this way should be kept in a separate account and careful records need to be kept on how the money has been spent.

The activities department may periodically receive cash or material donations or contributions from residents, their families, volunteers, or from friends of the facility. It is important that these individuals receive a letter of appreciation and that the gift is publicly recognized. In this way, others may also want to donate or contribute to the department. Occasionally, residents and/or families may want to purchase supplies for individual projects.

Activity Areas

In some long-term care facilities, rooms have been designated for particular activities such as a craft room, library, chapel, auditorium, game room, gift shop, kitchen, and snack shop. However, most facilities have limited space available for activities. Lounge areas, dining rooms, resident rooms, outdoor patios, and multipurpose rooms can all be used for activities (see Chapter 7). If this is the case, the multipurpose room should have proper lighting; be well-ventilated; be located near restrooms; be readily accessible to elevators; have plenty of electrical outlets; be equipped with either a telephone or call bell system; and have a folding curtain or moveable partition, darkening shades on windows, stacking or folding chairs, and a sound system. Regardless of the space that is available, careful planning and scheduling will ensure maximum room use. In addition, office space with a desk, telephone, and locked file cabinet are bare essentials. Adequate storage space is also a necessity. Shelving prevents items from being placed on the floor and/or too near to the ceiling (Mullen, 1979).

SUPPLIES AND EQUIPMENT

Scissors, knives, tools and valuables should always be kept in locked areas. Toxic and flammable substances need to be stored in locked, metal, vented cabinets. Food supplies need to be kept in sealed, plastic containers with labels identifying the contents and the date of purchase. It is the responsibility of the activities director to maintain all equipment in good working condition and to make arrangements for necessary service and repairs. Warranty and operating information should be readily available.

STAFFING

There are no definitive guidelines on staffing requirements for recreation personnel in long-term care settings. Some facilities use the ratio of one full-time equivalent staff person for every 60 residents. Much of this is determined by budgetary considerations and the philosophical orientation of the administrator/owner/operator of the facility. Other considerations include residents' abilities, physical layout of the facility, types of programs offered, other resources that are available (consultants, families, volunteers, student interns, and community involvement), and the specific duties and responsibilities of the activities staff (Bachner and Cornelius, 1978).

JOB DESCRIPTIONS

Bachner and Cornelius (1978) present the following guidelines for job descriptions. A job description clarifies responsibilities for both the employee and the supervisor. It also serves as an aid in recruiting and interviewing. A job description also provides each employee with a list of specific duties upon which he/she will be evaluated. Each activity staff member and volunteer should have a job description.

Preparing a job description involves three steps.

Step 1: Work Identification—Complete an overall analysis of the work and tasks that need to be covered. This involves determining whether the position requires a full-time or several part-time employees. Part-time employees often provide more variety to programming and better coverage especially for evening and weekend programs. However, it may be difficult to find part-time employees to fit scheduling needs since many qualified people prefer or require full-time employment.

Step 2: Writing the Job Description—Once the tasks needed to be performed are identified take time to review any existing job descriptions. They may be modified instead of having to create new ones.
Each job description should include:

Job Title: Titles must be consistent with other positions in the facility. For example, if department managers are referred to as "Directors", the title would be "Activities Director" instead of "Activities Coordinator". If possible, make the job title descriptive of the type of work to be performed, i.e. "Friendly Visitor".

Scope of Responsibility: This section outlines to whom the employee reports to and for whom the employee is responsible.

Qualifications: Any special training, skills, and/or educational requirements for the position.

Duties: A list of specific tasks be performed. A job description reflects the needs of the facility and its residents. Avoid trying to design a job description to fit the qualifications of a particular employee. When preparing and/or reviewing job descriptions, it may be helpful either to start with the top position and follow in order of level of responsibility, or you may wish to start with the simplest and advanced to the more complex positions, as you become more comfortable with the process.

Step 3: Job Description Review—Review all job descriptions as a whole to see it they work together without duplication of efforts and that no conflicts exist. All positions can be illustrated through the use of an organization chart which shows responsibilities and staff relationships.

Sample Job Description

Title: Activities Director

Scope of Responsibility: The Activities Director reports directly to the Nursing Home Administrator and is responsible for supervising the Activities Assistants and Volunteers. If not qualified, the Activities Director shall receive regular, periodic consultation from a qualified Activities Consultant.

Qualifications: Must have a minimum of the following:

1. High school diploma or GED.
   In addition, according to the OBRA regulations, "the activities program must be directed by a qualified professional who is:
   (i) A qualified therapeutic recreation specialist who is:
       (A) licensed or registered, if applicable, by the State in which practicing; and,
       (B) eligible for certification as a therapeutic recreation specialist by a recognized accredited body by August 1, 1989; or
   (ii) Has two years of experience in a social or recreation program within the last five years, one of which was fulltime in a patient activities program in a healthcare setting; or
   (iii) Is a qualified occupational therapist or occupational therapy assistant; or,
   (iv) Has completed a training course approved by the State (Federal Register, 1989).

Individuals who are certified by the National Certification Council for Activity Professionals (NCCAP) also meet these qualifications.

Duties:

1. Plans, coordinates, and directs a program of individual and group activities based on the residents' needs and interests.

2. Maintains a balance of individual and group activities including: physical, social, intellectual, spiritual, and creative programs.

3. Schedules activities for maximum resident involvement including evening and weekend programs and ensures proper staff coverage.

4. Records all necessary documentation in the resident's medical chart including: the activity section of the Minimum Data Set (MDS), an activity assessment, problems/needs, goals, and approaches on the care plan, and progress notes.

5. Serves as a member of the interdisciplinary care planning team.

6. Maintains all departmental records and reports including: daily record of resident participation in activities, monthly activity calendars, activity file and resources, resident council meeting minutes, record of in-service training, etc.

7. Publicizes activity programs by posting monthly activity calendars, maintaining bulletin boards, making daily announcements, circulating calendars and facility newsletters to residents, families, volunteers, and other staff, and by inviting appropriate parties to special events.

8. In some facilities, may be responsible for recruiting, orienting, placing, supervising and recognizing volunteers.

9. Schedules and conducts the monthly residents' council meeting.

10. Responsible for seasonal and holiday decorations.

11. Participates in the facility in-service program.

12. Participates in the quality assurance program and serves on various appointed committees.

13. Plans community programs held in and outside the facility. Makes necessary arrangements for transportation.

14. Is responsible for the activities budget. Maintains records of departmental income and expenses. Requisitions and/or purchases supplies, equipment and materials within established budgetary guidelines.

15. Maintains activity equipment and supplies.

16. Observes all facility safety policies and procedures.

17. Performs other related duties as directed by the administrator.

Activities Assistants and Volunteers

Job descriptions and an organization chart need to be reviewed with administration before they are presented to staff and volunteers. Periodic review will keep job descriptions current and up-to-date.

ROLE OF THE ACTIVITIES CONSULTANT

Occasionally, a long-term care facility may require the services of a qualified activities consultant. In addition to working with an activities director who might not be qualified yet, a consultant may be used for the following: to recruit and train new staff, to evaluate existing programs and make recommendations for program enhancement, and to assist in implementing new programs.

Initially, the activities consultant meets with the nursing home administrator to discuss the purpose and need for consultation services. At this point, a contractual agreement is prepared stating:

• type and extent of services to be rendered;
• hours of service each month;
• length of time the contract will be in effect;
• fees to be paid to the consultant;
• billing and payment procedures; and,
• format for reports.

The consultant then arranges to meet with the activities director at a mutually agreed upon time.

The basic duties of the consultant are to provide guidance in the following areas: program requirements as mandated by federal and state regulations, program ideas, documentation, resource materials, use of volunteers and community resources, in-service training, reports and record-keeping, program evaluation, personnel issues, and research developments.

PLANNING ACTIVITIES

One of the most important responsibilities of the activities director is scheduling activities. Bachner and Cornelius (1987) developed a systematic approach to this task. Here is a modified version of this approach.

Step 1: Establishing a "Scheduling Schedule"— Determining how much time you need to plan is the main task involved in this step. In some situations, you may be faced with printing deadlines for newsletters or calendars and planning will need to be done four to six weeks in advance. Other programs may need administrative approval, interdepartment involvement, or advanced reservations, all of which must be done early to ensure program success.

Step 2: Blocking Out the Schedule—Begin with a rough draft taking into consideration mealtimes, therapy schedules, beauty and barber shop hours, and any routine services and activities that will affect all residents. In addition, be sure to block out staff meetings, resident care conferences, and in-service training programs. This aspect of planning involves communicating with other staff members regarding room use so that space will be available for scheduled programs.

The rough draft should be indicative of residents' needs, interests, and time preferences. This task can be accomplished by matching programs with the resident profile. For example, if 20 percent of the resident population has been identified as nonparticipants, then a proportionate number of scheduled activities should be on a one-to-one basis. Although it is impossible to design a perfect schedule for everyone, appropriate programming for as many residents as possible is a realistic goal.

Step 3: Review—Review the schedule taking the schedules of other departments into consideration. In addition, residents' capabilities and staffing patterns are two other variables that affect scheduling.

Leitner and Leitner (1985) suggest several guidelines to follow in developing activity schedules:

1. Whenever possible, offer more than one activity simultaneously. In this way, residents of different functioning levels will all have opportunities to choose the activities they prefer.

2. Include passive and active activities throughout the day. Too many passive activities can lead to drowsiness, while too many physically active programs can cause fatigue.

3. Limit physically active programs to 30 minutes and schedule these programs in the morning and/or in the afternoon but avoid times immediately before meals.

4. Cognitive and intellectually demanding programs seem to work better in the mornings when residents are more alert.

5. In general, activities should be scheduled to last approximately 45 minutes due to limited attention spans of most people. More cognitively impaired residents will have an even shorter attention span.

6. Allow ample time between activities for preparation and set up, transporting, and clean up.

7. Schedule one main or special activity each day to give residents something to look forward to. Residents should also have input into the review process. Residents' Council meetings are an ideal forum for this review. Ask questions similar to those outlined in the interpretive guidelines of the OBRA regulations (Department of Health and Human Services: Health Care Financing Administration, 1989).

- Do available activities meet your interests?
- Are these activities similar to the kinds of things you were interested in before you came here?
- Are you satisfied with the:
  - times activities are offered (daily, weekends, and evenings)?
  - number of activities offered?
  - variety of activities provided?
  - use of community resources, both in side and outside of the facility?
  - assistance provided in fulfilling leisure interests (e.g., turning on tape recorders, putting activity supplies within reach)?
  - adaptations for residents' special needs (e.g., one-to-one attention, large print books, book holders, adaptive recreational equipment, age appropriateness of activities)?
- Do you enjoy the activities you take part in?
- Are they fun?
- Do the activities help you make friends?
- Do they help you feel good about yourself?

Document resident response and follow up on requests.

Although residents' needs, interests, and preferences all are important in scheduling activities, you need to be aware that some residents will only choose certain programs. These are generally activities that are fun and easy while more challenging and therapeutic programs may be avoided. As the activities director, you are responsible for structuring a schedule that provides a balance of both innovative

and routine program options. Structure also allows you to design programs for residents with similar needs such as a reading group for the visually impaired, or a special cooking class for residents with dietary restrictions. Structure need not imply rigidity and needs to be balanced with flexibility that can be enhanced by the use of part-time staff, volunteers, and student intern (Hamill and Oliver, 1980) (see Appendix C for Daily Schedule of Activities).

Step 4: Equipment and Supplies Review—Be sure that equipment and adequate supplies will be available. This step prevents last minute shopping trips for supplies. Have a contingency plan and be prepared to address, "What if . . . ?"

Step 5: Assigning Staff—After you determine staff requirements for each program, you can begin to assign staff based on work schedules. It may be helpful to look at the schedule of each individual staff member and assign programs based on staff availability, special skills, and qualifications. In general, schedule more qualified staff to do programs that require more intense resident interaction. Conversely, less qualified staff and volunteers may be able to handle the less demanding activities such as movies, church services, entertainment, and socials.

Step 6: Integrating the Schedule into the Total Facility Program—Review the schedule with the administrator and make copies available for all department managers. It should be understood that the schedule will be put into effect unless you are notified in advance of any scheduling conflicts or changes.

Step 7: Be Flexible—Even though you may prepare the schedule well in advance and can anticipate certain changes, other revisions may also occur. Learn to expect the unexpected and do the best you can regardless of the situation. This attitude will create a positive atmosphere within the department and residents and staff will benefit from it.

After the activities schedule has been finalized, large monthly calendars are developed including the time and location of programs. Block lettering using black ink on white or yellow paper maximizes visual acuity. Calendars are then posted on bulletin boards throughout the facility. Be sure to post calendars low enough for wheelchair-bound residents to be able to read them. Each resident should receive an individual calendar that can be included in the facility's monthly newsletter (if one exists).

Facility Newsletter

A facility newsletter is an excellent resource to promote in-house and community relations. A newsletter can be used to inform residents, staff, families, volunteers, and other interested parties about what is happening in the facility. It can also be used to profile selected residents, staff members, and volunteers; to highlight special events, and to explain timely topics of interest to these groups. In addition, the publication of a facility newsletter can be a way of involving residents in the activities program. Residents can assist in writing articles, typing, editing, proofreading, folding, and distributing newsletters.

NEWS RELEASES

Some activities are newsworthy enough to merit the submission of a press release to the local newspaper. These activities may include:
- A resident's 100th birthday,
- Special events or theme celebrations,
- Open house events, or
- Volunteer activities.

Press releases should be clearly written to answer the five W's of news reporting (who, what, where, when, and why). Indicate in the press release the name and telephone number of who should be contacted for more information and when the release is to be used. In most cases, the press release will read, "For Immediate Release." The administrator must approve all press releases before submission.

There are several reasons why it is important to obtain media coverage of activities. The morale of residents, staff, and volunteers is boosted when they see their work recognized, and the community perceives the nursing home in a more positive fashion when they see that nursing home residents are capable of productive pursuits (Bachner and Cornelius, 1978). Media coverage is also viewed favorably by administrators as it helps to create a positive image of the facility.

Summary

This chapter focused on the organization of the activities department and includes information on the organizational structure and purpose of the department. Benefits of recreation programs were discussed.

Specific details were given on how to structure an activities department including resources, staffing, budget, and equipment and supplies. A systematic approach to scheduling activities was presented as well as guidelines to consider in developing an activities schedule. Finally, newsletters and press releases were covered.

LEARNING EXERCISES

1. Review the organization of the activities department in a long-term care facility using the factors outlined by Teague and MacNeil (1987).
2. Obtain a copy of a job description for an activities director and an activities assistant. Review the duties and responsibilities for both.
3. Become familiar with activities program resources used in a long-term care facility including *Activities, Adaptation & Aging* and *Creating Forecasting*.

References

Atchley, R. C. (1977). *The social forces in later life*. Belmont, CA: Wadsworth Publishing Co., Inc.

Atchley, R. C. (1987). *Aging: Continuity and change* (2nd ed.) Belmont, CA: Wadsworth Publishing Co., Inc.

Bachner, J. P. and Cornelius, E. (1978). *Activities coordinator's guide*. (HCFA-HSQB 78-004) Washington, DC: Department of Health, Education and Welfare, Health Care Financing Administration, Health Standards and Quality Bureau.

Davis, N. B. (1982). The role continuity approach to aging: Implications for leisure programming. In M. L. Teague, R. D. MacNeil, and G. L. Hitzhusen (Eds.), *Perspectives on leisure and aging in a changing society* . Columbia, MO: University Printing Services.

DeBolt, N. and Kastner, M. E. (1989). *"I'm in here!" Strategies for one-to-one activities*. Torrington, WY: Lutheran Health Systems.

Department of Health and Human Services: Health Case Financing Administration. (1989, February 2). *Federal Register/Rules and Regulations, 54*(21). Washington, DC: U.S. Government Printing Office.

Department of Health and Human Services: Health Case Financing Administration. (1989). *Interpretive guidelines: Skilled nursing facilities and intermediate care facilities*. Washington, DC: U.S. Government Printing Office.

Hamill, C. M. and Oliver, R. C. (1980). *Therapeutic activities for handicapped elderly*. Rockville, MD: Aspen Systems Corp.

Incani, A. G., Seward, B. L., and Sigler, J. E. (1975). *Coordinated activity programs for the aged: A how-to-do-it manual*. Chicago, IL: American Hospital Association.

Leitner, M. J. and Leitner, S. F. (1985). *Leisure in later life: A sourcebook for the provision of recreational services for elders*. New York, NY: The Haworth Press, Inc.

MacNeil, R. D. and Teague, M. L. (1987). *Aging and leisure: Vitality in later life*. Englewood Cliffs, NJ: Prentice-Hall, Inc.

Mullen, D. A. (1979). *Recreation in nursing homes*. Arlington, VA: National Recreation and Parks Association.

Schneeweiss, S. M. and Davis, S. W. (Eds.). (1974). *Nursing home administration*. Baltimore, MD: University Park Press.

Teaff, J. D. (1990). *Leisure services with the elderly*. Prospect Heights, IL: Waveland Press, Inc.

Teague, M. L. and MacNeil, R. D. (1992). *Aging and leisure: Vitality in later life*. Englewood Cliffs, NJ: Prentice-Hall, Inc.

Tibbitts, C. (1960). *Handbook of social gerontology: Societal aspects of aging*. Chicago, IL: University of Chicago Press.

Documentation and Program Evaluation

Documentation—A Five-Part Approach to Written Communication

For many activities directors, documentation means something that must be done to meet federal and state requirements. Few of us fully realize the important role that the documentation process plays in program planning and in the everyday duties and responsibilities as healthcare professionals.

PURPOSE OF DOCUMENTATION

- Continuity of Care—provides a written record for others to follow.
- Communication—enables all staff to focus and clarify thinking.
- Justification—presents a written record of staff actions and purpose.
- Evaluation—shows if individual needs and interests are being met and measures the effectiveness of the program.
- Research—develops a data base for further reference.
- Reimbursement—assists in the payment for services rendered.
- Requirement—if it's not documented, it wasn't done (Cunninghis, 1982).

SOME GENERAL GUIDELINES FOR DOCUMENTATION

- The medical record is a permanent, legal document. All documentation on the medical record should be done in ink (blue or black) with full signature, title, and date. (Using initials and the month and year are not acceptable.)
- Errors should be crossed out with a single line and initialed. (Never use correction fluid to cover mistakes.)
- Medical records are thinned periodically and the extracted documents placed in a permanent file. These documents are retained for a period of seven years.
- Notes should be legible and easily read.
- Use only generally accepted abbreviations and symbols.
- Refer to residents by their full name and not by first name only.
- Describe behavior; do not label it. Example: "Mrs. Martin *has difficulty locating her room*" rather than "Mrs. Martin is confused."
- Avoid writing in the first person. Use the passive voice. Example: "*It was decided* to implement a program of one-to-one reality orientation (RO) . . . ."
- Try to describe behavior in a positive manner. Avoid the word NOT.
- Avoid writing in the absolute. Example: "Mr. Cooper *never* attends group activities."
- Remember that confidentiality of records is a rule in all facilities. Do not discuss the contents of the medical record with family members, other residents, or staff members on an informal basis, or with anyone outside the facility.
- Remember that you are reporting information for the benefit of others and not just to keep your own records. Be sure that others will understand what you are saying. Avoid jargon and terminology known only to your particular discipline (Cunninghis, 1982).

A FIVE-PART APPROACH

Documentation is a five-part process. According to (Olsson, 1986), the five major parts are:

1. Assessment;
2. Problem/Need Identification;
3. Setting Goals;
4. Plan of Approach; and,
5. Evaluation or Progress Notes.

These five parts play an integral role in the development of an interdisciplinary plan of care for each resident.

(1) Assessment

The process of collecting information to learn as much as possible about each resident is the function of the assessment. This is done to identify problems/needs, interests, activity preferences, strengths and capabilities.

Although the initial assessment is to be completed in a relatively short time period following admission or re-admission, (no later than 14 days after admission, or before the first interdisciplinary care conference), it is probably the most important part of the documentation process and is vital in the development of the care plan.

To prevent frustration in the completion of the assessment, it is important to remember that the initial assessment is merely *the evaluation of the resident at the time of admission.* The resident has not had time to adjust to the facility and may be suffering from depression, confusion, the trauma of relocation, anxiety (other disciplines will also be completing their assessments at the same time), or other medical problems.

Keep in mind that documentation is a process. The initial assessment will serve as a baseline to measure the effectiveness of care. Also, it is important to establish a relationship with each resident as soon as possible after admission. The assessment will aid in getting to know the resident.

The OBRA regulations state:

The facility must conduct, initially and periodically, a comprehensive, accurate, standardized, reproducible assessment of each resident's functional capacity, which is based on a uniform data set" (Federal Register, 1989).

This assessment is referred to as the Minimum Data Set (MDS) (see Appendix D for sample MDS).

Activity Pursuit Patterns section (Section I) of the MDS measures the amount and types of interests and activities that the resident currently pursues, as well as those activities the resident would like to pursue. This section includes the following subparts:

1. Time Awake—that period of a typical day when the resident is awake all or most of the time.
2. Average Time Involvement in Activities—the proportion of available time which the resident spends involved in group activities as well as independent activities such as reading magazines and writing letter.
3. Preferred Activity Setting—the activity setting in which the resident prefers and appears to be most comfortable.
4. General Activity Preferences—of those listed, the activities which the resident prefers regardless of his/her actual participation and the availability of the activity (Florida Association of Homes for the Aging, 1990).

Since the activity section of the MDS provides only limited information, it may be helpful to supplement another activity assessment form.

There are many different types of activity assessment forms available for your use (see Appendix E for sample Activity Assessment). The activity assessment should consider the normal everyday routine of the resident and his/her activity preferences. Other important areas to include are:
- *Medical Problems*—including dietary restrictions and allergies that may limit activity participation.
- *Physical Impairments and Functioning*— including exercise level, range-of-motion, mobility, coordination, ability to perform

activities of daily living, and any adaptive equipment needed.
- *Sensory Impairments and Communication*— any deficit in vision, hearing, or speech that might affect activity participation. Include any language problems and any corrective devices used or needed.
- *Mental and Emotional Functioning*— attention span, memory, mood, orientation to time, place, and person, intellectual ability.
- *Affective Functioning*—attitude, perception of problems and placement, coping and adapting skills.
- *Background*—social, educational, cultural, occupational, religious, and environment.
- *Social Functioning*—family, friends, meaningful relationships, and interpersonal skills.
- *Environmental Functioning*—how resident adapts and reacts to environment (Bachner and Cornelius, 1978). Any loss of function or potential loss of function, that would benefit from activity intervention (group or individual) must be addressed.

How To Get Information
Ask the resident. He/she may not be able to respond but it is still important to gather as much information as possible and to initiate a relationship with each resident.

During the first visit, it is important to introduce oneself and explain the role one plays in the facility. Avoid checklist-type assessment forms. Be prepared to ask different kinds of questions to complete the assessment. Questions such as: "What is your favorite holiday? How do you like to celebrate holidays? How did you use your free time? Tell me about your family," will elicit responses that will assist in the completion of the activity assessment.

Observe the resident. Make note of physical and behavioral functioning such as posture, gait, movement, grooming, eye contact, and response to others. Also, observe items and possessions surrounding the resident. These items will give clues as to how the resident feels about himself or herself, the environment, and other people.

Another helpful technique is to show the resident around the facility, possibly even to observe activities in progress. Note if anything seems to capture the resident's attention. Or, sharing a photo album of past activities will help to familiarize the new resident with what the facility offers.

Talk with other staff members. The nursing staff oftentimes has information that can be helpful in developing an activity plan.

Become familiar with the medical record. It may be helpful to read the admitting records, the physician's orders, and assessments completed by other disciplines.

Talk with family members, friends, and visitors. Again, be sure to introduce yourself and explain your role in the care of the resident. The activities director may want to invite family members to accompany the new resident to selected programs.

Do not become discouraged if the resident states, "I don't like activities," or "I don't want to do anything." More than likely, the resident's admission to the facility was precipitated by a number of medical problems or a sudden loss of a caregiver. The new resident may need time to adjust to the new surroundings.

It is important to be positive and supportive during this difficult period. Also, be careful not to make false promises of discharge or total recovery if these outcomes are not realistic.

Assessments must be conducted again if there is a significant change in the resident's physical, mental, or psychosocial functioning, and in no case less often than once every 12 months (Federal Register, 1989). Hospitalization, transfers, etc., may require a reassessment depending upon the length of stay, change in diagnosis, and/or facility policies.

The assessment should be as specific and individualized as possible. Assessments must clearly define problems/needs that are addressed on the care plan.

(2) Identification of Problems/Needs

The Resident Assessment Protocols (RAPs) are structured frameworks that organize the MDS components. By using a standardized worksheet to review the MDS, levels of measurement, known as triggers, identify problem areas that may affect the resident's level of physical, mental, and psychosocial functioning. The triggered problem/need areas designated on the RAP Trigger Legend serve as the basis for the care plan. Responsibility for completing both the RAP Summary sheet and initiating care plan action for the particular problem should be delegated to the discipline member who completed that section of the MDS (Florida Association of Homes for the Aging, 1990). (See Appendix F for sample RAP Trigger Legend and RAP Summary.)

The OBRA Regulations State:

The facility must develop a comprehensive care plan for each resident that includes measurable objectives and timetables to meet a resident's medical, nursing, and psychosocial needs that are identified in the comprehensive assessment.

A comprehensive care plan must be—

a. Developed within seven days after completion of the comprehensive assessment;

b. Prepared by an interdisciplinary team that includes the attending physician, a registered nurse with responsibility for the resident, and other appropriate staff in disciplines as determined by the resident's needs, and with the participation of the resident's family or legal representative, to the extent practicable; and,

c. Periodically reviewed and revised by a team of qualified persons after each assessment, no less than once every three months, and as appropriate" (Federal Register, 1989). (See Appendix G for sample Care Plan.)

(3) Setting Goals

After completing the RAP Summary, the care plan can be developed. Once problems/needs have been prioritized, the next step is to define appropriate goals for each problem/need that is to be addressed.

A goal is what the resident will be doing when the problem/need has been resolved. Each goal should be *realistic*, *measurable*, and *individualized* with an *expected target date*. (Oftentimes, it is helpful to select the next review date as a target date.)

There is much confusion about the difference between short-term goals and long-term goals. A long-term goal is a general statement of what is expected in the future. Short-term goals are the specific steps necessary to achieve the long-term goal. The long-term goal is the highest attainable level of independence. If the resident's status changes, rewrite the long-term goal.

Goals should be reviewed with each residents and he/she must agree to the treatment plan. If possible, it is also helpful to have residents take responsibility for meeting some or all of the goals. For this reason, it is important to write positive goal statements and avoid the use of maintenance goals such as "Maintain present level of activities." Instead, it is better to try to focus on action verbs such as prepare, respond, select, understand, describe.

(4) Plan of Approach

Goals are continually reevaluated, revised, resolved, or considered unresolvable. Due to the progressively deteriorating nature of some residents' conditions, it may be necessary to scale down goals to the simplest forms. For example, a goal for a nonresponsive resident might be to establish eye contact in response to the use of his/her name.

For each goal, the interdisciplinary care team must identify various plans of approach. A plan of approach is basically the staff interventions that will be tried to accomplish the goal. In this step, it is important to use information gathered during the assessment process, such as likes and dislikes, to develop an appropriate plan of action. It is also important to note the disciplines responsible for the plan. Here is where the concept of using of activities as therapy for residents and not just as diversionary uses of time becomes apparent.

Guidelines for Consideration in Developing a Plan of Approach

- Be specific as to type of activity to be utilized.
- Document expected frequency of participation.
- Explain type of approach to be used, i.e., friendly with much encouragement.
- Type of participation, i.e., individualized, small group, large group.
- Adaptive equipment needed.
- Others who may assist such as other staff members, volunteers, family, friends (Cunninghis, 1982).

Before developing a plan of approach, the activities director must check to see if the physician has ordered activities and if so, noting specific guidelines such as "resident may only participate in passive activities."

If a subpart of the activities section of the MDS triggers on the RAP Summary, it must be addressed on the care plan, unless otherwise indicated. If activities do not trigger on the MDS, activities can contribute to the care plan by assisting with another problem area or loss of ADL functioning, i.e., independence in ambulation, eating, grooming, range of motion, toileting. In this way, activities are a part of every resident's care plan.

Therefore a specific activity plan of approach must be documented for each resident unless otherwise indicated in the progress notes, i.e., "resident refuses to participate in planned group activities. Will continue to encourage resident to participate in individual and small group activities." Remember the content of the care plan is more important than the format. Care plans must be current and include all changes in condition (see Appendix G for sample Care Plan)

(5) Evaluation or Progress Notes

A progress note is the evaluation of the plan of approach. It is a statement of what is being done to help the resident solve his/her problems while meeting the established goals. The progress note documents progress or lack of progress for each specific plan of approach. All information on the care plan must be reviewed, evaluated, and documented in the progress notes.

If the approach was not successful and the goal was not met, the care plan should be revised and the new plan of approach described in the progress notes. If the goal was met, then a new approach should be introduced.

Although each state requires activity progress notes to be written at varying intervals, these standards are to be considered the minimum expectation, and not the maximum. Activity progress notes should be written at least every 90 days. A good practice is to write progress notes on or before the next care conference. In this way, care plans have been reviewed and progress notes are guaranteed to be timely. Any change in the resident's physical, mental, or social functioning must be documented. In addition, it is best to document any extraordinary incident that may occur such as a disturbing visit from a relative.

When documenting, remember to ask, "What is good practice?" as opposed to merely meeting regulatory guidelines. In writing progress notes, it may be helpful to consider:
- What was the resident's participation in the prescribed activity?
- How well has the resident achieved stated goals?
- What is the opinion of the activities director?
- What is the present plan of approach? (Post, 1986)

Another approach to writing activity progress notes might be:
- Who is the resident?
- What is the problem/need?
- What is being done to solve the problem/ meet the need?

(See Appendix H for sample Activity Progress Notes.)

OTHER FORMS OF DOCUMENTATION

It is important that the activities director also check for the following:
- Are there any dietary restrictions that should be noted?
- Is there a physician's order for outside activities?
- If alcoholic beverages are served, is there a physician's order?
- Did the resident and/or responsible party sign a permission slip for the resident to participate in outside activities?
- Did the resident and/or responsible party sign a photo release form to give permission for the resident's photograph to be used for educational or public relations purposes?

Record-Keeping

In addition to the required documentation on the medical record, the following items are also needed.

Calendars

Monthly calendars should be posted throughout the facility in conspicuous locations. Calendars should be neat and clearly written, stating the activity, scheduled time, and location.

Each resident should also receive a copy of the activity calendar as a reminder of upcoming events. Calendars should be kept on file for at least one year.

DAILY RECORD OF RESIDENT PARTICIPATION

To aid in future documenting, a daily record of resident participation is maintained. This form will assist in noting changes (increases/decreases) in resident involvement (see Appendix I for sample Daily Record of Residents Participation).

Resident File

A Cardex system can be utilized for easy access to important information. For this system to be effective, it is necessary to update this information periodically. The following is a listing of items that can be maintained in a cardex system.

- Birthday File
  Residents' birthdays can be listed on separate cards by month. In this way, monthly birthdays are listed together for ready use.
- Dietary Restrictions
  A separate card noting residents with dietary restrictions. This card can then be duplicated and distributed to staff, family members, and volunteers at special functions to avoid confusion regarding who may or may not have cake, ice cream, and so forth.
- Religion
  Separate cards can be used to identify the various religious affiliations of residents. Again, these cards can then be used by staff and volunteers who may be assisting in transporting residents to a particular religious program.
- Alcohol
  Maintain a card with the names of those residents who have alcohol restrictions.
- Outside Activities
  Maintain a card with the names of those residents who may not participate in outside activities.

REQUIREMENTS

OBRA represents significant changes in long-term care requirements. Two underlying themes are emphasized in the new regulations; empowerment of the resident and quality of care.

With the enactment of OBRA, surveyors are now instructed to put themselves in the place of the resident and to view the facility from that perspective.

The survey procedures for activities are as follows:

A. Observe individual, group and bedside activities.
  - If residents sit for long periods of time with no apparently meaningful activities, is the cause:
    - Resident choice;
    - Failure of staff either to inform residents when activities are occurring or to encourage resident involvement in activities;
    - Lack of transportation; and/or
    - Program design that fails to reflect the interests or ability levels of residents, such as activities that are too complex?
  - Are residents who are confined to their rooms provided with in-room activities in keeping with life-long interests (e.g., music, reading, visits with people with shared interests) and in-room projects that they can work on independently? Does staff assist residents with activities they cannot pursue independently?
  - Do activities occur as posted?
  - During the course of the survey, are all activities attended by the same residents or are activities designed to meet the functioning levels, needs, and interests of different residents?
  - What input do residents have in their schedule and type of activities?
  - Are adaptations made so that all residents can participate in the activity, including augmenting activities into simple steps for residents with dementia?
  - Are residents with Alzheimer's type dementia engaged in structured activities, such as music events, gross motor games, or outdoor walks?
  - Are residents provided with verbal cues and demonstration when unable to complete tasks by themselves?

For sampled residents, determine to what extent the activities reflect the individual resident's assessment (see especially MDS III.1 and Sections B, C, D, and I). For interviewable residents, ask them if they enjoy the activities in which they are involved.

B. Review the activity calendar for the month prior to the survey to determine if the activity program:
- Reflects interests identified by the comprehensive assessment;
- Offers activities at hours convenient to the residents (morning, afternoon, some evenings and weekends);
- Reflects the cultural and religious interests of the resident population;
- Appeals to both men and women and all age groups living in the facility;
- Takes place in a variety of locations (i.e., indoor/outdoor and community-based activities); and,
- Includes seasonal and special events.

C. Review medical records and activity attendance records of sampled residents to determine if:
- Activities reflect individual resident history indicated by the comprehensive assessment;
- Care plans address activities that are appropriate for each resident based on the comprehensive assessment;
- Activities occur as planned; and,
- Outcomes/responses to activities interventions are identified in the progress notes of each resident.

If there are problems with provision of activities, determine if these services are provided by qualified staff (Department of Health and Human Services: Health Care Financing Administration, 1992).

Additional changes that may affect activities include:
- The use of the word "patient" is no longer acceptable; all shall be referred to as residents.
- Resident rights have been revised (see Appendix B for sample Resident Rights).
- The use of physical and chemical restraints has been reduced. Restraints are used only when no other alternative is feasible. All staff must understand that wandering is acceptable if it is not detrimental to the resident or problematic to other residents.

- To ensure quality of life, many facilities have established a quality assurance committee and program.

Quality Assurance

What is quality assurance? Quality assurance is minimally defined as a process to ensure regulation compliance.

Conceptually, quality assurance is interrelated with quality of life. What is quality of life? It is the good life; it is living the best life one can. Sylvester (1989) noted five characteristics in his attempt to implement the concept of quality.

1. Autonomy and Control—being responsible for self;
2. Choice—choosing a certain kind of life;
3. Competence—leading to feelings of increased self-esteem and self-worth;
4. Virtue—using one's expressive qualities; and,
5. Community—sharing and contributing.

A basic component of a quality assurance program is in the identification of the important aspects of care the organization delivers.

The quality assurance program includes:
- Aspects of Care—standards;
- Indicators—outcome, criteria, or measurements; and,
- Threshold—range of acceptability; 0 percent to 100 percent

(see Appendix J for sample Quality Assurance Program for Activities.)

To establish a quality assurance program, it is important to:
- Review all pertinent regulations;
- Review literature on how to improve quality of care and services;
- Identify isolated problems;
- Look for trends or patterns of problems;
- Develop effective action plans to correct problems;
- Follow-up on action plans;
- Note improvement; and,
- Increase thresholds and standards on a regular basis.

PROGRAM EVALUATION

The quality assurance program is one way to evaluate the effectiveness of the activities program. However, there is still a tendency in long-term care facilities to try to fit residents into existing programs. It is important to look at the total environment and all available resources and then design a program to meet the needs and interests of all residents. Activities should be viewed as a means to providing quality of life and not just as blocks of time that must be filled.

Program evaluation can assist in this process. Some approaches to program evaluation include:

A. Evaluation Using Established Standards

Quality assurance is a method of establishing standards of care and then comparing the existing program with the established standard. You may wish to also compare your program with other established guidelines developed by professional organizations, or other standards found in research on long-term, aging, care and recreation (see Chapter 4).

B. Goal-Oriented Evaluation

This approach is similar to the process of developing resident care plans. Departmental goals are established based on problems/needs. Goals should be *reasonable*, *measurable*, and *individualized* with a *specific target date*.

It is important to discuss departmental goals with the administrator to ensure that the goals are in line with his or her expectations and the overall plan for the facility. Some organizations are currently basing salary increases on goal achievement.

When using this approach, it may be helpful to prioritize the goals. Remember to consider all aspects of the department.

A typical list of goals might include:

GOALS	TARGET DATES
1. Schedule remotivation therapy two times weekly	JAN 31st
2. Initiate monthly activities staff training program	FEB 15th
3. Plan volunteer recognition	APR 30th
4. Clean out storage areas and prepare inventory of supplies	JUN 30th
5. Revise and update policy/procedure manual	OCT 1st

This method also aids in continually motivating the staff for results. Remember to review and update goals on a regular basis.

C. Evaluation By Others

Sometimes it is helpful to find out how others perceive the activities program. Surveying others on the strengths and weaknesses of the programs may be helpful. Remember not to be defensive. Those individuals outside the department will give a different perspective. The following are some individuals who might be included in the evaluation process:

- administrator,
- director of nursing,
- activity consultant,
- other activities directors (peer review),
- staff of the activities department,
- residents,
- family members,
- volunteers, and
- recreation professional from recreation department of local college or university.

In addition, involvement in a local activity professionals group will provide opportunities for networking, sharing activity calendars and other resources.

D. Resident Needs Assessment

Identify several categories of residents; (i.e. alert, oriented; lacks motivation; confused). (You may select as many categories as necessary.) From the total resident population, determine the number and percentage of residents in each category. Then analyze the present activity schedule. Do the scheduled programs meet the needs/interests of these categories? For example, if you determined that

40 percent of the resident population were confused with a limited attention span, then the activity schedule should reflect the needs/interests of that group. Sensory training, reality orientation, reminiscing, simple games, music, cooking class, exercise class, etc., would be the primary types of activities planned (Bachner and Cornelius, 1978).

E. Time Management Approach

Have each staff member maintain a time diary for one week. Analyze the use of time, looking carefully for time-consumers.

Consider the following:
1. Reschedule and reassign duties based on staff strengths.
2. Utilize part-time activity aides instead of full-time staff.
3. Avoid the overlapping of duties.
4. Streamline extra work. Organize correspondence into that which is filed, discarded, or acted upon.
5. Monitor nonrelated duties.
6. Maintain lists of things to do (e.g., daily, tomorrow, next week, special projects).

F. Set Priorities

List all duties and responsibilities and set priorities of which are the most important.

Evaluation is a continual process. Always ask yourself, "Is this the best I can do? Have I done everything that I can?" Remember to start small and build rather than expecting too much all at once. Be flexible. You have the tremendous opportunity to shape the environment and contribute to the residents' overall well-being.

Summary

The focus of this chapter was on proper documentation techniques. The issue of documentation was approached as a five-part process that is essential for effective program planning. Practical suggestions were presented for the completion of required documentation.

In addition, suggestions were given for other types of record keeping. A discussion of the survey process helps the activities director understand how the requirements are interpreted.

The last section of the chapter addressed the issue of quality assurance and different methods of program evaluation were reviewed.

LEARNING EXERCISES

1. Review and analyze the forms that are presently used by the activities department in a long term care facility. What are the advantages and disadvantages of each of the forms? How can the documentation process be revised to be more effective?
2. What forms of record-keeping have you found to be useful?
3. Obtain several different quality assurance programs that are used in other facilities. Compare and contrast the activities section of each program. Make suggestions for improving the quality assurance program that you presently use.

References

Bachner, J. P., and Cornelius, E. (1978). *Activities coordinator's guide*. (HCFA-HSQB 78-004). Washington, DC: Department of Health, Education, and Welfare, Health Care Financing Administration, Health Standards and Quality Bureau.

Cunninghis, R.N. (1982). *The art of documentation: A "how-to" manual for activities personnel* (2nd ed.). Willingboro, NJ: Geriatric Education Consultant.

Department of Health and Human Services: Health Care Financing Administration. (1989, February 2). *Federal Register / Rules and Regulations, 54*(21). Washington, DC: U.S. Government Printing Office.

Department of Health and Human Services: Health Care Financing Administration. (1992). *Guidance to surveyors—long-term care facilities*. Washington, DC: U.S. Government Printing Office.

Florida Association of Homes for the Aging. (1990, June). *Resident Assessment Systems: Utilization Guidelines*. Tallahassee, FL.

Olsson, R. H. Jr. (1986). Managing your documentation: A systems approach. *Activities, Adaptations & Aging, 9*(1), 93-100.

Post, M. S. (1986). If it isn't written, it isn't done: How to formulate individual treatment plans. *Activities, Adaptations & Aging, 9*(1), 85-92.

Sylvester, C. (1989). Quality assurance and quality of life: Accounting for the good and healthy life. *Therapeutic Recreation Journal, 23*(2), 7-22.

Programming

What is a Good Activities Program?

A common concern among activities directors in long-term care facilities is the question, "What is a good activities program?" Too often, because of a lack of understanding, a good activities program is described as one in which large groups of residents are gathered together for bingo, entertainment, or a special party. Only after close scrutiny does one notice that this kind of program involves only a small percentage of higher functioning residents while the majority of residents receive little or no activity contact. The irony of this situation is two-fold. First, the residents who need the most stimulation receive the least. Second, if we were to compare our own leisure lifestyle with that of nursing home residents, we would find the situation to be unappealing, unnatural, and probably unacceptable.

A necessary ingredient to a good activities program is that it be based on the previous lifestyles of the individual residents and their current needs and interests.

The interpretive guidelines of the OBRA regulations state:

Because the activities program should occur within the context of each resident's comprehensive assessment and care plan, it should be multifaceted and reflect each individual resident's needs. Therefore, the activities program should provide stimulation or solace; promote physical, cognitive and/or emotional health; enhance to the extent practicable each resident's physical and mental status; and promote each resident's self-respect by providing, for example, activities that allow for self-expression, personal responsibility and choice" (Department of Health and Human Services: Health Care Financing Administration, 1992).

Therefore, a good activities program offers a variety of individual and group activities to meet the needs of all residents regardless of their physical, mental or psychosocial functioning.

The number of possible activities that are available is endless. Several texts including Bachner and Cornelius (1978), Hamill and Oliver (1980), Beisgen (1989), and Bowlby (1993) offer extensive lists of activities from which to choose. This chapter will focus on understanding activities and their importance and developing programs that make a difference.

ACTIVITY ANALYSIS

Often the selection of activities is done without much thought. Traditional and routine programs are carried over from one month to the next and others are chosen based on staff skills and interests, program availability, and budget considerations. Activity analysis is a systematic method of breaking down and examining the activity to find characteristics that contribute to program objectives. Activity analysis also makes us aware of what skills are required to be able to participate in the program and what modifications may be needed.

Gunn and Peterson (1984) offer suggestions for analyzing activities. They stress the importance of understanding the four behavioral areas (physical, cognitive, affective, and social) that are involved, regardless of the activity.

The physical aspects of an activity are complex and include sensory requirements, gross and fine motor abilities, coordination, strength, and endurance. Cognitive abilities are also important and include comprehension, memory, concentration, language, and intellectual skills.

There are no set affective or emotional requirements. Residents may respond to a particular activity in a variety of ways based on their own lifetime experiences. Carefully selected activities can facilitate appropriate expressions of emotion. Social interaction occurs in a variety of activity settings and requires different abilities including communication skills, cooperation and competitive skills (Gunn and Peterson, 1984).

In addition to using activity analysis to accurately select appropriate programs to meet the residents' predetermined goals and objectives; other factors to consider include the age-appropriateness of the activity; number of residents to be served; available facilities, supplies, and equipment; staff skills; and the carry-over value of lifestyle habits (Gunn and Peterson, 1984).

Although the activities director typically does not have the time to analyze each activity, a basic understanding of the process is essential. The behavioral aspects of activity analysis need to be considered when completing resident assessments and when selecting programs (Gunn and Peterson, 1984).

As resident's skills improve or deteriorate, the level of participation and the activity may need modification. Activity analysis will determine the actual participation requirements and level of functioning will be assessed to ascertain the amount and types of modification needed. Regardless of the modification, remember to:

1. Keep the activity as close to the original version as possible.
2. Modify only the aspects of the activity that need to be changed.
3. Adapt to the specific needs of each individual (Gunn and Peterson, 1984).

Changes can be made in the materials, equipment, or method of presentation to enable residents with various limitations to become more involved in the activities program. For example, large print can be used for residents with fine motor skill problems, and simple, repetitive instructions can be used for residents with memory impairments (Bowlby, 1993).

AN ACTIVITIES PROGRAMMING MODEL FOR NURSING HOME RESIDENTS

Tedrick has developed a model that sums up the necessary components of an activities program in a long-term care facility. It includes three levels: the resident, the recreation professional, and the environment (see Figure 6.1). In addition to the resident's needs, the following are aspects of the first level of the model:

- Impairments—physical, sensory, mental, and psychosocial impairments that may affect functional abilities.
- Personal skills—functional abilities that have remained intact.
- Environmental skills—perceived control, choice, and responsibility as well as adaptive and coping skills.
- Background—family, social, educational, cultural, occupational, religious, and leisure history.

This information is part of the assessment process (see Chapter 5).

The second level of the model is the influence of the recreation professional which includes the following factors):

- Professional background—knowledge of activities and their use, knowledge of the aging process, and knowledge of available resources.
- Personality—ability to motivate and to establish relationships with residents, their families, and staff members (see Chapter 4).
- Cohort effect—personal values and attitudes of the recreation professional.

The third level is the influence of the environment which includes:

- Physical environment—available space, equipment, and supplies.
- Role of recreation within the organization—status and importance placed on the recreation program.

- Overall atmosphere—presence of employee motivators (recognition, accomplishment, advancement, growth opportunities, and level of responsibility) and employee maintenance factors (salary, benefits, interpersonal relationships).
- Constraints—regulations and policies that restrict or limit program options.

UNDERSTANDING THE CONCEPT OF LEISURE

The field of gerontology has long recognized the relation of leisure to the well-being and life satisfaction of older persons. Ragheb and Griffith (1982) determined that the higher the frequency of participation in leisure activities, the higher the leisure satisfaction; and the greater the leisure satisfaction, the greater the life satisfaction. They also suggested that leisure satisfaction (the meaning or quality of leisure) contributed more to the life satisfaction of older persons than did leisure participation (the quantity of leisure).

Cutler and Hendricks (1990) note that often the concept of leisure is defined either as a specific time or as an activity. The problem with this approach is that leisure is not looked upon as an integral part of life but more as time left over after work. With the changing nature of work (who works, for how long, and in what capacity) and the increased value that is placed on leisure activities, it is even more imperative that we redefine leisure and begin to look at the concept as a dynamic part of the entire life course. Leisure experiences may change throughout life in their meaning and in time spent. However, many age-related changes in leisure patterns, preferences, and experiences are not determined by developmental changes in the individual but by the opportunities that are available to the person. The same authors make reference to the work of Riley (1987) who suggests that activity participation reflects the individual's expectations and the expectations of others, the individual's social roles, and resources.

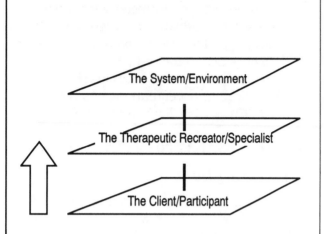

**An Activities Programming Model for
Nursing Home Residents**

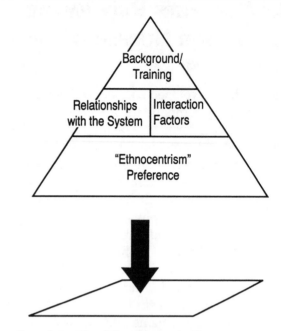

**Level 2: The Therapeutic Recreator/
Specialist**

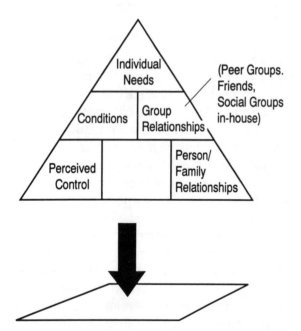

Level 1: The Client/Participant

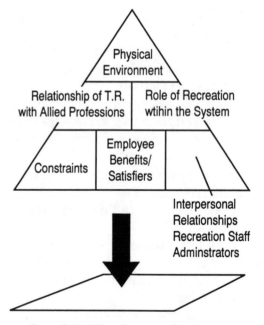

Level 3: The System/Environment

**Figure 6.1
A Model of Exploring Leisure Activity and Older Adults**

Social Theories of Aging

Social roles are addressed in the numerous theories that have been proposed to explain the adjustment to the aging process. These theories also help to explain the relationship of activity participation to life satisfaction.

The disengagement theory formulated by Cumming and Henry (1961) described a mutual withdrawal of older persons and society which resulted in decreased social interaction. While some older persons may respond by withdrawing, it appears that disengagement is neither universal nor inevitable (Atchley, 1977).

Havighurst, Neugarten, and Tobin (1968) proposed the activity theory. According to this theory, adjustment and life satisfaction are related to the individual's ability to maintain the activities of the middle years for as long as possible (Kart, 1980). This approach may be somewhat unrealistic for some older persons and may result in feelings of failure and uselessness (Atchley, 1977).

Atchley (1977) suggests that individuals develop habits, preferences, and other qualities that form their personalities. As they age, individuals tend to maintain continuity in habits, associations, and preferences. This approach is referred to as the continuity theory. Throughout the life course, these characteristics adapt to changes in physical and psychological capabilities, opportunities, and resources. Atchley further added that individuals define themselves by their social roles, and these roles have an impact on self-concept, how the person sees himself or herself, and on self-esteem, how the person feels about himself or herself. According to Davis (1982), leisure activities provide opportunities for role continuity among older persons.

Seleen (1982) offers yet another explanation of the leisure patterns of older persons. Her "congruency theory" predicts that life satisfaction and leisure satisfaction are related to how well leisure patterns fit leisure needs. In essence, the theory states that life satisfaction depends on how well actual use of time matches the desired use of time.

Program Planning

One way to approach program planning is to look at the age cohort factor. This factor refers to the tendency of people born during the same time period to share common behavioral, attitudinal, and value characteristics. This occurs because people of the same age have typically shared similar experiences (such as historical events and social conditions), and these experiences help to shape behaviors, attitudes, and values. Even though each individual may have unique experiences due to personality and cultural differences, the age cohort factor is useful as a basis for activity program planning (Walz and Blum, 1988).

According to the same authors, those individuals born in the early part of the twentieth century typically share some of the following characteristics:

1. A strong work ethic;
2. A religious, family, and patriotic orientation;
3. Distinct sex roles;
4. A view of leisure as rest from work;
5. A respect for food as a necessity for survival;
6. Sex as a private, personal matter for reproductive purposes;
7. Time restricted by weather and seasonal changes and not ruled by clocks;
8. A respect for nature; and,
9. A belief in rugged individualism.

Based on these characteristics, Walz and Blum (1988) developed guidelines for activity programming that include:

1. Work-based activities including service projects and activities that produce functional and useful items such as baking, needlework, and woodworking.
2. Food-centered activities and holiday and special event celebrations that incorporate family traditions, customs, and patriotism.
3. Religious activities including music, Bible classes, clergy visits, and the recognition of religious holidays.

4. Time allotted for rest and reflection which is viewed as leisure time by older persons.
5. Respect for gender differences by including same sex as well as mixed group activities. Also, offering gender-appropriate activities for men and women.
6. Encouraging self-directed activities rather than strict adherence to time schedules.
7. Intergenerational and family-oriented activities.
8. Nature-based activities including the care of house plants, gardening, and pets.

These kinds of programs not only afford older persons the opportunity to use their existing skills and expertise, but they also can elicit comforting memories of past experiences.

Although these guidelines suggest programs that are familiar to the activities director, their value is often overlooked. This may be due to the fact that the activities director represents a different cohort group with a much different orientation to leisure. Also, residents' cooperation and compliance with scheduled programs may be due to a respect for authority and not an indication of enjoyment and satisfaction (Walz and Blum, 1988).

Cutler and Hendricks (1990) report that it is sometimes difficult to distinguish between leisure activities and obligatory activities when the activity is viewed from a perspective other than the participant's actual perception. Therefore, it is not surprising that the activities director's perception of resident satisfaction may not always reflect what the resident may actually report. This problem can be minimized by involving residents in the program planning process and using the residents' council meetings as a forum to question residents about their satisfaction with the time, number, and variety of activities offered.

The attitudes of those working with the older persons, according to Beisgen (1989), also influences the older person's own attitudes. By conveying a positive attitude, the older person will make an increased effort to maintain his or her independence and level of activity. The activities director is challenged to maximize the strengths and minimize the weaknesses of the nursing home resident.

Both Miller (1965) and Lawton (1985) suggest that the expectations of older persons may, in fact, limit their leisure pursuits to passive activities. The older person in a nursing home setting may have limited leisure interests; he or she may be at a point in time when competency is questioned and when feelings of inadequacy, embarrassment, or the prospects of failure need to be minimized.

LEISURE EDUCATION

Leisure education is an important aspect of programming activities in a long-term care facility. Programs are planned to meet the needs of the residents. Sometimes these needs are to increase functional abilities. In this situation, activities are therapeutic and are designed to maintain or restore abilities. If the resident needs to have opportunities to express and use existing skills, activities are planned for recreational purposes. And, at times the activities director becomes a teacher and counselor by encouraging the resident to learn new leisure skills and attitudes. This process is known as leisure education (Gunn and Peterson, 1984).

According to Gunn and Peterson (1984), the process of leisure education includes four major areas:

1. developing an awareness of leisure values and attitudes;
2. developing social interaction skills;
3. developing leisure activity skills; and,
4. developing knowledge of leisure resources.

In developing an awareness of leisure values and attitudes, the individual must address feelings about leisure, skills, abilities, and limitations. To do this the activities director uses counseling techniques to facilitate conversation. In developing social interaction skills the activities director again uses counseling techniques to give the individual feedback on his or her ability to interact in small or large groups, either cooperatively or competitively. The activities director can also serve as or make available appropriate role models. In developing leisure activity skills, the activities director teaches specific activity skills that are suitable for the participant based on needs, interests, and limitations. In developing knowledge of leisure resources, the activities director guides the individual to available in-house and community resources that can be used independently and/or offers assistance, supervision, or necessary adaptations.

Leisure education enables the individual to acquire meaningful skills and attitudes. This process is especially important in long-term care facilities because it promotes resident independence and fosters feelings of control. Numerous studies, Langer and Rodin (1976) and Iso-Ahola (1980), have shown that increasing nursing home residents' perceived responsibility and control enhances their physical and psychological well-being, mental alertness and interpersonal activities. Seligman (1975) has shown that a person may feel helpless in situations where he or she has no control. This feeling, which he called "learned helplessness" can lead to despair, apathy, and dejection. Recreation programs in long-term care facilities are not simply a means of occupying residents' time but are a way to help residents look forward to a future of enjoying life in a supportive social environment.

PROGRAM SUGGESTIONS

Beisgen (1989) offered the following program suggestion for the mentally impaired. These suggestions have application to any long-term care setting:
- Plan activities that rely on old skills and result in success.
- Take a break between programs.
- Simplify each activity and give instructions one step at a time.
- Demonstrate or show an example of the completed project.
- Repeat successful programs.

- Match the activity to the resident's abilities.
- Adapt the activity to the resident's needs.
- Offer assistance when needed and anticipate difficulties.
- Give praise and compliment efforts.
- Plan daily activities around a specific theme.
- Provide a calm, supportive, nonthreatening environment.
- Ask for resident input in planning programs.
- Be flexible.
- Incorporate variety into programming by including the following kinds of activities:
    Physical
    Competitive
    Mentally/Intellectually Stimulating
    Personal Care
    Spiritual
    Health Maintenance
    Social
    Sensory
    Service Projects
    Intergenerational
    Cultural
    Pets
    Creative
    Community (In or Out of the Facility)
    Entertaining

It is also important to encourage independent activities as well as to offer small group, large group, and one-to-one activities. Independent activities provide residents with opportunities to continue lifelong pursuits such as reading and hobbies. Small group activities offer intellectually stimulating conversation, competition, and cooperation which leads to improved self-esteem. Large group activities create a sense of community and provide entertainment and social interaction (DeBolt and Kastner, 1989).

For those residents who are unwilling or unable to participate in group activities, one-to-one programs enable these individuals to receive stimulation and the attention they may need to participate in activities. One-to-one activities should be part of the activity schedule and may also include residents who do participate in group activities but may require more individualized care. Many of the group activities offered can be provided in a one-to-one format. The basis of one-to-one activities is the establishment of a trusting, accepting, and understanding relationship between the staff member and the individualized resident (DeBolt and Kastner, 1989).

THE AGING PROCESS AND ITS IMPLICATIONS FOR ACTIVITIES

In order to plan an activities program based on residents' needs, it is important to have a basic understanding of the aging process. Although certain aspects of aging are common to many older persons, Atchley (1987) cautions the reader to remember:

Aging is not one experience but many.

The elderly are typically capable.

Aging can have both positive and negative results.

Aging is greatly affected by the individual's sex, social class, race, and place of residence.

Physical Aspects

Numerous theories have been proposed attempting to explain the aging process. These theories focus on age-related declines of the major body systems and organ reserve capacity due to either genetic or external factors. No one theory has yet to explain the cause of physiologic aging of why certain physical changes occur. The first signs of aging are changes in the individual's appearance (such as skin, hair, and body shape). Such changes affect the self-concept of the older person. Although aging and disease are not synonymous, there are age-related declines in the major body systems, organ reserve capacity, and immune system. These changes make older people more susceptible to chronic illness and extends the recovery time (Berger, 1988).

Changes in the central nervous system may affect sleeping patterns and reaction time. These changes are normal and are highly variable. Reaction time depends on individual's past experiences, his or her motivation to perform the task, and the complexity of the task. The overall impact of slower reaction time is minimal and results in only slight alterations in function (Clarke-Stewart, Perlmutter, and Friedman, 1988).

Degenerative changes occur in the functioning of the cardiopulmonary system. The system operates less efficiently and chances of heart attacks and strokes increase because of insufficient blood supply to the heart and brain. Poor diet, lack of exercise, smoking and weight problems all contribute to these changes (Clarke-Stewart, Perlmutter, and Friedman, 1988).

The musculoskeletal system which facilitates movement and protects and supports the body also experiences decline with age. Muscles begin to atrophy; bones become more porous and less hard; and the connective tissues around joints loses strength and elasticity. The effects of these changes can be minimized by a regular exercise regimen including: stretching, weight-bearing, and strengthening activities (Teague and MacNeil, 1992).

Sensory Aspects

With increasing age, sensory impairments become more problematic. Declines in vision, hearing, taste, smell, and touch can severely restrict a person's mobility, communication, self-care, and sense of independence. Medical technology has advanced the prevention and treatment of sensory impairments, but sensory decline is still a major problem for older persons (Teague and MacNeil, 1992).

The following can help in understanding sensory impairments:

1. Sensory changes are gradual and rarely occur suddenly except in the case of an accident or serious illness.
2. Multiple losses (vision and hearing) are more difficult to cope with than single losses.

3. Older persons develop compensatory mechanisms to adapt to their losses and declines.

4. Even though most older persons have some degree of sensory loss, this does not imply dysfunction.

Kart (1990) gives a thorough explanation of age-related sensory changes which include:

Vision

- Diminished ability to focus on near objects (farsightedness)
- A yellowing effect creating difficulty in distinguishing certain colors, especially blue, green, and violet
- Cataracts resulting in blurred or dimmed vision
- Glaucoma, a response to increased pressure within the eyeball, can lead to optic nerve damage and blindness
- Loss of peripheral vision (tunnel-vision)

Hearing

- Decreased selective attention, the ability to focus on particular stimuli in the environment while ignoring others. This may affect the individual's ability to screen out distractions.
- Presbycusis, a loss of ability to distinguish high frequency sounds which affects communication skills
- Accumulated ear wax may impair hearing ability
- Genetic conditions, exposure to loud noise, certain drugs, and chronic ear infections which can cause conductive or perceptive types of hearing losses

Taste, Smell, and Touch

- Disease, certain drugs, smoking habits, and other environmental conditions which may cause a diminished ability to discriminate smells and tastes
- Loss of taste resulting in food complaints and poor appetite
- Loss of smell resulting in body odor and inability to discern spoiled food, smoke and other hazards

- Some decline in touch sensitivity may result in tendency to drop objects or difficulty in grasping items
- Increased tolerance for pain

Vision and hearing losses are much more critical than losses in taste, smell, or touch to functioning ability. Careful consideration to size of print, placement of objects, and use of color can help the older person deal with the loss of vision. Hearing loss may lead to social isolation and depression. Proper fit and maintenance of a hearing aid can compensate for some of the hearing problems. For other individuals with problems in discriminating sounds, hearing aids only offer amplification of sounds and not clarification. In addition, the older person may have grown accustomed to abnormal hearing and may find the normal sounds of daily living to be annoying. Speaking clearly and distinctly; avoiding glare from the sun or from artificial lighting; and using gestures may help the older person overcome the effects of hearing loss. Removing noisy distractions and minimizing background sounds can also aid in communicating with the hearing impaired older person. Encouraging residents to season food and adjusting menus to their specific food preferences may reduce the number of food complaints. Special cooking programs can provide "home-style" treats to please even the most discriminating appetite. Personal care activities can stress the importance of good hygiene habits and the need to change clothing often. Good grooming habits affect self-esteem and social interaction. A loss of feeling may result in residents being unaware of cuts, scrapes, and bruises. Be sure to report any noticeable injuries to the nursing staff.

As was previously stated, some of the physiological changes related to the aging process are inevitable. Fortunately, these changes do not significantly interfere with functional capabilities. Other changes that are part of physical aging can be minimized by modifying lifestyle habits such as diet, exercise, stress management, and rest. Recreation programs provide enjoyment and this is what motivates the individual to continue doing activities that promote good health in later years (Teague and MacNeil, 1992).

COGNITIVE ASPECTS

There appears to be some decline in cognitive abilities associated with advancing age. However, this decline, unless associated with disease, is slight and only affects some individuals. The decline in sensory abilities may be responsible for some of the changes in learning, thinking and remembering (Clarke-Stewart, Perlmutter, and Friedman, 1988).

Cognitive abilities may also be affected by a reduction in the supply of oxygenated blood, a decrease in the number of neurons in the central nervous system, disease, chronic pain, poor nutrition, social isolation, and other age-related conditions (Teague and MacNeil, 1992).

The same authors noted several misconceptions about changes in the cognitive functioning of older persons. These misconceptions suggest that older persons experience a reduction in learning ability, increased forgetfulness, and increases in confusion and disorientation.

Given the above observations about cognitive functioning, there are several instructional considerations to be taken into account:

• Older persons need more time to learn and process information.
• The more anxious the individual feels, the less likely he or she will perform well.
• Older persons are especially vulnerable to distraction.
• Older persons are more cautious and less willing to take risks.
• Continual reinforcement and practice is necessary.
• Motivation influences performance.
• Memory abilities decrease slightly with increasing age (Clarke-Stewart, Perlmutter, and Friedman, 1988).

Learning can be enhanced by using certain techniques such as repetition, continual reinforcement, practice, focusing on one item at a time, oral presentations, and avoiding disruptive stimuli (Teague and MacNeil, 1992).

Some decline in cognitive abilities is a normal aspect of the aging process. A small percentage of older persons have brain disorders that interfere with their functioning abilities. These disorders may be functional disturbances caused by personality factors or life experiences. There may also be organic disturbances which have physical causes. Regardless of the cause, brain disorders have similar symptoms whether slight or profound with slow or rapid progression (Teague and MacNeil, 1992).

According to Butler and Lewis (1982), the symptoms of brain disorders include:
1. Impaired memory—problems registering, retaining or recalling information.
2. Impaired intellectual function—difficulty understanding facts.
3. Impaired judgement—difficulty understanding personal situation.
4. Impaired orientation—to time, place or person.
5. Exaggerated or shallow emotions.

The most common cause of organic disorders is senile dementia, which includes Alzheimer's disease, a progressive, irreversible illness that results in alteration of the brain cells. The disease is characterized by a proliferation of abnormalities in the cerebral cortex, called plaques and tangles, that impair the brain's functional ability. Other causes of organic disorders include multi-infarct dementia (obstruction of the blood vessels preventing sufficient blood circulation to the brain), brain tumors, and Parkinson's disease (Berger, 1988).

Nonorganic problems, often misdiagnosed as some form of senile dementia, are considered to be reversible because the disorientation, restlessness and other symptoms are generally alleviated when the causative factors are removed. Some of the factors that contribute to nonorganic problems include head trauma, drugs, alcohol, infection, diabetes, and congestive heart failure (Teague and MacNeil, 1992).

PSYCHOSOCIAL ASPECTS

Functional disorders have no physical (organic) cause and their origin seems to be emotional relating to personality factors or lifestyle experiences (Atchley, 1987).

Anxiety, paranoia, schizophrenia, and depression are considered functional disorders. Depression is the most common functional disorder associated with older persons, yet it is not often diagnosed. Depression can vary in duration and degree and may be triggered by the multiple losses older persons suffer—such as health, spouse, family and friends, status, roles, income, residence (Kart, 1990).

The symptoms of depression include mood changes, loss of interest in daily activities, loss of appetite, disturbance of sleep, agitation or lethargy, feelings of worthlessness, guilt and suicidal thoughts or behavior (Atchley, 1987). Functional depression is treatable. Drug therapy is the most popular treatment of depression in older persons (Kart, 1990).

Functional disorders in older persons may actually be a carry over from earlier years. Atchley (1987) relates depression in the elderly to what Erikson calls the final stage of psychosocial development, ego integrity versus despair. Integrity involves being able to look at one's life as having been meaningful and accepting the positive and negative dimensions of one's self. Despair is the result of rejection of one's self and results in the potential for depression. In addition, Atchley points out that if older people are satisfied with present and past lives, they have adapted to aging.

Berger (1988) explains that for many older persons the later years are a time for greater enjoyment of nature and the arts. Heightened appreciation leads to active expressions in various creative endeavors. In addition, individuals tend to become more philosophical as they age.

Life review or reminiscence is a process in which the older person recalls various aspects of his or her life and compares the past with the present. For some people the life review process leads to resolution of conflicts and is a way of putting one's life into perspective. The life review, done either as an oral history or written autobiography, is a valuable psychological experience for the older person, as well as family members (Berger, 1988).

SPECIALIZED PROGRAMS

Most of the activities offered in nursing homes tend to be familiar programs that would be suitable for individuals of any age regardless of their place of residence. As a result, few programs are truly unique to this setting.

There are a number of different therapies such as music, horticulture, movement, and creative arts that are sometimes used in the rehabilitative process. Specific therapies such as these are generally initiated by specially trained individuals, but some of the techniques can also be incorporated into the activities program (Weiner, Brok, and Snadowsky, 1978).

Both Beisgen (1989) and Bowlby (1993) offer suggestions for various therapeutic activities that can be used. The quarterly journal, *Activities, Adaptation & Aging*, is also another reference for therapeutic activity ideas. In addition, it may be helpful to contact local colleges and universities that offer courses in the different therapies for program suggestions and to recruit volunteers and/or student interns.

In addition, several rehabilitation approaches have been designed especially for the nursing home resident who has some type of cognitive disorder. Sensory stimulation, reality orientation, and remotivation are treatment modalities that are geared to the lower functioning resident (Weiner, Brok, and Snadowsky, 1978). Another modality is the validation technique which was developed by Naomi Feil and is based on her work with nursing home residents (Beisgen, 1989).

Sensory stimulation is a structured activity for individuals who have difficulty relating or responding to their environment. Cognitive, visual, and hearing impaired, as well as, bedridden residents may benefit from this approach (Beisgen, 1989). Sensory stimulation can be incorporated into other programs or done on a one-to-one basis or in a small group setting. The technique involves using meaningful and familiar objects from the environment to stimulate the five senses. Sensory stimulation activities increase the individual's awareness of the environment and helps the individual recall past memories (Bowlby, 1993).

Reality orientation (RO) is a two-part, consistent, repetitive approach used in orienting confused residents to time, place, and person. One part of RO is a 24-hour approach used by everyone who has contact with the individual resident (Teague and MacNeil, 1992).

This a common sense approach to dealing with cognitive impairments and includes the following guidelines:
- Repeat basic information e.g., (time, day, date, place, name) in conversations.
- Address residents by name.
- Give clear, simple directions to guide residents.

In addition, large-print calendars, easy-to-read clocks, posted daily schedules, up-to-date RO boards, and other environmental cues serve as memory aids and reminders for the confused resident (Beisgen, 1989).

A typical RO board includes:

The facility is:

The city is:

Today is:

The date is:

The year is:

The weather is:

The next holiday is:

The second part of reality orientation is scheduled classes which are usually the responsibility of the activities department. Either one-to-one or small group RO classes should be scheduled for residents who have a need for this type of program. Some residents appear to benefit from constant reminding by all staff who are using a consistent approach.

On the other hand, the validation technique was developed after efforts to reorient confused residents resulted, at times, in withdrawal, hostility, and abusiveness. Validation involves accepting what the person says and empathizing, rather than being argumentative or judgmental (Beisgen, 1989).

Remotivation is a structured program of group discussion used with mildly confused residents and those who lack motivation. The purpose of remotivation is to promote independence, to stimulate residents' interest in thinking and talking about topics in the real world, and to boost their self-esteem. Remotivation topics should be objective and relate to issues that are both familiar and interesting to the residents (e.g., sports, holiday celebrations, school work, fashions, vacations). Avoid using emotionally-charged issues and controversial topics (Weiner, Brok, and Snadowsky, 1978).

To encourage socialization and improve memory, Berliner (1991) offers a list of fifty topics that are guaranteed to increase interaction among residents and staff. The topics are varied and designed to stimulate the senses of nursing home residents.

Each of these rehabilitation techniques is designed to meet the needs of the cognitively impaired residents. Due to the differences in functioning abilities, it is important to match residents with the appropriate program. All of these programs can benefit residents who are unable or unwilling to participate in the regular activities programs. By improving social interaction skills, it is hoped that residents will be able to benefit from other programs that are available (Weiner, Brok, and Snadowsky, 1978).

Teague and MacNeil (1992) offer activity suggestions that relate to the various needs of the older person. They are:

Social needs—the need for companionship and friendship. Examples are parties, trips, dining, entertainment, and coffee hours.

Intellectual needs—the need for stimulation and learning experiences. Examples are quizzes, games, discussion groups, current events, and book reviews.

Creative needs—the need for self-expression, control, and achievement. Examples are arts and crafts, hobbies, and woodworking.

Work-oriented needs—the need for accomplishment and a sense of purpose. Examples are gardening, volunteer service projects, and cooking.

Physical needs—the need for exercise and fitness. Examples are exercise classes, games, and walking.

Recreation needs—the need for fun, enjoyment, and relaxation. Examples are movies, shopping, entertainment, and games.

MEALTIME ACTIVITIES

One-to-one activities were previously discussed as a way to meet the needs of nonparticipants. Another approach is through mealtime activities which offer unique opportunities for involving nonparticipants. Mealtimes involve all residents and offer routine as they occur at the same time every day. In addition, fond memories of family traditions and celebrations generally center around food. Low functioning residents may benefit from one-to-one interaction prior to mealtimes, sensory stimulation using food as the stimuli, and adaptive techniques may increase residents' self-feeding abilities. Higher functioning residents enjoy the social interaction of dining experiences and mealtimes are an opportune time to discuss upcoming programs. Special events may also be incorporated into mealtime experiences.

RESIDENTS' COUNCIL

Residents' Council is a way for residents to be more actively involved in the quality of care which they receive. It is also an opportunity for the activities director to include residents in the program planning process. Minutes of the Residents' Council meetings should be maintained for future reference. The minutes should include date, attendance, staff in attendance, review of Resident Rights, old business,

new business (issues, concerns, problems), and administrative response to old business.

A BALANCED PROGRAM

Every activities director strives for a balanced program of activities. Kaplan (1979) offers some suggestions for a balanced program based on observational evaluations of traditional programs. He suggests that simple, routine, familiar, and peer-oriented programs need to be balanced with complex, novel, varied, and intergenerational programs. These balances along with perceived choice and responsibility can contribute to enhanced quality of life for nursing home residents.

Summary

This chapter addressed the question, "What is a good activities program?" and discusses several approaches that can be used in program planning. The application of activity analysis, the age cohort factor, and leisure education are reviewed.

Part of the chapter focused on the concept of leisure and its relation to life satisfaction and the effects of the aging process. These are essential ingredients to understanding the leisure needs of the older person.

Various program suggestions were incorporated throughout the chapter including therapies, specialized programs, mealtime activities, and Residents' Council as well as an offering of program ideas that address specific resident needs.

LEARNING EXERCISES

1. Select two activities and complete an activity analysis for each one. How can activity analysis be used in program planning?

2. Using the leisure education model, interview a nursing home resident and make recommendations regarding his or her participation in the activities program.

3. Evaluate the existing activities program using Tedrick's model.
4. Make a list of innovative program ideas that can be implemented throughout the coming year.

References

Atchley, R. C. (1977). *The social forces in later life.* Belmont, CA: Wadsworth Publishing Co., Inc.

Atchley, R. C. (1987). *Aging: Continuity and change* (2nd ed.). Belmont, CA: Wadsworth Publishing Company, Inc.

Bachner, J. P. and Cornelius, E. (1978). *Activities coordinator's guide.* (HCFA-HSQB 78-004). Washington, DC: Department of Health, Education, and Welfare, Health Care Financing Administration, Health Standards and Quality Bureau.

Beisgen, B. A. (1989). *Life-enhancing activities for mentally impaired elders: A practical guide.* New York, NY: Springer Publishing Company, Inc.

Berger, K. S. (1988). *The developing person through the life span* (2nd ed.). New York, NY: Worth Publishers, Inc.

Berliner, H. (1991, January/February). Let's talk! *Geriatric Nursing,* pp. 21-22.

Bowlby, C. (1993). *Therapeutic activities with persons disabled by Alzheimer's disease and related disorders.* Gaithersburg, MD: Aspen Publishers, Inc.

Butler, R. and Lewis, M. F. (1982). *Aging and mental health.* St. Louis, MO: The C. V. Mosby Company.

Clarke-Stewart, A., Perlmutter, M., and Friedman, S. (1988). *Lifelong human development.* New York, NY: John Wiley & Sons, Inc.

Cumming, E. and Henry, W. (1961). *Growing old.* New York, NY: Basic Books, Inc., Publishers.

Cutler, S. J. and Hendricks, J. (1990). Leisure and time use across the life course. In R. H. Binstock, and L. K. George (Eds.), *Handbook of aging and the social sciences* (3rd ed.), (pp. 169-185). San Diego, CA: Academic Press, Inc.

Davis, N. B. (1982). The role continuity approach to aging: Implications for leisure programming. In M. L. Teague, R. D. MacNeil and G. L. Hitzhusen (Eds.), *Perspectives on leisure and aging in a changing society,* (pp. 298-318). Columbia, MO: University Printing Services.

DeBolt, N. and Kastner, M. E. (1989). *"I'm in here" Strategies for one-to-one activities.* Torrington, WY: Lutheran Health Systems.

Department of Health and Human Services: Health Care Financing Administration. (1992). *Guidance to surveyors long-term care facilities.* Washington, DC: U.S. Government Printing Office.

Gunn, S. L. and Peterson, C. A. (1984). *Therapeutic recreation program design: Principles and procedures* (2nd ed.). Englewood Cliffs, NJ: Prentice-Hall, Inc.

Hamill, C. M. and Oliver, R. C. (1980). *Therapeutic activities for handicapped elderly.* Rockville, MD: Aspens Systems Corporation.

Havighurst, R. J., Neugarten, B. L., and Tobin, S. S. (1968). Disengagement and patterns of aging. In B. L. Neugarten (Ed.), *Middle age and aging,* (pp. 161-172). Chicago, IL: University of Chicago Press.

Iso-Ahola, S. E. (1980). Perceived control and responsibility as mediators of the effects of therapeutic recreation on the institutionalized aged. *Therapeutic Recreation Journal, 14,* 36-43.

Kaplan, M. (1979). *Leisure: Lifestyle and lifespan: Perspectives for gerontology.* Philadelphia, PA: W. B. Saunders Company.

Kart, C. S. (1990). *The realities of aging: An introduction to gerontology* (3rd ed.). Needham Heights, MA: Allyn & Bacon, Inc.

Langer, E. J. and Rodin, J. (1976). The effects of choice and enhanced personal responsibility for the aged: a field experiment in an institutionalized setting. *Journal of Personality and Social Psychology, 34,* 191-198.

Lawton, M. P. (1985). Activities and leisure. In M. P. Lawton and G. L. Maddox (Eds.), *Annual review of gerontology and geriatrics, 5,* 127-164. New York, NY: Springer Publishing Company, Inc.

Miller, S. J. (1965). The social dilemma of the aging leisure participant. In A. Rose and W. Peterson (Eds.), *Older people and their social world* (pp. 77-92). Philadelphia, PA: Davis.

Ragheb, M. and Griffith, C. (1982). The contribution of leisure participation and leisure satisfaction to life satisfaction of older persons. *Journal of Leisure Research, 14*(4), 295-306.

Riley, M. (1987). On the significance of age in sociology. *American Sociological Review, 52,* 1-14.

Seleen, D. R. (1982). The congruence between activity and desired use of time by older adults: A predictor of life satisfaction. *The Gerontologist, 22,* 95-99.

Seligman, M. E. P. (1975). *Helplessness: On depression, development and death.* San Francisco, CA: W. H. Freeman & Co., Publishers.

Teague, M. L. and MacNeil, R. D. (1992). *Aging and leisure: Vitality in later life* (2nd ed.). Dubuque, IA: Brown & Benchmark.

Walz, T. H. and Blum, N. S. (1988). The age cohort factor in activities programming for the elderly. *Activities, Adaptation & Aging, 12*(1/2), 1-12.

Weiner, M. B. Brok, A. J., and Snadowsky, A. M. (1978). *Working with the aged: Practical approaches in the institution and community.* Englewood Cliffs, NJ: Prentice-Hall, Inc.

The Activity Room: Establishing the Proper Psychosocial Environment In the Long-Term Care Setting

To what extent does the environment—physical, social, and psychological—affect the outcome of leisure programs within long-term settings? The answer is obvious, but the topic of the physical environment where activities are conducted has not received extensive examination from the perspectives of both programming guidelines and research questions and issues within the field of leisure programming for older adults in nursing homes and other long-stay facilities.

Program or activity directors working under less than ideal physical space requirements can easily describe difficulties in programming where adequate space is not provided or when the multiuse concept is carried to the extreme making it difficult to place or store ongoing projects. Improper levels of lighting, excessive noise, and poor ventilation are other problems which affect both staff and program participants. Conversely, activity personnel fortunate enough to be working in a setting where much attention has been paid to space and the organization of people within that space should be able to describe how such factors enable them to do a better job of programming. Residents, the most important link to the physical surroundings and also those most susceptible to the negative impact of a poorly designed environment because of chronic conditions associated with aging, are either assisted with programming in a well-designed area or must overcome barriers presented by a poorly designed activity area.

While the literature describing the process of programming for older, institutionalized adults has not discussed environmental effects in great detail, the topic has been and is being explored by various professional groups.

Gerontologists, environmental psychologists, human factors engineers, and architects are all paying more attention to the design needs of older adults. While much of this work is still in its infancy, progress is being made, and research is being conducted to expand the knowledge base so that improved environments will exist for those elderly living in long-term care and community settings. Articles and studies reviewed for this chapter covered disparate areas of the physical environment ranging from guidelines for an ideal bathroom or bedroom to how hallways and other public places within a rehabilitation hospital or nursing home create a social interaction pattern; to specific recommendations on colors, color contrast, levels and types of illumination, and other suggestions related to sensory deficits associated with aging. This work is exciting, and, while guidelines are not entirely based upon empirical studies, these recommendations are a move in the right direction. It is hoped that the activity room, or whatever space in which activities are conducted, will receive attention by the design specialist just as the total design of long-term settings and specific areas like bathrooms and hallways are being analyzed now. Certainly there are specific objectives and outcomes associated with activity programming (the goal of assisting socialization is a frequently mentioned objective) which are tied to the relationship of the physical, psychological, and social characteristics of the activity area. This area should be the focus of analysis by activity specialists and environmental engineers.

Returning to the "Activities Program Model for Nursing Home Residents" presented in Chapter 6 (page 75), the system or environment is explored in level three of the paradigm (see Figure 6.1, page 76). Of particular importance here is the physical environment as a part of other factors operating within the total long-term care facility. Some of these factors are organizational/bureaucratic such as the role and importance given the recreation or activity program within the pecking order of departments or divisions within the setting. Others might

be classified as human/social, the manner and nature of relationships between the activity department and other allied professions (such as nursing or occupational therapy). The activity room or rooms, the furniture and supplies available, how those pieces of furniture are placed and used by residents, and how the senses are able to process information within that specific setting must be considered as well as the physical environment in which programming occurs. Those physical, psychological, perceptual, and social factors come together through the activities undertaken and with the human interaction of staff and residents to create an assistive or problematic environment. If activity specialists can become more keenly aware of this interaction, becoming actively involved in the process of planning and evaluating the physical environment for activities, and if residents are considered the most important aspect of the environment, their input should lead to activity areas which assist, rather than detract from, the achievement of desired outcomes.

A few considerations regarding the physical environment for activities must be noted. First, the activity room does not exist as an independent entity in terms of function, process, or location. It does exist as a part of a larger system which greatly influences the psychological and social tenor of residents. Where the activity room is physically located may have much to do with ease (or unease) in getting residents to the setting. Stuck down in a basement without a large or reliable elevator nearby, an activity room might be expected to entice few people. Located strategically near easily accessible areas and planned so that traffic flow leads to the activity room, success may be ensured if scheduling and programming are appropriate.

A second factor to consider is that guidelines and recommendations are geared most often to a normative or "typical" older adult likely to be found in a long-term care setting. Often this typical resident is hard to find. As with all older adults, those residing in long-term care facilities are quite heterogeneous. While anthropometic data giving mean heights, weights, and limb measurements for elderly persons are a starting point for design considerations for tables, chairs, and closets, they are by no means a guarantee that a specific individual will have no difficulty in using that piece. Even with groups that appear to be relatively homogeneous—working with a number of older blind clients or programming for those with Alzheimer's disease—the interplay of the aging process with various stages of illness or disease makes it almost impossible to create an activity setting ideal for all. Adaptability and the ability to reach or satisfy those most in need of environmental assistance are paramount. Since nearly all activity rooms are multipurpose, the ability to change or modify certain elements (e.g., seating or furniture arrangements, location and levels of certain lighting, amplification level of sound) is often possible. This modification principle is a key, however, and implements such as light switch dimmers, the availability of low vision aids for these who require them, adjustable height tables or tables of different heights, and the ability to amplify sound are all useful devices in attempting to assist individuals. The guidelines based upon normative considerations are a solid starting point, but as with any standard, they must be considered in relation to specific individuals who participate in the activity program.

It must also be kept in mind that many activity rooms (and total facilities for that matter) were designed and constructed before attention was given to these ergonomic/environmental considerations, and it is unlikely they would be considered state-of-the-art. Similar to public facilities built prior to the legislative mandates that guarantee accessibility and in need of retrofitting to meet current standards, many activity settings are less than ideal. This situation is not without positives, however. There are many products available today which do not require major construction projects to be useful. If funding permits, these products (e.g., tables, chairs, types of lighting, portable humidification devices) can be assistive. Activity staff working under less than desirable conditions know what does not work or what needs to be improved

should any type of future planning take place. Staff should be used as consultants when new buildings or activity rooms are being considered. Starting from the perspective of what barriers must be overcome can be an important contribution to the planning process.

An additional point worthy of consideration is the notion that the activity room is not and should not be considered the only area where leisure or recreation occurs within the facility. In fact, staff may be guilty of perceiving activity or leisure for residents only during the time there is resident-staff contact. Halberg (1987) raised this point in noting that most of a resident's leisure takes place outside of a specific activity program conducted by an activity department. Residents watch television, socialize with others on their own, use the library, and become volunteers. This consideration emphasizes the earlier point that the activity room must be viewed as part of a larger system. Leisure will and should occur in places, both inside and outside the facility, and a goal of the activity department should be to encourage such independent, self-selected experiences. This perspective also favors a total design of the facility where units and rooms are integrated with one another and the primary activity room is located with accessibility in mind.

This chapter will proceed with an analysis of the environment, or the interplay of the physical, psychological, and social forces upon older adults. The activity setting as a part of the total environment will be discussed. Age-related sensory changes will also be noted, as will the needs of older adults with cognitive impairments. Guidelines or recommendations for creating a supportive environment within the activity setting will be offered at the end of the chapter.

MacNeil (1982) has provided an excellent review of the work on the relationship of the natural and manmade environment with human social forces as they link to an institutional setting. Using the term "motivational wasteland" to describe the unattractive features of nursing homes, he noted the negative image created of the nursing home industry from studies and hearings done in the 1950s, 1960s and early 1970s which revealed over medication, abuse, unsanitary conditions, and often an environment where little meaningful activity was available. In regard to the physical environment, he concluded that research clearly supports the notion that the physical environment greatly affects behavior and even personality. One study cited (Zarlock, 1975) found that schizophrenic behavior was more common in medically-based living environments, as contrasted with environments geared to occupational or recreational activities. Overall, the synthesis revealed direct effects of the physical, manmade environment on important human factors such as the nature and extent of social interaction, the degree and type of motivation, and even the ability to assist with prosocial behavior or to reduce negative behaviors. He stressed that nursing homes often represent a closed environment and that attempts must be made to design living environments that are suitable to older residents, rather than those that are constructed with administrative efficiency in mind. Choice and independent functioning must be emphasized.

Environmental Theories

Hiatt (1986) advocates an environmental approach for the elderly classified as "holism". According to Hiatt "holism" is the combination of human and nonhuman factors into a total system. She notes a number of important results of the interaction between older adults with their physical environment: self-image is shaped through the environment (i.e., competence or incompetence may be seen depending upon the level of complexity present); quality of life can be improved through a well-planned environment; and poor environments may hasten or worsen the aging process (i.e., unwanted background noise may complicate hearing deficits leading to withdrawal). Conversely, proper

environments may help to prevent disability (i.e., risk of falls or disorientation are reduced when adequately illuminated cues are present); even agitation and wandering can be reduced by utilizing proper design.

There are a number of reasons why attention to the physical environment for frail older adults has only recently been addressed (Hiatt, 1986). Often, the training of those who design spaces for the elderly has been inadequate in this area. Many of the codes or design standards have been established for specific disabilities without considering the aging process in a developmental scheme or without regard to the combination of specific disabilities or chronic illnesses of the aging process. Often, designers have opted for managerial effectiveness or aesthetic appeal while relegating functional utility for residents to a second or third design priority. Starting with the capabilities of older adults in the areas of vision, hearing, touch, balance, mobility, and agility, Hiatt (1986) recommends a number of considerations in the creation of an ideal physical environment for older long-term care residents: fitness must be encouraged (i.e., safe places to walk and move appropriate to one's senses); differing levels of mental and physical abilities must be recognized while at the same time encouraging the practice of interaction (this challenge is one typically facing the activity programmer); design factors like complexity, safety, and routine for the increasing number of Alzheimer's patients; and the reduction of stress or agitation must also be a goal for older, frail adults. These goals must be applied to the area where activities take place just as they are applied to the total setting and personal living spaces.

From the perspective of environmental psychology, Pastalan (1985) has discussed a number of critical design issues which can be applied to the activity room. Complexity and levels of stimulation need to be addressed when considering older adults. Planners must seek to make a match between the level of stimulation present and that required by the client to produce an interesting and pleasant environment while at the same time affording safety and easy mobility without creating dull and uninteresting spaces. The task becomes complicated when one considers the varying levels of fitness, both mental and physical, present within the long-term care setting. Does the designer aim for the lowest denominator at the risk of boredom for the higher functioning residents? Again, clients with Alzheimer's disease are becoming more prevalent in long-term care facilities, and routine activity within a low-level complexity environment is essential to their ability to function. Pastalan (1985) raises the significant point that judgments about the mental competence of frail older adults are linked to behavioral observations, and the worst case scenario would be one in which a poor manmade environment leads to confusion or the inability to move about appropriately for an older resident resulting in inappropriate diagnosis and an improper treatment plan.

Important principles to remember according to Pastalan (1985) are that space must be organized and landmarks must be present to guide ambulation. Applied to the activity area, this would call for landmarks being available so that residents can easily locate the room where recreation occurs. It should be located along a prominent hallway with color-coded walls and near large elevators for accessibility. The orientation process must also be simplified within the room where location and type of tables, the colors used (colors may signify placement or location), and textures can combine to create a supportive system. Complexity also relates to social interaction, and Pastalan (1985) cautions that creating groupings of large numbers of people may lead to a sensory overload for certain residents. One would expect activity specialists to be keenly aware of this. Another point to remember is that the size of the room itself may present problems, and if administrative dictum favors heavy attendance figures from the activity department leading to larger groupings, problems may arise.

Activity programmers considering the physical environment must also consider environmental stressors and hypostimulation (i.e., under

stimulation) (Pastalan, 1985) as potential issues concerning residents. Since, by nature, many activity areas or rooms are multipurpose and serve different groups or individuals perhaps at the same time, environmental stress created both by the physical surroundings and by the confluence of differing activities may create some level of discomfort for the participants. Background noise (i.e., fans, music, television) creates difficulties for those with certain audiologic problems. Different people talking at the same time or a mixture of sounds when activity groups are underway could result in overstimulation. Those with Alzheimer's disease are particularly susceptible to distractions in the environment or changes in pattern or routine which can easily produce an agitated state. Awareness on the part of the activity director of those attending given programs and what might be going on at the same time is essential so that these potential problems can be avoided by proper planning. Understimulation may also be a situation dealt with by activity specialists although, hopefully, not as a physical environment issue within the activity room. Many nursing homes residents, often classified as unmotivated, do, however, spend a great deal of their time room-bound, and the level of stimulation within that setting may be limited. Programmers often seek to provide that stimulation through bedside activities, by suggesting library materials, or by hanging new plants or paintings within the room. Hypostimulation may make these clients prime candidates for the experiences found in the activity room, but the nature of their involvement (e.g., small group activities with persons they know), and the level of stimulation present (e.g., too much in the early stages may be a danger) must be planned for accordingly.

Human factors engineers, according to Fozard (1981), must account for human development and progression, while at the same time acknowledging sensory deficits seen in later life, as the most compatible environment for aging adults is planned. While there is orderliness in the stages that adults pass through, the difficulty is that not all encounter or cope with those stages at the same pace. Stages of retirement, grief, or acceptance to disabling conditions have been identified by scholars studying older adults facing those situations, yet there is no easily applicable developmental sequence which can be applied to those residing in long-term care settings. Older adults in such settings are perhaps among the most heterogeneous of all adults. Fozard (1981) states that the optimum environment for the aged "will promote independence of activity and provide challenges to the individual, as well as, maximize safety and physical comfort." Two additional factors mentioned are that changes in routine or placement/location can create major problems for the elderly (particularly those with short-term memory loss) and that stimulus-response incompatibility due to environmental factors are particularly bothersome to the frail elderly. For example, older adults are usually bothered much more by glare than are younger persons. A central idea of many design experts is to provide a stimulating and challenging environment while at the same time recognizing that many levels of ability will be apparent within this population. This is not an easily accomplished task.

Parsons (1981) has synthesized both the chronology of those groups exploring physical design with the aging and the approaches and limitations of relatively current and past efforts. Each group: human factors engineers; architects; gerontologists in the areas of psychology, sociology, and human behavior; government agencies attempting to create design standards; and organizations whose primary focus is those with a specific disability has presented a slightly different perspective on the issue, and what is encouraging is the fact that there has been more collaboration among the groups as the elderly population has grown.

Four sets of critical considerations (Parsons, 1981) are features that distinguish older adults from others and from each other; the behavioral aspects directly affected by the physical environment; the analysis of what specific and singular features exist within the environment that are directly responsible for behavioral change; and, what must be considered in functionally distinct areas such as bedrooms, lobbies, bathrooms. A constantly changing population—constantly changing individuals are viewed in both a developmental scheme and with recognized deficits which accompany the aging process—and few empirical studies to draw upon are apparent problems. One important effort by a task force of the Gerontological Society (Sherwood, 1975) focused on six areas of user functioning:

1. anthropometic measurements;
2. physical functioning;
3. cardiorespiratory and metabolic;
4. sensory;
5. cognitive; and,
6. social characteristics.

These six functions were related to tasks performed using specific architectural elements such as drawers and furniture heights.

A useful paradigm has been developed by Parsons (1981) for assessing the interplay between environmental and behavioral aspects. It is applicable to older, frail adults. Among the environmental factors are resources, the spatial arrangement, communication devices, appearance, consequation, protection, ambient conditions, and the entire setting. Presented in a matrix, each of the environmental factors are analyzed regarding their impact on nine behavioral areas: activities, locomotion, social interaction, feelings, perceptions, motivation, health and safety, learning, and manipulation. Using the paradigm, Parsons (1981) selects the bedroom in a long-term care setting as an illustration of how design features can be analyzed with regard to behavior of older adults. The number of beds and how those beds are arranged, the kinds of furniture present in the bedroom, the types of lamps or lighting, and how communication elements assist or detract from successful ambulation within the facility are all discussed with regard to how each affects the relevant behavioral characteristics of older adults in a long-term care setting. It is a model appropriate for assessing the physical characteristics of the activity room (see Figure 7.1, pages 114-117).

To summarize some of the major issues in environmental design for long-term care settings, it is apparent that the phenomenon of focusing on the physical space needs of the frail aged is a relatively new one. Designers, gerontologists, psychologists, and behaviorists have studied the issue from differing perspectives. There is general agreement supported by studies that the physical, man-made environment does indeed affect human behavior. Developmental and holistic theories suggest that growth is just as much a part of aging as sensory decline, yet the elderly living in long-term care settings are heterogeneous, and sequencing and timing of stages become very difficult to predict. Holistic theory implies that the total physical, social, and psychological environment must be considered as a system affecting humans. The activity room and department, therefore, must be viewed as part of all other physical, social, and psychological components in the residence. While the problems outnumber the neatly packaged recommendations with regard to design, principles are emerging, and the continued focus on the issue using the strengths of various concerned groups should result in further advancements.

Assisting With Independence Through the Psychosocial Environment

A special edition (Vol. 3, No. 1, 1987) of the journal, *Topics in Geriatric Rehabilitation*, dealt with the physical, social, psychological, and cultural aspects of rehabilitation and extended care settings as they relate to older persons. Beyond just the physical environment, the impact of the social structure of facilities and the way in which therapists are able to manipulate various elements (e.g., what activities are chosen and how adaptations can be made) were examined. Broader environmental theories were tied to the rehabilitative context.

Independence is a crucial cultural value according to Kiernat (1987), one which is often compromised by the aging process and the loss of which is primarily responsible for residents being placed in nursing homes. Once located in that situation, however, the combination of manmade environmental features, the manner in which staff and residents interact, and the degree to which personal initiative results in goal-oriented behavior, create a system in which aged adults are to function.

Much has been written in the negative vein about those nursing home environments which are sterile, structured to support regimented operational activities, and offer little in the way of sensory or behavioral challenges for residents. This type of setting many times is responsible for institutionalized behaviors on the part of residents or for what Seligman (1975) has termed "learned helplessness." When one is told when to wake, at what time to eat, and under what conditions social interaction is permitted, it can be expected that conditioning will occur, and independence is often relinquished in favor of an approach focusing on passivity, compliance, and allowing others to make choices. Learned helplessness (Seligman, 1975) in its most damaging form involves severe depression, loss of appetite and other physiological changes, and a complete paralysis of the will. Clearly the role of the activity department and staff is to create an atmosphere where choice is inherent and control, to whatever degree is permitted by resident circumstances, is maintained by the participant.

Surveys cited by Kiernat (1987) reveal that residents are aware of and are demanding greater amounts of control. Again, allowing control would seem to be ideally suited to leisure activities. How can staff provide for resident control? A starting place is a well-designed, total system approach to the long-term care setting itself. The ability to dress, ambulate, bathe, toilet, and socialize must be enhanced through design. Staff must plan opportunities for individual selection: applied to leisure programs this can be represented through the use of resident councils, by allowing residents to select specific activities, and by offering alternatives themselves. By consciously working against a mentality of administrative convenience first and resident independence second, staff may be able to head off problems that can lead to institutionalized outlooks on the part of residents.

A frequently cited study by Langer and Rodin (1976) demonstrated that allowing choices can lead to feelings of control. Residents who made choices of and cared for plants proved to be more active and in better spirits than those who were not given such choices. The positive effects were relatively long-lasting, as well. Thus administrative perspective, one which stresses residents' abilities to select, control, and be responsible, can be a significant factor when combined with a challenging and assistive physical environment when the goal is to optimize resident feelings of competence.

From a rehabilitation perspective Levine and Merrill (1987) discussed the interplay of the psychological and social worlds linked to a recovering client. Perhaps the foremost goal of rehabilitation is to see that the client can interact successfully, again, in his or her environment. If one is surrounded with supportive friends and family members who themselves stress independence and force the selection of alternatives, recovery time may be lessened. Adaptive devices are central to rehabilitation, and the ability to modify an activity or movement is a tool specialists often utilize. Such factors indicate that activity personnel must be keenly aware of the social influences present in long-term care settings. Are staff or family members too sympathetic, leading to the early stages of institutionalized behavior on the part of residents? Are friends within the nursing

home encouraging and accepting, or do cliques prevent the active socialization of some residents? Do special events and other elements of the program bring together people in social atmospheres? All of these must be explored in examining the social forces present.

One question which arises throughout this discussion is the degree to which the match is made between the older adult and that total environment in which he or she is functioning. While the physical planner often views the issue in the collective sense and focuses upon how to design an entire nursing home used by many groups of people, the activity therapist and the resident desire an environment which works for each individual. In their review, Yerxa and Baum (1987) highlight Lawton's (1982) environmental press theory. Here the physical, interpersonal, and social environments are weighed against the competence of the person. The goal is to create a match between those forces outside the older individual and how that person is able to navigate within his or her environment. By focusing on strengths, by planning programs which challenge but do not frustrate, and through using adaptation principles, activity staff may play a role in ensuring that the match is a suitable one.

Other psychologists have attempted to explain the interplay of human, social, and psychological elements within a framework of systems theory. Rather than focusing on specific cause and effect relationships, this group of theories is broader from a systems perspective. Applied to the nursing home environment, an integrated approach analyzing various parts of the physical setting, the manner in which staff interact with residents, the social network present, and what opportunities are available for growth would all be utilized in understanding how a particular older person would interact. The goal would be to make the system "fit" in the best way possible with the needs and competencies of the resident under consideration. The contribution of the activity program here could be highly significant.

Specific elements in the physical environment such as well-balanced and supportive chairs; cognitive devices such as clocks, calendars, and other reality orientation aids; color coding which assists with orientation, and appropriate color contrast which can help with visual impairments and mobility patterns should all be considered (Yerxa and Baum, 1987). Studies have indicated that greater personal responsibility, greater levels of social interaction, and a quickened rehabilitative period (Yerxa and Baum, 1987) can be the result of a physical environment which attends to the needs of aged adults. As mentioned before, a crucial problem facing activity personnel is the disparate abilities and levels of functioning of the clients with whom they interact. Yet by planning an activity room which accommodates the agility, mobility, and sensory needs of most frail older adults and also allows adaptations (seating arrangements that can be changed, low vision aids for those who need them), a situation can be created which suits the majority of those who participate. The other key element at the discretion of the of the activity specialist is the process of selecting and conducting programs which permit a match between a client's abilities and what he or she undertakes.

Assessing the Environment

The question arises, "are there specific measures which can be used in assessing the physical or social or psychological environment existing in a nursing home or, specifically, in an activity room?" Approaches have been made and some tools developed to deal with this complex issue. Architects and planners use standards as a starting point, and when dealing with physical properties, such standards provide a minimum level of acceptance. However, individual differences do create problems in reaching that ideal match between the person and the environment. It is much easier to specify a minimum width needed in a doorway for a wheelchair to easily

pass than it is to specify the correct level of illumination needed in an activity setting when visual acuity will differ tremendously on a person-by-person basis.

According to Spencer (1987), there are a variety of ways in which the environment can be measured. Measurement of physical properties (e.g., heights, widths, distances.), naturalistic observation, self-reporting by older participants, reporting by all who come in contact with the environment (e.g., staff, residents, volunteers, family), and judgments by experts can all be techniques used in measuring the physical, social or psychological environment present. Organizations like the American National Standards Institute (ANSI) and other professional societies have created standards dealing with access and mobility of those with disabilities. The specific anthropometic requirements of the elderly combined with chronic and multifaceted health problems require that such standards based upon physical disabilities be reviewed carefully and adapted to specific needs. In attempting to evaluate the mood or atmosphere present within a long-term care facility both naturalistic observation and resident reports can be useful. Spencer (1987) cites an evaluation tool by Moos (1974) which measures the atmosphere of the facility and can be used by clients and staff. Discrepancies between what is present and what is desired can be discussed and corrective steps taken. Likewise, a structured observation approach can be used by staff and could be employed in various areas. Behavioral observations can chart how residents move within the facility or within the activity room, how persons socialize or interact with one another, or under what conditions disruptive behavior occurs. Visitors and family members can also play an important role in assessing the psychological or social climate of a nursing home. Removed from a 24-hour-a-day presence, their views will provide a perspective different from that of residents or staff. Expert opinion is another frequently used technique and one which is associated with periodic reviews by state health departments or certifying bodies. Linked to the activity program, this method would use other activity directors to observe and comment upon what is taking place, the nature of the program, how outcomes are determined, and other important factors. These outside professional views can be particularly useful to those recently assuming their positions or to those who have been at their jobs and sites for a number of years and are seeking freshness. Included later in the chapter is a discussion of specific environmental considerations for the activity room.

ARCHITECTS' PERSPECTIVES

The psychological, social, and physical space needs of elders who will reside in long-term care institutions must be turned into a design program complete with specifications, size and space requirements, and actual blueprints. This challenging task faced by professional design specialists will eventually result in the construction of a building. Thus, the physical structure will provide the foundation within which the social and psychological environment will be created.

Mentioned previously was the concern given to the design needs of the elderly by architects. Most acknowledge that their science is not perfect, but that strides are being made. Noakes (1988), an early and prominent advocate in design for elders, noted the inadequacies of current design standards (ANSI) relative to the elderly and called upon architects and gerontological specialists to be active in the revision processes of the ANSI's criteria in 1991. Noakes (1988) cites the tendency of architects to plan for the typical or "average" older person without accounting for diversity. This averaging process often results in individual problems (e.g., reaching, sitting, ambulation), and adaptability is desireable where possible (such as adjustable shelves in closets, or adjustable drawer pulls). By eliminating problems from the outset such as outside steps, narrow doors, and narrow hallways, costs can be kept in line, and the overall environment will be much improved (Noakes, 1988).

This concept of adaptability has been stressed by Raphael (1987). In discussing residential housing for seniors, he notes that maximum accessibility should be an initial consideration. Beyond that, he has planned kitchens and baths that become wheelchair accessible should the resident require it. Also stressed is the role that staff who work in long-term care settings should play in the design process. From healthcare workers, to maintenance employees, to activity specialists, special expertise must find its way into the planning process. Raphael (1987) would define an activity room as a semiprivate space which should be clearly identifiable, offer a sense of territory, and be reached through a transition point from a public space such as a corridor. It would appear that the concept of adaptability would be particularly well-suited to the activity room. Since activities vary and multipurpose functions must be served, the room must be suited to change. The ability to move furniture and to accommodate specific activities such as needlework or board games are prime objectives. The social order of those who participate in activities will surely undergo change with time, and the need to shift from larger group to smaller group seating arrangements may become apparent. Adapting or modifying activities, a programming principle which should be within the talents of the activity director, can be extended to the physical environment. Awareness of the types of activities to be utilized and knowledge of the environmental needs of all residents serve as two planning factors for the modification of physical space within activity settings.

Sensory Loss As a Design Consideration

This section will review sensory changes within older adults as related to environmental accommodations designed to improve functioning. As in previous sections, the danger must be reaffirmed of applying means or averages from large groups to individual persons. Similar to other psychological or biological areas, each older adult will experience sensory maintenance or decline in a singular fashion.

An attempt will be made to keep the review as nontechnical as possible, yet some statistics or figures must be used for comparative purposes. The intent is not to have the reader become an expert in sensory loss associated with age, but rather to provide an understanding of problems created by sensory losses and how the physical environment can be modified to assist those with deficiencies. The effects, psychological and behavioral, of sensory declines will also be addressed particularly as they may affect activity participation.

At this time there are many areas within the realm of design accommodations related to the sensory mechanisms of older adults that are only in the beginning stages of empirical testing. Types and levels of lighting to assist with visual declines have been subjected to experiments, although often workers, rather than the elderly, serve as study participants. Very few studies were reviewed that specifically used older, frail adults in testing environmental changes designed to improve functioning. Guidelines or recommendations can be found relative to improving the physical environment as a result of sensory input, but the effectiveness of these suggestions needs to be substantiated thorough scientific testing. Lighting has probably received more attention than other areas.

This review will begin with vision problems in later life, followed by the topic of hearing. Balance and the problem of falling will be covered next. The special concern of the elderly with cognitive impairments will be addressed in the last section of this chapter.

VISION

It is apparent that vision is linked to nearly all of the activities which might be undertaken in the activity program. Kirchner (1985), noted that visual impairments are four times more likely in the elderly as compared to all persons. Problems resulting from poor vision can force

major changes in the pattern or type of activities engaged in during life. These changes or withdrawals from long-held activity patterns can have profound psychological effects upon long-term care residents already aware that choices are being made for them, and losses are readily apparent. One study (Branch, Horowitz, and Carr, 1989) of noninstitutionalized elderly found that not only was there an expected decline in vision with advancing age, but that many instrumental activities of daily living such as climbing stairs and doing housework were given up by those with poor vision. More important, perhaps, was the finding that poor vision was also associated with poor morale and greater depression. Thus, the ability to perform favored pursuits can be significant in warding off negative psychological distress.

Declining vision impacts leisure participation, as well (Heinemann, Colorez, Frank, and Taylor, 1988). Older attendees at a low vision clinic were found frequently to give up particular leisure activities as vision problems grew, and few (3 percent) reported developing new interests to replace pursuits lost. Thus, activity directors must be aware of changes related to vision and be prepared to accommodate those changes so that maintenance of enjoyable activities will result.

Vision, related to the aging eye, involves much more than acuity. While a sharp image is central to the performance of many tasks, the concerns with sight among the elderly extend to levels of illumination, problems with glare, adaptability to darker areas (or moving from dark to bright areas), and the ability to distinguish color. Keep in mind that the more the physical environment can assist those in long-stay facilities with ambulation, the less the chance will be for the unfortunate situation to arise whereby residents will become confused, disoriented, or become room-bound due to poor visual cues or inadequate levels of lighting in hallways or semipublic areas.

Greater levels of illumination are required for older adults to perform effectively (Fozard, 1981), yet the source and distribution of lighting must be considered as well. Older adults can be expected to take much longer to adapt to lighting while moving from a darker area (their bedroom in the late afternoon or evening, for example) and glare will be particularly bothersome. Falls have been related (Archea, 1977) to glare near stairways (having a window near the top of stairways). The movement from a darker area (stairway) to a brightened, glaring spot in a relatively short time may not give the aging eye ample time to adjust. The reasons for these adaptability and glare problems are tied to biological changes (Dye, 1983). The eye's lens tends to cloud and thicken with age, and usually light will scatter or diffuse when it enters the older eye (Dye, 1983). About 66 percent less light reaches the retina at the age of 60 (Hughes and Neer, 1981). Thus, the effects of glare are magnified for the elderly. Cataracts occur more frequently in later life and cloud the lens as well.

Other changes seen in the eye include a flattening of the cornea creating an irregular image, a decrease in the size of the pupil causing less light to enter initially, and a weakening of the muscles surrounding the eye (Dye, 1983). Older persons also will process visual information more slowly (Fozard, 1981). Activities requiring quick movements of the eye and changing visual patterns (a video arcade game operating at top speed) would likely cause problems for many older residents.

Color discrimination is another area related to functional problems. The ability to perceive accurate color becomes more difficult in later life, and the ability to discriminate between two objects of a similar shade are tasks more troublesome to the elderly. This latter situation can create many practical problems in daily living. The inability to distinguish items on a nightstand, or colors of socks in a dark drawer, or where the door to a room meets the frame or the wall can result in much frustration. This type of problem creates a much greater impact on living than does simply seeing a color in a slightly different shade than the normal eye would.

Engineers speak of "spectral power distribution," or the ability to reflect accurately true colors in the spectrum (Hughes and Neer, 1981). With the clouding of the eye's lens, certain waves of light become distorted (Dye, 1983). Blues and violets are particularly affected. Yellow shades are difficult to distinguish, and reds lose some vividness. It is clear that the type of lighting available will affect color representation. Standard florescent bulbs, for example, do a poorer job than regular incandescent bulbs in representing true colors of the spectrum (Hughes and Neer, 1981). These bulbs can be judged on a color rendering index (CRI) and high CRI bulbs, differing from standard florescent, do a much better job of illuminating color accurately. One study conducted with older subjects (Boyce and Simons, 1977) indicated higher CRI bulbs assist in the ability to discriminate colors.

In addition to the type of illumination, color contrast has been explored to assist with functional daily living tasks. Cooper (1985) has developed an 11-step model analyzing tasks to be performed and how color contrast can be applied to create greater visual discrimination in the elderly. The objective of the task is identified, existing colors and background shades are noted, any limitations mentioned (e.g., the inability to paint an entire room) and finally, recommendations given that would maximize color contrast. Of importance here is the recognition on the part of personnel that the environment in which the residents are living may be less than ideal for color discrimination. By analyzing the environment and noting problem areas, minor changes can be made which may greatly assist the performance of certain tasks. See Figure 7.2 (see page 118) for application of this model to the activity setting. Simple awareness by activity staff of color contrast principles can often create a better environment for activity participants.

One final note relative to vision is the role that the activity department may play in rehabilitation efforts with residents suffering from vision impairments. Activity staff working with doctors and nurses may be called upon to assist in maintaining or developing visual skills. Smith and Aston (1989) highlight a number of leisure activities appropriate for this purpose. Writing, reading, and craft activities, often of an adapted or modified nature, may be used for this purpose. The type of environment and available lighting sources are critical factors with this type of rehabilitative activity. The American Foundation for the Blind[†] is an excellent source of low vision aids and activities for older adults with vision problems.

ASSISTING VISION WITH OLDER ADULTS: THE ENVIRONMENT

Based upon the previous discussion of changes in vision with age, the following suggestions may be used in correcting problems in the environment or in creating a more supportive visual environment. Activity professionals are urged to apply these principles within the activity setting and also to be consciously aware of their application to the total long-term facility and to specific personal spaces (e.g., bedrooms and bathrooms) as frequented by each resident:

- *Provide an adequate level of illumination.* Simple observation and awareness will begin this process. Older adults need more light. Make sure that maintenance staff replace bulbs regularly. Several kinds of light will most likely be used in the activity room.
- *The level of illumination should be consistent and balanced throughout the area.* Avoid dark and bright areas—consistency is required. If sections are noticeably darker, provide more lights.
- *Local, focused lighting is a good idea for the activity room.* Projects underway on a table may need a focused light source. A 60-watt bulb in a adjustable lamp will often suffice.

- *Eliminate glare to whatever degree possible.* The sun may present problems depending on the orientation. Glare is a problem for older eyes. Glare from manmade sources should be controlled as well. Matte surfaces and window shadings will ease the problem.
- *Use bold, large print with color contrast whenever possible.* Go beyond just providing large-print books in the reading area. Instructions from staff or any printed message should be in large, bold typeface as should any print on games or devices used for activities.
- *Modification and adaptability may be necessary with activities to assist with vision.* Enlarging the size may be called for. Larger needles or brushes may be needed by some residents. A larger, softer ball may improve the abilities of those engaged in games.
- *Have low vision aids such as magnifying glasses, stand magnifiers, and reading stands available.*
- *Use color contrast where needed.* Edges of doors, or tables, or changes in levels of the floor will all benefit through appropriate use of color contrast. Handles and implements on tables should be contrasted. Cooper (1985) recommends complementary color contrast (those colors opposite one another on a color wheel such as blue-orange or red-green contrast). Color coding of areas, or tools may also prove useful.

A number of these recommendations do not require major outlays of money or staff time—two commodities which are at a premium in most activity departments. By assessing the visual environment and by making minor changes, staff may greatly improve the activity area as related to the vision of their residents.

HEARING

Most older adults will experience a loss of hearing. Hearing loss ranks within the top five chronic conditions reported by older adults and tinnitus (ringing in the ears) falls within the

---

[†] Contact the American Foundation for the Blind at 15 West 16th Street, New York, NY. 10011

top ten chronic problems (Senate Special Committee on Aging, 1989, p. 81). It is a problem which greatly affects the quality of life, and, compounded with other losses, the inability to discriminate among sounds can lead to profound psychological and behavioral changes for residents of long-term care settings. If avoidance of social situations and an undesired turning inward are the adaptations to hearing loss, the resident affected may be expected to experience a world much different from the one previously encountered. Activity professionals, then, must view hearing loss not only in terms of its potential impact on the conduct of programs, but also they must be vigilant for changes in behavior or morale which may be the result of poor adaptations to hearing loss.

The loss of tones in the upper frequency range often signals the beginning of "presbycusis," a term typically associated with hearing loss in later life (Kiernat, 1983). Causes of auditory ineffectiveness for the elderly are many; trauma from the environment, changes in the outer and inner ear, and conductive problems can all be linked with hearing loss. As with many symptoms "associated" with older age, hearing loss should not be dismissed by medical or program staff as an accepted part of living. Testing and prescriptive measures should be sought.

In a nontechnical vein the modifications affecting hearing can include less elasticity of the ear drum, greater translucency of the drum, degeneration of important hair cells within the ear, fewer and more inefficient cells which are important in carrying messages along the central nervous system, greater rigidity of the small bones within the ear, and a general slowing of the central nervous system (Dye, 1983, pp. 147-149; Fozard, 1981; Kiernat, 1983). Many negative changes associated with older cells are thought to be responsible for difficulties in late life audition.

The practical impact of the above changes is a loss of tone and quality for auditory messages. Clarity is often lost; higher-pitched sounds blur; and consonants become indistinguishable. The spoken word becomes a guessing game. Ringing in the ears may create a constant annoyance or outside, environmental noises may be magnified. Simply increasing the level of sound may not help, and the end result of these frustrations is an older resident who becomes confused or agitated.

It is imperative that activities professionals understand the type of hearing loss experienced by each resident. Audiological exams should be conducted on a regular basis and staff must review medical records so that different approaches can be planned to accommodate the variety of losses. If, for example, the loss results from problems in the acoustic nerve which do not allow the brain to interpret the message (Shore, 1976), simply speaking slowly or shouting will do little good. Shore (1976) has indicated that paranoia and depression are found much more often in older, hearing-impaired individuals.

From a socioenvironmental perspective, the following guidelines are offered for activity staff:

- *Do not confuse hearing loss with senility*. Hearing examinations are important and the source of the problem must be determined.

- *Be mindful and on the look out for behavioral changes*. Could hearing loss be a cause of poor morale, a stoppage in social functioning, or depression?

- *Hearing aids will benefit some*. Make sure they are worn, regularly inspected to guarantee proper functioning, and checked to see if batteries are working.

- *Some suffer from the magnification of normal sounds (recruitment)*. Sounds appear to be much louder. Check for background noises, motors, fans, or even voices in rooms. Sound may need to be dampened for those with this problem.

- *Use good communication procedures*: face those to whom you are speaking; have adequate light for those who use lip reading for assistance; speak slowly and clearly; reduce the distance between yourself and

those who have impairments; do not shout—this may distort the message even more.
- *Assess the activity area for acoustics*: How is the furniture arranged? What type of materials are present? Is sound easily absorbed? Is sound too easily reflected? Is illumination adequate to see the speaker? Do you have an amplification system? Are you aware of specific hearing impairments and are you able to make the appropriate accommodations?

PREVENTION OF FALLS

The elderly as a group are at much greater risk than others to suffer falls and are much more likely to suffer serious consequences as a result of the fall (Cardea and Tynan, 1987; Tideiksaar, 1987; Yerxa and Baum, 1987). Broken hips are the most common type of fracture for the elderly, and, for 30 percent, the fall may prove fatal within a year's time (Cardea and Tynan, 1987). The inability to recover from falls is a frequent cause for placement in a long-term care facility, and nursing homes have a responsibility to create an environment whereby every step is taken to prevent residents from falling.

Much of the analysis of falls among the frail, older population has been the result of investigations into the home environment (Belkin, 1984; Cardea and Tynan, 1987; Salmen, 1988; Tideiksaar, 1987). Experts have recognized the severity of the problem and have attempted to determine some of the hazards which are partially responsible for falls in one's home (Belkin, 1984; Cardea and Tynan, 1987). As with other biological factors of aging, the cause of falls in the elderly can be varied. Diminished sight, poor balance, drug interactions, and a poor environment, may all combine to create a hazardous situation when older adults are ambulating at home (Cardea and Tynan, 1987; Tideiksaar, 1987). While the long-term care environment differs somewhat from the home setting, there exists a number of similarities so that investigating the causes of home falls will prove instructive. Galton (1976) noted

that 50 percent of all falls are due to a poor physical environment, and problems associated with flooring are a specific negative factor. Inadequate lighting and poor traffic patterns can also result in trips or falls.

A survey of elders' homes in the Philadelphia area (Belkin, 1984) revealed a number of hazards linked to floor surfaces. Furniture covering wires, wires directly on the floor in accessible areas, inadequate lighting, scatter rugs, frayed or worn carpeting which could be snagged by a shoe, and steps in poor condition without lighting or handrails were all potential risk factors found by surveyors. Since carpeting, furniture, and lights are found in long-term care settings, either in private rooms or in congregate spaces, the implication for activity personnel is to recognize potential causes of falls and to correct them. The activity department should be well-aligned with the maintenance staff so that repairs can be quickly handled.

Another contributory factor to older adult falls is the effect of medication, or over medication (Cardea and Tynan, 1987). Since medication should be carefully monitored in the long-term care environment, two important guidelines for activity professionals are to have a knowledge of the medication taken by residents and to be aware of possible side effects. Certain activities may be contraindicated, and all ambulation within the activity area must be carefully monitored.

The following recommendations are offered relative to assessing the environment surrounding activity areas with particular attention to fall prevention. Many of the suggestions in the section on vision impairments are also applicable here. Be aware of the following:
- *Watch the placement of furniture*. Keep aisles clear, make aisles wide, be sure legs of chairs or tables do not jut out into areas used for movement.
- *Use sturdy chairs at all times*. A solid base is essential for any chair in the activity area. Chair arms should be in good repair. Chairs used for movement or exercise programs should be checked carefully for sturdiness.

- *Proper illumination is a must.* Hallways, activity areas, and personal living areas need adequate lighting. Avoid glare and be sure blown bulbs are replaced promptly.
- *Use color contrast where appropriate.* All slopes should be designated by a cue for the resident. Color contrast will signal a change in elevation.
- *The American Association of Homes for the Aged (1985), however, cautions against using color contrast where there is no change in elevation.* A contrast where there is no slope or decline may be perceived by the resident as a change in height, and a misstep may result.
- *It is assumed that steps are typically not used by residents.* Staff, however, may use them to access certain areas. Keep stairs clear, well lit, and have handrails for support.
- *Should handrails be used in the activity area, be sure that the grip area is appropriate for older hands.* A thumb and finger grip will work well, and rails should not be too wide.
- *Any carpeted area can be a potential hazard.* Carpet must be in excellent condition without frayed areas. Regularly check all seams. Contrasting colors can designate perimeters or exiting areas.
- *Scatter or throw rugs should not be used.* They are frequently cited as a cause of falls in homes. Policy should be set as to their use in bedrooms. Avoidance is the best approach.
- *Noncarpeted flooring surfaces need to be checked also.* The key issue here is slickness. While aesthetics and cleanliness are obvious concerns in a long-term care setting, safety must not be compromised by having slippery surfaces. Always be sure that spills are cleaned up quickly in the activity room.

The focus here has been the area under the control of the activity coordinator or director. Personal space, particularly the bedroom, has not been discussed but clearly architects and staff have a responsibility to design for and monitor safety in all areas. Those interested in personal spaces may wish to examine the following sources: American Association of Homes for the Aging (AAHA); Cardea and Tynan, 1987; 1985; Parsons, 1981; and Salmen, 1988; Tideiksaar, 1987.

The Physical Environment and Cognitive Impairments

An issue raised earlier in the chapter was the possibility of a confusing, poorly designed physical environment contributing to behavioral change on the part of older residents (decreased movement within the facility taken to the degree of becoming room-bound). Agitation, restlessness, or wandering on the part of aged residents who cannot successfully manage the existing physical environment may even result in psychological or other types of therapeutic interventions. Anything that can be done from the physical design standpoint to create logical spaces, areas which can be easily recognized, and a comfortable flow of traffic must be provided so that unnecessary confusion is eliminated. Experiments with architectural modifications for Alzheimer's patients (Lewin, 1990) are beginning to test what may or may not lead to successful adaptation to an indoor environment.

Some of the central debates which face older adults in general are applicable to design consideration for residents in long-term care settings who suffer from cognitive impairments. These issues may be framed as the degree to which the physical environment encourages or discourages the following:

organization_____	disorganization
socialization_____	singular activities
independence_____	dependence
choice_____	nonchoice
innovativeness_____	dullness

Each pair of terms can be thought of as representing a continuum, and each physical space within the long-term care setting could be evaluated relative to these criteria. One must not assume, however, that the left hand column is in all instances the ideal, or preferred status. Each resident will vary in the ability to function cognitively, and therefore the environment must be processed individually. The safety of all residents and staff must always be a prime consideration. It is safe to assert that organized space is preferable to that which is difficult or confusing to navigate. Certain places (the activity room as an illustration) will be designed for socialization, yet residents can be expected to spend time alone, and personal spaces, such as bedrooms, must accommodate the individual. Independence and choice are hallmarks of the leisure experience, yet cognitive impairments may create a situation where options become restricted. A top priority for an Alzheimer's client, for example, may be the ability to walk down the hall and return to her room. Here choice and independence are viewed differently from those of the resident who exhibits excellent cognitive skills. The innovativeness - dullness issue also creates practical problems. Spaces need to be alive and interesting, yet also rate highly on safety and functional scales. Thus, cognitive abilities add one more consideration to an already heterogeneous profile of residents when the physical environment is planned.

MacNeil and Teague (1987) have summarized the cognitive process and associated problems with aging. Perception, storage, retrieval, and the ability to respond appropriately are all key ingredients relative to mental functioning in later life. Personal history factors, one's biological status, the social and physical environment, medications and day-to-day living patterns create a mix directly tied to cognitive functioning.

Processing information first entails reception or stimulation from the environment. The senses provide a key here and, as discussed earlier in the chapter, vision and hearing inaccuracies often plague older adults. The sensory information is next transferred to the brain via neural impulses. These impulses are involved in a process of selection by the brain and are often assigned to short-term memory. Some are acted upon immediately and generate a response (e.g., answering a question), and others are sent for long-term memory storage (MacNeil and Teague, 1987).

A primary function of long-term memory is to transform the impulses into an orderly, conceptual mode (encoding) which can be used at later times. Often it becomes difficult to access such stored information (MacNeil and Teague, 1987). If needed, stored information must be brought through short-term memory and acted upon, and a response generator could start body movements. Problems may appear in a number of processes: initial perception, transfer and encoding, searching and retrieving stored material, and activating an appropriate motor response.

Cognitive problems associated with old age are broadly classified as functional (not physical in nature but related to personality or background of the adult) or organic (a physical cause is present), yet the symptoms displayed as a result of the two causes may be similar (MacNeil and Teague, 1987). Organic disorders are linked to impaired brain tissue and are characterized by faulty memory, poor intellectual functioning, poor judgment and orientation, and flat affect (MacNeil and Teague, 1987). Acute Brain Syndrome (ABS) can be attacked through intervention and is marked by confusion, restlessness, delusions, or stupor. Chronic Brain Syndrome (CBS) is more frequent in the aged and is generally regarded as irreversible; hardening of the blood vessels in the brain, nerve cell damage, and senile plaques in the brain typify its status (MacNeil and Teague, 1987).

It is significant for activity professionals to understand that not all cognitive dysfunctions are irreversible. Activity staff are frequently called upon to aid in the mental assessment of clients or residents, and the role they play in activating and encouraging mental functioning is a valuable one. MacNeil and Teague (1987) strongly assert that the use-it-or-lose-it philosophy holds with mental performance. In situations where the cognitive level of the resident cannot be expected to improve (i.e., an organic brain syndrome which will not respond to medical or pharmacological approaches), the issue becomes not one of use-it-or-lose-it but rather one of using mental stimulation, be it reality orientation or other activities, in an attempt to maintain the present level of mental functioning. Understanding the nature and causes of cognitive problems with residents is vital in establishing program treatment plans and conducting activity analyses. The physical environment must also be assessed for aiding (or impeding) intellectual functioning.

The AAHA (1985) has noted a number of important design considerations which would compliment reality orientation programs and generally assist older, mentally impaired adults. They remind staff to eliminate contradictory information—clocks set at different times, plastic plants which offer no scent, or other mixed signals used in interpreting the environment are to be avoided. Unplanned disruptions and a lack of structure in time and place are problematic. Recommended are color contrasts to signify change, symbols with large figures, and grouping furniture to help create social situations. Multipurpose rooms (as is often the case with activity areas) may present difficulties for those with mental confusion; care should be taken to keep furniture arrangements in familiar patterns, to locate residents who are confused at the same tables every day, and to bring them to the activity program at the same time each day. These simple measures will lessen the chance for confusion. Excessive pacing and wandering of confused residents are frequent problems which have been addressed through design techniques. Figure eight or circular traffic patterns have been planned and utilized in some nursing homes (AAHA, 1985; Brent, 1984), as to wandering the AAHA (1985) states:

> Not all mentally impaired residents wander. In deciding how to deal with this problem, therefore, the facility must consider the effects of its decision on both wanderers and nonwanderers, and also look at the relative numbers of each in the program.

Obviously, security becomes a problem when wanderers have the ability to leave the residence and enter outside areas. Some type of behavior management may be tried (AAHA, 1985), and electronic devices attached to those who roam have also been used. Such devices can alert staff when patients leave the residence.

Environmental modifications are a common consideration in programming for older cognitively impaired adults (Levy, 1989; McClannahan, 1973). Activity assessments call upon therapists to analyze the cognitive and motor skills required to complete an activity, and planning for adaptations becomes a part of the job activity professionals are required to do. Using a cognitive disability theory developed by Allen (1985), Levy (1989) has addressed environmental and activity modifications to assist those with mental dysfunctions. The approach divides impairments into six levels (one being the most severe, six being the absence of disability) and focuses on the sensory cues, sensorimotor associations, and motor actions required of an activity. Therapists are forced to examine individual abilities, types of thinking required, decision making as part of the activity, and whether sequencing is required. The end result might mean that adaptations are required in structuring and leading the activity and that adaptive devices are present to ensure success. Even those activity directors with minimal experience are aware of modifying traditional rules or activity implements to better suit the population of concern. Sponge balls of different sizes and weights, larger buttons or thread, and altered table games are frequently found in supply closets of activity specialists. The value of the Levy (1989) model is in combining the physical and cognitive state of the client while at the same time analyzing the physical environment used for the activity as well as examining specific adaptations to devices manipulated by the older participant.

Older adults suffering from Alzheimer's disease have recently begun to receive scrutiny from the standpoint of determining the most compatible physical environment (Lewin, 1990). At the Corrine Dolan Alzheimer's Center in suburban Cleveland, the Robert Wood Johnson Foundation has funded experimental research designed to answer some of the questions as to how the physical environment may better serve those with Alzheimer's. Lewin (1990) describes the facility:

> The center looks more like a rustic corporate conference center than a residence for senile people, with its peach and terra cotta colors, skylights, quilts on the walls and two big country kitchens opening out into dining areas. There is a puppy wandering around the living room, where classical music is playing, and out back, on a hill, is a fenced two-acre garden landscaped with nontoxic plants.

Two identical sections were designed at the center to allow researchers to manipulate certain environmental features so that a control and experimental group design could be undertaken. While experimentation is in the preliminary stages, researchers have noted that placing familiar objects near the entrances to residents' rooms has helped the more severely impaired adults to find their way back. One experiment attempted to keep wandering residents away from an exit to the outdoors. A grid pattern was painted in front of the doorway. Instead of keeping people away, it attracted more attention. It was also found that covering a panic bar on doors tended to keep residents away because most Alzheimer's clients could not recognize what was behind the cloth.

The above example provides a most interesting approach to the interaction of design, living space and those who suffer from one type of cognitive impairment. Every attempt was made to create a home-like environment which would also allow residents to be relaxed, safe, independent, and functioning to their maximum. It is hoped that research like that being conducted at the Dolan Center will result in guidelines to create activity areas which are highly functional for activity staff and the residents they serve who suffer from cognitive dysfunctions.

Summary

The purpose of this chapter was to create an awareness on the part of activity professionals of the relationship between the environment in which activities occur and in which residents live and the experiences gained through leisure programs. The psychosocial link of humans with the physical environment has been much discussed.

The model presented earlier in this book and in this chapter showed the physical environment as a part of the system within which activity directors operate. The role of the activity department within the long-term care setting, the relationship of the activity department with other allied professions (e.g., nursing, physical therapy), and everything which constitutes the physical environment are combined to create this system.

The activity room is an essential part of the total long-term care facility. Issues of location, ease in access, and compatibility with the total design are significant concerns. In both a functional and an aesthetic sense, the activity setting must complement other public and private spaces.

A frequent problem in designing for older adults residing in nursing homes and other long-stay facilities is that generalizations and norms are used where averages don't always apply to specific individuals. The aging process varies tremendously on a personal level; added to this are the varieties of conditions experienced by many elders. The status of physical, emotional, and cognitive health as represented by residents is constantly changing in a long-term care facility. It is understandable that designers are faced with a challenging, if not impossible task conceiving a single plan to meet the needs of all.

A number of theories were reviewed highlighting the relationships of behavior and personality with the physical environment. Holism (Hiatt, 1986) analyzes the interplay of humans with man-made and natural features in the environment. Pastalan (1985) views the design task as seeking an appropriate match between the complexity level each person can handle and the physical elements present. Both over or understimulation in the sense of environmental challenges can be problematic.

Fozard (1981) reaffirmed the heterogenity of the older population and the difficulty in establishing cycles or stages that all frail older persons pass through at similar chronological points. Parsons (1981) has developed a matrix which examines environmental factors affecting nine behavioral areas.

Learned helplessness (Seligman, 1975) can be the result of a physical and social environment which demand passivity and compliance. In its worst form residents see themselves as only accommodating to the wishes of staff. Kiernat (1987) emphasized that designers and long-term care personnel must allow control to exist in the hands of residents. Independence and choice are to be fostered.

Sensory loss and the aging process was reviewed. A theme throughout was the possibility that sensory deficiencies may lead to behavioral and morale changes. Activity and medical staff must not assume that loss (sensory) is to be accepted because of old age. Examinations are to be undertaken and prescriptive devices used where appropriate.

Vision problems are typical in later life. Sensory input through the eye is central to most leisure activities. Environmental concerns to assist with poor vision may take the form of greater levels of illumination, reduction of glare, use of bulbs which help to render exact color, use of color contrast, and having low vision aids in the activity room. Activity directors may also be called upon to plan specific activities which may aid in the rehabilitation of those with vision problems.

Declines in hearing are experienced by large numbers of those who live in long-stay settings. Causes of hearing problems are many; dysfunctional cells, trauma to ears or eardrums, conductive problems, and changes in the structure of the inner ear can all result in decreased levels of audition. The types of hearing problems are numerous, as well. Blurring of sounds, loss of high-pitched tones, loss of consonants in speech, ringing in the ears, and magnification of normal background noises may be experienced by aged adults. Staff must understand the type of hearing problem experienced, and suggestions were offered to create a setting where sound can be transmitted with a minimum of environmental interference.

Safety within a nursing home is always a priority. Fall prevention is a goal related to indoor and outdoor spaces which aligns with safety. Falls are often the cause of physical impairments which lead to placement in a long-stay facility. Similar to vision and hearing, the cause of falls may be multifaceted. Poor sensory input, poor balance, medication, and hazards in the environment are responsible for falls among the elderly. The placement and type of furniture, kinds and levels of illumination, nature of floor surfaces, and prompt clean-up of spills are all considerations under the control of the activity directors which may lead to a safer environment.

The concluding area discussed relative to design and space was that of cognitive impairments. The degree to which organization of space is present and the ability of the environment to encourage socialization, independence, choice, and innovativeness are factors crucial to those with cognitive problems. The process of cognition was reviewed. Messages must be perceived correctly, and transferred to the brain for encoding. Later, a search and retrieval process will occur and a proper response, verbal, motor, or both, will be required. Breakdowns can occur in any of the processes which may lead to problems in cognition.

Two main categories are used in classifying cognitive impairments: functional and organic.

Activity staff are required to understand the type of cognitive impairment present, and low expectations in this area must not be associated with normal aging.

The physical environment is extremely important to the functioning of those with deficits in cognition. The ability to navigate the physical environment successfully and safely is a criterion related to mental functioning. The need for well-planned spaces which allow accurate information to be processed is apparent. Residents suffering from Alzheimer's disease are becoming more common in long-term care settings. Experimentation with elements of residential space may lead to guidelines which will offer a supportive environment.

PRACTICAL EXERCISE

Activity Area Assessment

The following tool has been developed for activity personnel to be used in evaluating the physical environment in which activities take place. The intent is to examine the primary room or area used for activities; other personal spaces such as residents' rooms could be analyzed using elements within the assessment or by creating a tool for personal spaces based upon comments in this chapter.

Rather than viewing each statement or criterion as an absolute standard which must be measured and quantified, the assessment may prove more useful in creating an awareness of how the physical environment interacts with persons and programming and in noting any obvious weaknesses.

Activity staff and residents, volunteers, and others familiar with the activity setting can be called upon to join in the assessment.

I. **General Assessment**
    1. Draw a diagram of the room and show the placement of furniture, entrances/exits, storage areas, and offices.
    2. If the room serves multipurpose functions, list the different types of programs which will take place in it.

3. How is the activity room linked with other areas in the facility? Where is it located? Are there problems getting residents to the area because of its location?
4. Is the space organized within the activity room? Are certain parts of the room used for specific purposes?
5. What type of furniture, chairs, tables, etc. are used? Are they at the proper height to serve most residents? Are chairs sturdy and do they offer good back support?
6. Is furniture arranged to create social groupings? Are both small and larger groupings of persons found in the room? Could any change be made to encourage different types of social interaction?
7. Have provisions been made for assisting with certain deficits? Are design elements present to aid sensory, mobility, or cognitive deficits?
8. Were residents and staff consulted in the initial design of the activity room? If so, in what ways were their suggestions incorporated into the physical environment? If not, what recommendations would you favor to create an improved design for the existing activity area?

II. **The Environment and Vision**
    1. Are staff aware of the different types of vision problems experienced by residents? Are these problems considered when program plans are developed, and are adaptive devices such as low vision aids available for those who require them?
    2. Rate the level of illumination. Are both natural and man-made sources used? Is illumination consistent and balanced throughout the area; are dark spots present? Do any residents/staff complain of poor lighting?
    3. Is glare a problem at all? Are sections of the room oriented so that

natural light causes glare at certain times of the day? Can this be corrected? Do any surfaces (e.g., tabletops) reflect light causing glare?

4. Are incandescent or florescent (or other type) bulbs used as the primary source? If florescent are used, are they high CRI bulbs to help in accurately rendering true color?

5. Is color contrast used throughout the room? Are edges of doorways set apart from walls, are knobs or drawers and doors of contrasting color, are tabletops of a different color than implements or tools placed on them? Are sections of the room denoted by different colors?

6. Are low vision aids apparent? Adjustable, focused light sources, magnifying glasses, etc.? Does the library have large-print books and is contrasting, large print used on signs, posters, etc. within the activity room and throughout the facility?

III. The Environment and Hearing

1. Can staff detail the specific type of hearing problems experienced by residents? Are these deficiencies accounted for in program plans? Has the activity room been designed to support the accurate transmission of sound?

2. Are excessive background noises apparent (e.g., ventilation motors, air conditioners)?

3. Are sound amplification devices used when appropriate? Is there a public address system in good working order? Is there a sound loop for the severely hearing impaired?

4. Do activity personnel check to see if hearing aids are in good working condition and are being worn by residents who have them?

5. Are staff aware of good communication techniques, and are they used? Are they facing those spoken to,

speaking at a reasonable pace, and reducing distance between speaker and receiver?

6. Can problems be identified in the activity area which would either dampen sound or cause sound to bounce or reflect? Heavy carpet and drapes will dampen sound whereas stark surfaces may reflect sound.

7. Do staff consider hearing as a cause when behavioral changes are noted in residents? This is particularly important when social activities are noticeably reduced.

IV. Falls

1. Is furniture arranged so that aisles are clear and large enough to accommodate walkers, wheelchairs, and other assistive devices?

2. Has color contrast been used to designate changes in slope or surface? Does a pattern in the flooring cause residents to perceive a change in slope where one does not exist?

3. Are handrails in place within the activity room for residents who need them? Are they such that they can be easily grasped?

4. If carpeting exists in any area within the activity room, is it of high quality and kept in good repair?

5. Is the tile flooring kept clean and maintained so that slips will not occur?

6. Do staff monitor personal spaces, bedrooms, for example, as part of an overall plan to create a safe environment where falls will be minimized?

V. The Environment and the Cognitively Impaired

1. Are staff aware of the differing types of cognitive impairments experienced by residents? Do program plans include cognitive skills needed to complete the activity?

2. If reality orientation programs are used, are all devices such as clocks,

calendars, weekly schedules, etc., adjusted to reflect the same information?

3. If the activity room is multipurpose (as it most often is), is there a way of designating the use of the room by such things as the arrangement of the furniture, or having music playing prior to a music program? Are such signs or signals available to assist the cognitively impaired?

4. Has the entire facility been designed to accommodate wandering? Is there a figure eight or circular pattern available for wandering? Do staff have a plan to deal with wandering in the activity area?

5. Are adaptive devices used in activities to assist the cognitively impaired? Are multiple clues, such as combining colors and shapes, used to modify activities? Are activities continually reviewed to analyze cognitive requirements?

6. Is color coding used in the activity room to symbolize function? Example: yellow designating storage space, green as a dominant color where a specific activity occurs (e.g., music or painting).

VI. The Psychological Environment

1. Is there a philosophy present which is expressed in the way that all staff treat residents? What are the characteristics of this philosophy? Is the physical environment compatible with this philosophy?

2. Evaluate the entire facility and the activity room in particular according to the criteria discussed earlier:

organization _____	disorganization
socialization _____	singular activities
independence _____	dependence
choice _____	nonchoice
innovativeness _____	dullness

3. The concept of "learned helplessness" was noted as an undesirable condition often reinforced by the structure of the long-term care facility. Are there any ways in which activity staff encourage "learned helplessness" on the part of residents? Identify specific problems and suggest ways to address them.

4. Discussed at length was the notion of attempting to make a match between the demands of the physical environment and the abilities of each resident. Assess the physical characteristics of the activity setting, the types of programs offered, and the way recreation staff interact with residents in regard to making this desirable match.

References

Allen, C. (1985). *Occupational therapy for psychiatric diseases*: *Measurement and management of geriatric disabilities*. Boston, MA: Little Brown & Co.

American Association of Homes for the Aging. (1985). *Guide to caring for the mentally impaired elderly*.

Archea, J. (1977). Personal conversation with J. L. Fozard (See Fozard reference).

Belkin, L. (1984, August 14). *Making life safer for the elderly*. Rochester Times Union, p. 3E.

Boyce, P. and Simons, R. (1977). Hue discrimination and light sources. *Lighting Research and Technology, 9*, 125-140.

Branch, L., Horowitz, A., and Carr, C. (1989). The implications for everyday life of incident self-reported visual decline among people over age 65 living in the community. *The Gerontologist, 29*(3), 359-365.

Brent, R. (1984). Advocacy design in the nursing home: Cultivating public and private spaces for the newly admitted resident. In S. Spicker and S. Ingham (Eds.), *Vitalizing long-term care* (pp. 159-176). New York, NY: Springer Publishing Company, Inc.

Cardea, J. and Tynan, C. (1987). Home safety and health: A quality of life issue. *Lifestyles: A Journal of Changing Patterns, 8*(3/4), 106-115.

Cooper, B. (1985). A model for implementing color contrast in the environment of the elderly. *American Journal of Occupational Therapy, 39*(4), 253-258.

Dye, C. (1983). Sensory changes in aging. In N. Ernst and H. Glazer-Waldman (Eds.), *The aged patient*. Chicago, IL: Year Book Medical Publishers, Inc.

Fozard, J. (1981). Person-environment relationships in adulthood: Implications for human factors engineering. *Human Factors, 23*(1), 7-27.

Galton, L. (1976). Drugs and the elderly. *Nursing, 76*, 39-43.

Halberg, K. (1987). Leisure programming in long term care facilities: Far more than the monthly calendar of activities. In M. J. Keller and N. J. Osgood (Eds.), *Dynamic leisure programming with older adults* (pp. 107-119). Alexandria, VA: National Recreation and Park Association.

Heinemann, A., Colorez, A., Frank, S., and Taylor, D. (1988). Leisure activity participation of elderly individuals with low vision. *The Gerontologist, 28*(2), 181-184.

Hiatt, L. (1986). The environment's role in the total well-being of the older person. In G. Magau and E. Haught (Eds.), *Well-being and the elderly: An holistic view* (pp. 23-37). Washington, DC: American Association of Homes for the Aging.

Hughes, P. and Neer, R. (1981). Lighting for the elderly: A psychobiological approach to lighting. *Human Factors, 23*(1), 65-85.

Kiernat, J. (1983). The effect of hearing loss on the activities of older persons. *Activities, Adaptation & Aging, 4*(1), 39-47.

Kiernat, J. (1987). Promoting independence and autonomy through environmental approaches. *Topics in Geriatric Rehabilitation, 3*(1), 1-6.

Kirchner, C. (1985). *Data on blindness and visual impairment in the U.S: A resource manual on characteristics, education, employment, and service delivery*. New York, NY: American Foundation for the Blind.

Langer, E. and Rodin, J. (1976). The effects of choice and enhanced personal responsibility for the aged: A field experiment in an institutional setting. *Journal of Personality and Social Psychology, 34*, 191-198.

Lawton, M. P. (1982). Competence, environmental press, and the adaptation of older people. In M. P. Lawton, P. Windley, E. T. Byerts (Eds.), *Aging and the Environment: Theoretical Approaches*. New York, NY: Springer Publishing Company, Inc.

Levine, R., and Merril, S. (1987). Psychosocial aspects of the environment. *Topics in Geriatric Rehabilitation, 3*(1), 27-34.

Levy, L. (1989). Activity adaptation in rehabilitation of the physically and cognitively disabled aged. *Topics in Geriatric Rehabilitation, 4*(4), 53-66.

Lewin, T. (1990, May 2). Alzheimer's and architecture: A search for order. *New York Times*, p. A14.

MacNeil, R. (1982). The nursing home as a motivational wasteland: Perspectives on the design of a therapeutic environment. In M. Teague, R. MacNeil, and G. Hitzhusen (Eds.), *Perspectives on Leisure and aging in a changing society* (pp. 256-297). Columbia, MO: University Printing Services.

MacNeil, R. and Teague, M. (1987). *Aging and leisure: Vitality in later life* (pp. 96-119). Englewood Cliffs, NJ: Prentice Hall, Inc.

McClannahan, L. (1973). Recreation programs for nursing home residents: The importance of patient characteristics and environmental variables. *Therapeutic Recreation Journal, 7*(2), 26-31.

Moos, R. (1974). *Evaluating treatment environments: A social ecological approach.* New York, NY: John Wiley & Sons, Inc.

Noakes, E. (1988, September/October). Buildings that work for people, and not against them. *Perspective on Aging*, 14-15.

Parsons, H. M. (1981). Residential design for the aging (For example, the bedroom). *Human Factors, 23*(1), 39-58.

Pastalan, L. (1985). The physical environment and the emerging nature of the extended-care model (pp. 245-261). In E. Schneider, et al., (Eds.), *The teaching nursing home.* New York, NY: Raven Press.

Raphael, C. (1987). An architect's viewpoint. *Topics in Geriatric Rehabilitation, 3*(1), 19-25.

Salmen, J. (1988). *The do-able, renewable home.* Washington, DC: American Association of Retired Persons.

Seligman, M. (1975). *Helplessness: On depression, development, and death.* San Francisco, CA: W. H. Freeman & Company Publishers.

Sherwood, S. (1975). Long-term care: Issues, perspectives, and reactions. In S. Sherwood (Ed.), *Long-term care: A handbook for researchers, planners, and providers.* New York, NY: Spectrum Publications, Inc.

Shore, H. (1976). Designing a training program for understanding sensory losses in aging. *The Gerontologist, 16*(2), 157-165.

Smith, A. and Aston, S. (1989). The use of activity in rehabilitation of elders with vision impairments. *Topics in Geriatric Rehabilitation, 4*(4), 45-52.

Spencer, J. (1987). Environmental assessment strategies. *Topics in Geriatric Rehabilitation, 3*(1), 35-41.

Stoudt, H. (1981). The anthropometry of the elderly. *Human Factors, 23*(1), 29-37.

Teaff, J. (1985). *Leisure Services with the Elderly.* St. Louis, MO: Times Mirror/Mosby College Publishing.

Tideiksaar, R. (1987). Fall prevention in the home. *Topics in Geriatric Rehabilitation, 3*(1), 57-64.

United States Senate, Special Committee on Aging. (1989). *Aging America: Trends and Projections.* Washington, DC: U.S. Government Printing Office.

Walz, T., Harper, D., and Wilson, J. (1986). The aging developmentally disabled person: A review. *The Gerontologist, 26*(6), 622-629.

Yerxa, E., and Baum, S. (1987). Environmental theories and the older person. *Topics in Geriatric Rehabilitation, 3*(1), 7-18.

Zarlock, R. (1975). In T. Smith (Ed.), *The Shangri-la effect: A view of the psychology of aging.* Paper presented at the University of Northern Colorado, Title IV Workshop on Aging, April, 1975.

Figure 7.1: Parson's Environmental/Behavioral Matrix Applied to the Activity Room

<table>
<tr><td rowspan="11" style="writing-mode: vertical-rl;">POTENTIAL BEHAVIORAL EFFECTS</td><td colspan="2">THE ENTIRE ACTIVITY ROOM</td></tr>
<tr><td>Concerns</td><td>
• Overall design of activity room.
• Where it's located within the facility.
• Type of furniture, chairs.
• Size of the room.
• Shape of the room
• Planning process used.
</td></tr>
<tr><td>Activities</td><td>
• What activities can or can't be undertaken?
• Can residents easily reach the activity room?
• Is furniture appropriate for activities?
• Does the design hamper or assist with activities?
</td></tr>
<tr><td>Locomotion</td><td>
• Does the room permit easy movement?
• Are aisles wide?
• Can transfers be made for those with wheelchairs?
• Are floor surfaces appropriate?
</td></tr>
<tr><td>Social Interaction</td><td>
• Is the room designed for specific social interactions?
• Can the arrangement of furniture accommodate large and small groups?
• Is social interaction a goal of programming and how is this linked to the physical environment?
</td></tr>
<tr><td>Feelings</td><td>
• Do color and other ambient factors create a mood in the room?
• Do staff members create a tone or atmosphere in the room?
• Are programs designed to uplift or create social interactions?
</td></tr>
<tr><td>Perception</td><td>
• Does the room permit accurate perceptions (e.g., clocks, calendars)?
• What is the shape and size of the room?
• Is the room designed to aid sensory input?
</td></tr>
<tr><td>Motivation</td><td>
• Does the room encourage or discourage certain interactions (due to shape, size, furniture arrangement)?
</td></tr>
<tr><td>Health and Safety</td><td>
• Is accident prevention a design consideration?
• What is the level of illumination?
• Are there mobility problems?
• What is floor surface?
• How is maintenance handled?
</td></tr>
<tr><td>Learning</td><td>
• Is learning a goal of activity program?
• Does the activity room assist with learning?
</td></tr>
<tr><td>Manipulation</td><td>
• Does the participant exhibit control?
• Is choice emphasized?
• Is there manipulation of objects/materials in the program?
</td></tr>
<tr><td></td><td colspan="2">RESOURCES</td></tr>
<tr><td></td><td>Concerns</td><td>
• How do furniture and control devices affect behavior?
• Is storage space available?
• What type of lighting is used?
• Are tables suitable for activities?
• Are materials adequate for programming?
</td></tr>
<tr><td></td><td>Activities</td><td>
• Can activities be undertaken due to proper furniture, lighting, storage, etc?
• Are necessary materials available?
• Are chairs appropriate for activities undertaken?
</td></tr>
<tr><td></td><td>Locomotion</td><td>
• Does furniture assist locomotion?
• Are considerations made for those with mobility problems or aids?
• Are aisles wide enough?
• Are handrails present for those who require them?
</td></tr>
</table>

Adapted From: Parsons, H. M. (1981). Residential design for the aging (For example, the bedroom). *Human Factors, 23*(1), 39-58.

Figure 7.1: Parson's Environmental/Behavioral Matrix Applied to the Activity Room
(continued)

POTENTIAL BEHAVIORAL EFFECTS		**RESOURCES** (continued)
	Social Interaction	• How does furniture and placement of furniture affect social interaction? • What type of tables are used? • Are different social interactions possible?
	Feelings	• How do furniture, lighting, etc., create a mood? • How would residents describe the activity room?
	Perception	• Is the room perceived as cluttered or barren? • Is furniture organized to create a perception of control, neatness, coziness, etc?
	Motivation	• Do chairs, tables and other elements encourage or discourage certain interactions?
	Health and Safety	• Do chairs, tables and other types of furniture assist with safety? • Are chairs and tables sturdy? • Are materials in the room stored safely? • Is an appropriate level of illumination present?
	Learning	• Are chairs, tables and other types of materials appropriate for learning activities?
	Manipulation	• Does the participant manipulate objects in the room? • Are any adaptations made to permit manipulation?
		SPATIAL ARRANGEMENT
	Concerns	• How does the arrangement/location of furniture and objects affect behavior?
	Activities	• Is furniture arranged for specific activities? • Are windows used in activities?
	Locomotion	• Does the arrangement of furniture permit easy locomotion?
	Social Interaction	• How does arrangement of furniture affect social interaction? • Are large and small group activities undertaken?
	Feelings	• What is the mood of the room due to the arrangement of objects?
	Perception	• How are physical elements arranged to create a perception on the part of participants?
	Motivation	• Is furniture arranged to encourage or discourage certain activities?
	Health and Safety	• Safety concerns related to furniture arrangement—adequate aisles, etc.
	Learning	• Is the arrangement of physical properties related to learning activities?
	Manipulation	• Is there a link between arrangement of chairs/tables, etc., and manipulation of objects in programs?
		COMMUNICATION
	Concerns	• How do elements in the physical environment communicate information about the environment? • How does the environment assist with communication among persons?
	Activities	• Are reality orientation devices accurate? • Does the physical environment assist with personal communication? • Does the room assist the cognitively impaired to understand purpose/function?
	Locomotion	• Is accurate information (color coded doors, contrasting color to indicate slope, etc.) communicated to assist locomotion?
	Social Interaction	• Is personal communication assisted to promote social interaction?
	Feelings	• Does the accurate/inaccurate transmission of information about the environment affect feelings of participants?
	Perception	• Are accurate perceptions gained due to how information is communicated (e.g. knowledge of storage areas, activity calendars)?

Adapted From: Parsons, H. M. (1981). Residential design for the aging (For example, the bedroom). *Human Factors, 23*(1), 39-58.

Figure 7.1: Parson's Environmental/Behavioral Matrix Applied to the Activity Room (continued)		
COMMUNICATION (continued)		
POTENTIAL BEHAVIORAL EFFECTS	Motivation	• Is there a link between the level of personal communication and motivation of residents?
	Health and Safety	• How is the emergency communication system related to safety? • Is information about the physical emergency equipment accurate to eliminate accidents?
	Learning	• Are techniques (e.g., color, size or shape) used to communicate information? • Are cognitively impaired assisted through reality orientation devices, etc?
	Manipulation	• Is there a connection between manipulation and how information about the physical environment is • communicated?
	APPEARANCE	
	Concerns	• How does color affect behavioral areas? • Is a stimulating environment present? • Is cleanliness present?
	Activities	• Does the appearance of the activity room (e.g., color, cleanliness) affect the provision of activities?
	Locomotion	• Does color affect locomotion? • Is color contrast used for safety in ambulating?
	Social Interaction	• Is a cheerful atmosphere present in color scheme, etc., to promote social interaction?
	Feelings	• How do color and cleanliness affect the mood of the room?
	Perception	• Does color contrast affect perception? • Do confusing patterns or designs negatively impact on perception?
	Motivation	• Does the appearance of the activity room help to motivate participants?
	Health and Safety	• How is cleanliness in the activity room related to health? • Does color (coding or information-related) assist with safety?
	Learning	• Is color used to denote function, etc? • Does color coding assist the cognitively impaired?
	Manipulation	• Do residents manipulate by way of displays or exhibits?
	CONSEQUATION	
	Concerns	• Are there design elements which strengthen or weaken behaviors? • Are certain activities encouraged or discouraged because of elements in the physical environment?
	Activities	• Is there a lack in the physical environment which does not permit certain activities? • Are certain activities encouraged because of the environment?
	Locomotion	• To what degree does design assist with mobility?
	Social Interaction	• Are persons encouraged to interact because of the physical environment (available seating patterns, etc.)?
	Feelings	• Are feelings linked to prohibitions or ecouragements from the environment?
	Perception	
	Motivation	• Is motivation encouraged/discouraged due to the physical environment?
	Health and Safety	• To what degree does design aid safety?
	Learning	• Is the room structured to encourage learning?
	Manipulation	• Are choice and active mastery available to residents?

Adapted From: Parsons, H. M. (1981). Residential design for the aging (For example, the bedroom). *Human Factors, 23*(1), 39-58.

		PROTECTION
POTENTIAL BEHAVIORAL EFFECTS	Concerns	• How do design elements related to safety of residents affect various behaviors?
	Activities	• Are elements in the physical environment designed to assist with the safe conduct of activities? • Are the floor surfaces safe for activities? • Are edges on tables rounded—safe for activities?
	Locomotion	• How do flooring, spacing of equipment assist locomotion? • Are slopes easily identified to assist locomotion? • Is adequate space available for locomotion?
	Social Interaction	• Does safety in the sense of design elements affect social interaction?
	Feelings	• Is safety one of the factors in the overall impression of the activity area?
	Perception	• Do residents perceive the activity area as safe?
	Motivation	• Do design elements (e.g., flooring, furniture arrangement) related to safety encourage or discourage certain actions (are safe behaviors encouraged due to design)?
	Health and Safety	• Analyzing the physical environment in relation to health and safety.
	Learning	• Are safe behaviors learned or encouraged due to the environment?
	Manipulation	• When using objects in activities, does the environment encourage safety? • Are objects themselves (scissor, etc.) designed for safe use?
		AMBIENT CONDITIONS
	Concerns	• To what degree do features such as heat, ventilation, illumination, sound, and odor affect the conduct of activities?
	Activities	• Is the room comfortable for activities? • Does a good lighting source assist activities? • Are temperature and humidity appropriate?
	Locomotion	• Do sound and illumination affect locomotion?
	Social Interaction	• Does the degree of comfort encourage social participation?
	Feelings	• How do ambient conditions in the activity room relate to feelings about the area?
	Perception	• Do residents perceive comfort in the activity room?
	Motivation	• Does lighting, heat, humidity, sound, odor, etc., encourage or discourage certain behaviors?
	Health and Safety	• Does illumination create a safe environment? • Is ventilation adequate (e.g., health concerns)? • Can people easily be heard, to warn or to give direction?
	Learning	• How do ambient conditions help residents to learn about their environment?
	Manipulation	• Are choice and mastery related in any way to ambient features?

Figure 7.1: Parson's Environmental/Behavioral Matrix Applied to the Activity Room
(continued)

Adapted From: Parsons, H. M. (1981). Residential design for the aging (For example, the bedroom). *Human Factors, 23*(1), 39-58.

Figure 7.2:
Application of the Cooper Color Contrast Model to an Activity Setting

OBJECTIVE: LEISURE ACTIVITIES		
	ITEM	
	PAINT BRUSHES	EASEL WITH WRITING PAD
Existing Color	Wooden, light color	White pad, wooden easel (light)
Background	Wood color formica table	Cream colored walls near windows
Ideal Contrast	Good light–dark contrast; opposite color hues	Dark matte colors
Limitations	Different table top not feasible	None
Final Color	Brush handles white	Dark blue wall
Method	Use black matte poster board on table top; paint handles white	Move existing easel near windows to inside blue wall

Adapted from: Cooper, B. A., (1985). A model for implementing color contrasts in the environment of the elderly. *The American Journal of Occupational Therapy, 39*(4), 253-258

Personal and Personnel Relationships

Human interactions in the nursing home or long-term care facility are shaped by a variety of players—residents, caregivers or staff, family members, and visitors from the community. These relationships occur in formal and informal ways, and the meanings attached to them vary from each person's perspective. Each day, social interactions are affected by not only the desires of individual residents, but also by a host of environmental or institutional factors such as established routines and time schedules, staffing patterns which allow or prevent a visit with a resident, or crises which occur and disrupt the normal regimens of all. Relations among residents are also affected by personal characteristics: ethnicity, physical and mental conditions, and longevity—whether the resident is newly admitted or a veteran of the facility.

It must be emphasized that the activity department's role in fostering socialization is a key one. A glance at individual activity goals or objectives of a given leisure offering will most often reveal the component of social opportunities or skills. Activity directors plan and direct experiences where individuals can come together to share interactions and perhaps to initiate or build friendships. Activity staff may operate in a formal manner as the deliverers of a program, but, in addition, they function as a part of the system of informal relationships. They joke, they kid, they sit and listen, they share in a song. This chapter focuses on the connection of personal relationships with the activity department.

This chapter explores interactions among residents and friendships, and their meanings are discussed. Relations with family members and friends outside of the long-term care residence are reviewed followed by an examination of staff interactions with older residents, focusing particularly on the activity department. Volunteers from the community are an important part of activity programming, and their supervision often falls to the activities director. Residents can be volunteers, as well, and this role is addressed. Community resources are detailed as ways of bringing vitality into the nursing home. In the last section, personnel relationships both within and outside of the activity unit are explored.

Personal Relationships: Resident-To-Resident

One measure of quality of life is the type and number of friendships one has. In Chapter 3, "Institutional Living," a number of points were raised about how adaptations are made to a long-term care environment and the particular difficulties faced by the newly admitted in approaching a level of comfort in the existing social milieu. One case study of a nursing home (O'Brien, 1989) revealed these themes pertaining to adjustment and social linkages. The resident on entering the nursing home faces a world turned upside-down, one characterized by loss, confusion, often unsure feelings about family and frequently accompanied by a change in physical condition, the reason for the placement. Social interactions forced too soon can be difficult for new residents. Most face a period of adjusting to new personalities and routines. Becoming comfortable with one's own situation is the major issue. Over time most do develop friendships with a few others, and there is a tendency to view certain staff as more than caregivers. Certain workers are valued for their caring attitudes, and they are perceived as a type of "friend" (more on this aspect in the next section). Family friendships are important although these relationships may be strained due to the circumstances surrounding placement.

One analysis of friendships among the elderly (Adams, 1986) found general support in the research literature for a positive connection between friendship and psychological well-being. Two types of friendship categories were noted: primary, or those characterized by emotionally close relationships and the number of friends; and secondary, friendships based on proximity, frequency of visits, and often new acquaintances. While Adam's (1986) sample consisted of older, nonmarried females living in the community, some findings bear scrutiny when considering the long-term care environment. The secondary friendships were correlated with positive affect or outlook in the older women. In fact primary relationships were linked to negative affect—feelings of restlessness, boredom, or depression, perhaps, because problems of their friends were internalized, or conditions no longer allowed the type of friendship known in earlier years. As related to nursing homes, however, proximity or closeness, frequency of interaction, and newness (coming in contact with recently admitted residents) are factors relevant to the social interactions of residents. Close friendships will develop among those living in long-term care facilities, but activity staff should be aware of the secondary type of friendships which they promote through their activity offerings.

Another issue involved in friendships and social interactions is the presence of cliques. It is natural in any setting where large numbers are gathered to form smaller groupings based upon interests or common backgrounds. O'Brien (1989) made reference to them in her examination of Bethany Manor. Activity staff must decide when such groupings become closed and destructive to others. The "card players" are a group often associated with the notion of a clique. The nature of the game itself lends to pairings or small groups. Staff observation is necessary, however, to determine if some are being excluded. Control exists in the hands of staff to structure situations which will bring smaller groups together or allow the reticent observer to feel welcome within the larger setting. Environmental factors such as using larger round tables instead of smaller square ones can also assist in creating desired social interactions. The key issue here is awareness and making a decision as to when the positive side of small groups (e.g., identification, familiarity) begins to become overshadowed by the negative aspects (e.g., exclusion, splintering).

Length of stay and personal physical and mental conditions greatly affect social networking in a nursing home. As in any situation where one begins a venture as a "novice" and remains for a period of time until the label of "veteran" is earned, the individual timeline in a nursing home may start with the typical state of confusion on entering, move to a period (perhaps lengthy) of adjustment and routine, and shift again at the last phase to placement in a new wing necessitated by a weakened condition whereby "patient" rather than "resident" becomes descriptive of treatment and interaction. A settling period must occur for anyone newly arrived in a long-term care setting. The elder has been wrenched from possessions and community friends. Staff swarm in initially in a probing, formal way—reports must be completed, goals established, and routine structured. A complete stranger within arm's reach may suddenly be sharing all of one's waking hours. Strides toward establishing friendships may be understandably tentative during this time. As distancing from the prior lifestyle proceeds, the nature of interactions changes. Once again, staff, particularly those providing activity services, can ease the transition and encourage interchanges. An assessment tool—looking at the resident's life history of leisure and the nature of social engagements during free time—can give direction to staff. A person preferring solitary leisure pursuits stands in contrast to one who always enjoyed social gatherings where large numbers were present. Past interests may signal introductions to various groups at the home—the card players or volunteers, for example.

It is common for "special" friends to be identified by residents (O'Brien, 1989). One or two individuals will fit the category of primary friendships (Adams, 1986). Health changes impact significantly upon the formation and maintenance of friendships. Residents are aware of those who suffer from cognitive deficiencies, and this group is seen as distinct from others in the residence (O'Brien, 1989). The fear of entering this group is pervasive.

To summarize, social interactions among older adults in long-term stay residences are influenced by a variety of factors, some under the control of staff. Personal history and background, physical and mental ability, the circumstances of admittance, length of stay, and personality factors are likely to shape how social interaction is approached. Environmental factors including staff, daily routine, and physical features such as areas accessible for small group interaction or the design and placement of furniture affect the process. Astute activity professionals will recognize their role in this area of daily life and offer assistance in developing positive social relationships among residents.

Family and Friends From the Community

Relationships with family members and friends living in the community represent another type of social network for older persons living in nursing homes. Family and friends are links to both the past and the present (O'Brien, 1989). They can serve as conduits for news and information between residents and their former neighborhood communities. This function or role, however, is likely to change when viewed from a perspective of a few months to a few years to a period of many years. Conflicting feelings on the part of both new residents and loved ones may exist which might be responsible for how this type of link to the past is handled. Family (or residents newly arrived) may wish to get on with the present, and an approach of negating the immediate past may be taken. Such a strategy may not be helpful or necessary. Guilt may be a factor, also. The here and now of the current situation in the nursing home may be stressed while associations with home or community may be blocked/avoided. Activity staff can be useful in giving a "read" on the situation from the view of "mom" or "pop." To dwell completely on the former life is not desirable in moving toward a positive transition, yet "transition" signifies a shift from the former to the current and the future, and to disregard completely the near past is not realistic. It can be expected that the activity director or leaders will be called upon for advice during this transition.

The circumstances surrounding the decision of placement in a long-term care setting establish the tone of resident-family relations at the outset. Both the negative ("I've been dumped") and the not so negative ("I don't want to be a burden and this is the best solution for all") are expressed by those in nursing homes (O'Brien, 1989). Staff can be proactive here in stressing the positive aspects of life in their facility and seeing that special attention is given to new members. Residents should be reassured of their family's love for them; and the variety of opportunities (especially in the activity department) available should be presented. Some residents try to "cover" for family members who are less than regular with their visits; excuses focused on time pressures are not uncommon (O'Brien, 1989).

Beliefs about nursing homes and the willingness to provide care by family members was the topic of a study by Biedenharn and Normoyle (1991). Their sample consisted of adults over the age of 60 in the midwest who were living in the community. The results concerning perceptions about the willingness of family to care for elders and the elder's ability to ask for assistance are instructive. About half of the respondents felt that their families would be willing to provide them care in their homes if needed; about one-quarter felt families would not be receptive to such a situation. Nearly 70 percent of the community elders expressed a reluctance to ask for such care if the need ever arose. A relationship was found between the perception of family members' willingness to provide care to

an elder and the fear of entering a nursing home—those who saw family as unwilling in this regard had higher levels of fear of entering a nursing home. Another aspect of the survey measured perceptions about resident care in nursing homes, and between 40 and 50 percent of respondents viewed care in the areas of staff concern for residents, the availability of interesting activities, and family interest in resident's care to be a problem. The implication here is that aging adults who may at some time enter a nursing home obviously see a connection between their family's willingness to provide assistance to them and the actuality of being admitted to a long-term care residence. New residents will express a range of emotions concerning family members—some perceptions may be accurate, others not. If the vast majority is reluctant to ask family to care for them, how does this change when one actually enters a nursing home? The point to be made is that each aged adult who enters a nursing home brings a history of interactions with loved ones. Past relations may be overshadowed by the recent events leading to placement, and staff may be challenged to deal with conflicting emotions of confusion, guilt, resistance, acceptance, fear, and anger held by family members or elders when moved to a care facility.

How can long-term care staff assist with relations between residents and family members or friends from the community? Experience has shown that members of the activity department are frequently called upon to act in an intermediary role. Loved ones want to know about adaptation, daily routine, and physical condition of their older family member. Residents may be more than willing to let staff know about their lack of visitors. For some, forgetfulness may be a problem, and personnel can remind residents that it has not been forever since their last visit. One rule should be observed, and that pertains to honesty in such matters. Even with patients/ residents who are cognitively impaired, expectations should never be raised or signals given that visitations may be planned without full knowledge and confirmation. Likewise, staff should discuss problems or issues faced by residents (difficulties in dealing with certain residents or the tendency to avoid all social occasions) in a forthright manner with family. Some requests may enter the domain of ethical consideration, and staff should be clear as to any information which should remain in-house. For example, if information being sought about a resident's condition goes beyond what can be given in a general description, activity personnel should defer to medical specialists.

The activity department has at its disposal a number of tools which can assist family or friend and resident interactions. Special events are commonly used to serve this purpose—holiday festivities, birthdays, picnics, and other celebrations of a group nature are situations where socialization is inherent. Families may display awkwardness in dealing with loved ones at two particular times, on admittance to the home and when cognitive decline such as senile dementia affects the ability to respond. Activity staff need to be sensitive in these situations. If family members can be given a task—purchasing a lemonade from the snack shop or bringing some photos for a discussion group—their anxiety may be eased.

Whenever possible, friends and family should assist with department activities. Anything from helping with music or arts programs to bringing in the Sunday paper and reading to a group of residents should be encouraged. After the activity has concluded, a quiet time may be shared with the family member residing in the home; having a structure to the visit may help ease anxieties. Most activity directors are aware of the value of such volunteer involvement.

Activities within the long-term care facility are often directed toward keeping those in the community informed of what takes place and who has done something of interest. Staff can help residents write letters or short notes to friends and family. A pen pal relationship with a student from the nearby neighborhood can keep information flowing. One successful writing project initiated by many activity depart-

ments has been the autobiography. Life histories are taken, either orally or in written form, and these are presented to family members or friends. Newsletters or photo booklets showing resident participation in events are techniques to share life with those outside the facility.

A final role which links residents and their family members is that of advocacy, either directly within the home via some type of ombudsperson effort, or, at a state or national level, dealing with reform or new legislation. The success of these programs varies depending upon intent, the structure of the committee or group, and the willingness of administration to accept recommendations or change. One survey of ombudsperson programs and their effects in nursing homes was conducted recently in Missouri (Cherry, 1991). Such programs fall under the general concept of community presence and include any type of involvement in long-term care facilities by those living outside of such settings. Board members, volunteers, and family members are all viewed as comprising community. Only one-third of facilities had ombudsperson programs operating, and their make-up, role, and success varied greatly. A correlation was found between having an ombudsperson and alleviating poor care for older residents. Some residents view such advocacy as an important way of having their views known, while others don't wish to jeopardize their current status by initiating an investigation of their environment. Family advocates realize this is often not easy. It is, however, another link between loved ones in a long-term care setting and those working to improve the quality of life for all residents.

Resident-Staff Interactions

Interactions between staff and residents take on characteristics both formal—completing an assessment, assisting with a shower, and informal—stopping to chat while walking down the hallway. This is particularly evident when considering the activity department. The process of providing service is derived from many informal interactions—conversing, listening, smiling, encouraging fun, and so forth. In fact this emphasis upon the informal may be one reason activity staff are referred to as the "fun and games" group, and this, as viewed by other workers/professionals, can be a negative since those providing leisure programs in long-term care settings strive toward professionalism themselves (See Chapter 10, section on Professional Issues).

Residents are keenly aware of these informal contacts, and a number of surveys reveal good staff attitudes form the basis for quality of life within a nursing home. Grau (1984) reported that two-thirds of residents saw kindness and caring as the most important qualities of staff. Residents will even make excuses for staff performance which is less than top rate if it is perceived that kindness characterizes their relationship. O'Brien (1989), however, hinted that such views (excuses for staff performance) may stem from feelings that staff-resident ratios would not improve in the nursing home, and the likelihood of better service through additional personnel was remote.

Systemic factors, high turnover, burnout, lack of career options are a few of the influences resident and staff relationships as well. Meager salaries and inexperience describe the situation for many activity specialists (see Chapter 10). In her study of Bethany Manor, O'Brien (1989) found turnover, particularly for aides and others at the lowest pay scales, to be a serious issue. Holidays and weekends were prime times for staff to call in ill. These factors impede the development of friendships, and are responsible for placing severe limits on the scope and the nature of work as performed by many employees in long-term care. O'Brien (1989) observed that most who provide direct care in nursing homes do so for convenience or because of a lack of other job options. Perceiving themselves as part of the profession of gerontology or viewing their work as a career was absent.

In spite of these drawbacks staff perform in ways beyond the formal job description; one study (Fisk, 1984) found interactions with residents to be the highest reward of nursing aides. Activity directors in one survey (Pieper and Gray, 1992) noted their greatest satisfactions to be the smiles on residents' faces. Clients were viewed as surrogate grandparents and benevolence described their attitudes toward those served. O'Brien (1989) in interviewing aides discovered that selected residents were described as "my babies." While such infantilization may have obvious negative outcomes (little in the way of expectations as to what residents can do for themselves or equating their opinions/views with those of small children), it was felt that genuine loving feelings existed and close bonds developed between certain staff and residents.

Another phenomenon of social interactions in long-term care settings is labeled "the underground" (Oliver and Tureman, 1987/1988). Here workers whose job titles are low-status ones—e.g., aides, housekeeping—make friendships with residents and offer that humanness which can be so prized in an institutional environment. At times it was a group of workers who adopted the more "difficult" residents and made the time to visit or bring them a snack. Another example (Oliver and Tureman, 1987/1988) was the initiative of staff in obtaining furniture which was used for a counseling area when family members needed a space to reflect and meditate after the death of a resident. Cumulatively these interactions stemming from the kind-hearted spirit of the least rewarded employees set the emotional tone of the residential environment.

The nature of formal versus informal actions from personnel toward residents frequently is dictated by location within the facility or type of care called for at a given time. O'Brien (1989) noted the distinction between how a resident was treated after being moved to a critical care wing (when a physical condition demanded specific treatment and professional attention from nurses) as opposed to areas of the nursing home where the daily routine allowed for greater informal contacts from staff. It is this mix of job responsibilities and functional demands coupled with the desire to spend more "informal" time with residents which often frustrates staff who enter gerontological service fields.

The following reflect considerations as to how activity department staff can approach interactions with residents:

1. *Process*, or how programs are delivered to residents, weighs heavily when it comes to quality. More than the number of events on the activity calendar, or the diversity of groups brought in from the community to perform, it is the consideration shown and caring attitudes which matter most to participants. Use the built-in strength of social contact focused on pleasurable experience. Fun and recreation are legitimate goals of leisure—and should be pursued.

2. *The competing demands of job responsibilities*—scheduling, planning, coordinating volunteers, paperwork, assessments—along with the need to spend time, perhaps one-on-one, with residents is guaranteed to be a stress-producer for activity directors. Many days the "To Do" list far exceeds time available. However, make sure that time is allocated for building relationships with selected residents. Some will need less time than others; many require more time than you can give, but devote time within the week to personal contact. Hints on effective time management appear in Chapter 10.

3. *Too much sympathy* leading to infantilization can impede the goals of an activity program. Caring and kindness are most desirable in staff, but the objective must be to maintain and challenge the abilities of residents. Never do for participants what they are capable of performing themselves. Always establish reasonable expectations and offer encouragement, but be wary of the smothering approach which borders on condescension.

4. Everyone is susceptible to *the undesirable consequences of ethnocentrism*, or allowing personal history, background, preferences, and cultural influences to color their view of a situation to the exclusion of others. Often this occurs unknowingly. O'Brien (1989) indicated that residents of Bethany Manor were primarily Catholic and of European descent, while the majority of direct-care staff consisted of Protestant African-Americans. Occasionally these differences caused difficulties. Taking the time to learn personal histories makes sense. In a study (Pietrukowicz and Johnson, 1991) where two groups of nursing staff were given medical charts—one accompanied by a life history and the other containing only comments on physical condition—those given a patient's life history expressed a much more positive attitude toward that patient. It seems that a history focused on leisure throughout the life cycle including pertinent characteristics (whether individual or group pursuits dominated, was there a balance between passive and active engagements?) gives direction to activity staff and at the same time sensitizes them to the uniqueness of the individual providing the history. This effort should short-circuit future problems based on ignorance or a lack of information.

VOLUNTEERS

Volunteers, community residents or others, who willingly devote their time to long-term care settings also form relationships with elderly clients. This bond is frequently a two-way street. The volunteer expects to offer something to the nursing home, or specifically to the residents, and at the same time he or she expects to receive something in return. This payoff does not take the form of financial renumeration. It may be as simple as feeling good about doing something useful while providing some structure during the day to a retiree, and it may culminate in a special friendship with a nursing home resident. Volunteers engage in their pursuits for a purpose, and surveys have shown (Gallup, 1982; Ozminkowski, Supiano, and Campbell, 1991) that they receive benefits in return.

The purpose of this section is not to describe how to manage a volunteer program at a nursing home, although general comments will be made here since volunteer operations frequently fall under the duties of the activity director or department (Clagett and Schillis, 1990). Instead, the focus will be on volunteer-resident interactions, issues which surface concerning volunteers, and characteristics of successful volunteer programs in long-term care. Examples will be noted of staff serving in volunteer capacities and, to conclude the section, the role of resident volunteers will be examined.

One study of volunteers in a long-term care facility (Shield, 1988) used the descriptors "ambiguity and ambivalence" to label the roles and operation of volunteers. It was noted that adult volunteers were much more willing to help financially than to provide the needed one-on-one contact with residents. Three groups—students, homemakers, and retirees—dominated the pool of volunteers. Another examination of volunteering in a nursing home (O'Brien, 1989) discovered benefits to residents as being singled out as someone special (and for those who had no family or other support network this was particularly significant) and developing a friendly relationship with another. Volunteers stated that they felt better about themselves and that they were clearly able to experience feelings of gratefulness and affection on the part of residents. A further study (Ozminski, Supiano, and Campbell, 1991) found volunteers much more likely to describe their contacts in a positive fashion (e.g., happy, rewarding, fun, and worthwhile) than in a negative manner (e.g., depressing, producing anxiety). An adequate training program was seen as important.

The roles of volunteers and their relationships with residents are indeed varied. In many cases lack of staff time for coordination and creative planning severely hampers the effectiveness of volunteers. What specifically do volunteers provide? Hopefully at the top of this list is a genuine desire to assist older adults, but some will deliver this help not through personal contact with residents—an office placement or some functional task such as editing a newsletter is what they desire. Others will have outstanding recreation skills—it may be teaching a class, leading a square dance, or assisting as an activity aide. It is the director's task to identify strengths and use talents in the most effective way.

Residents perceive community volunteers as providing many positives. Volunteers are a link to the world outside the institution; information sharing can be an important function and residents may enjoy hearing about families or children of volunteers (Moss and Pfohl, 1988). Mentioned previously was the situation that for some (without family or friends) contact with a volunteer represents the totality of their interactions with anyone outside the nursing home. Community volunteers also offer the opportunity for residents to give back something. All want to feel that they can contribute something. An example from an intergenerational program (O'Brien, 1989) was an elderly adult sharing a particular type of sewing or stitching with a teenager, a skill not found at home or in school. Volunteers are sometimes sounding boards, as well. They may be the only outlet (beyond those working in the facility) available to receive a gripe or complaint. Simply being available to listen is a valuable role played by volunteers.

STAFF AS VOLUNTEERS

Besides community volunteers who come into the long-term care facility, an additional category of those who donate their time without pay is staff. The motivation for this stems from the fact that many workers within a nursing home or long-term care setting have positions which don't bring them in contact with residents in an individual manner. Thus, programs have been started (Greenblatt, 1988; Moss and Pfohl, 1988) where employees donate their time, during lunch breaks or before or after the work day, and develop a friendship with residents. The effort at the Philadelphia Geriatric Center (Moss and Pfohl, 1988) operated independently of the existing department of volunteer services. Staff received an orientation and spent about half an hour weekly with a selected resident. The elders received the program favorably, especially that someone had singled them out for special treatment; their status within the center was improved. Staff participants viewed the program in positive terms, also. It allowed them to have a more holistic view of their place of employment, and most continued with the program.

An issue which surfaces in such instances is union support or opposition (where applicable). Even beyond staff serving as volunteers, unions will not always be receptive to those who offer their services for nothing. Groundwork must be laid to specify times when staff can volunteer. The overriding issue is that someone is performing a task without reimbursement when the job could be occupied by a union member. A further issue noted by Moss and Pfohl (1988) was that because one worked within the facility, one was sometimes exposed to problems or situations which called for him or her to exert pressure or to ask a favor for their resident friend. The fact that not all residents were afforded equal opportunity in this way posed an ethical concern for some. Another example noted by Shield (1988) was the middle-aged volunteer assigned to cleaning duties who was overzealous in the performance of duties and whose standards brought union opposition. After a transfer to another area, the volunteer relinquished his role.

QUALITY VOLUNTEER PROGRAMS

What factors are responsible for top-notch volunteer programs? The answer to the question can be approached in a generic sense (considering volunteer efforts in all types of organizations or settings) and with particular focus on long term-care settings. The field of volunteer management has been growing in recent years, although survey or empirical studies analyzing volunteersism in nursing homes and other extended-stay facilities is scant (Ozminkowski, Supiano, and Campbell, 1991). Curricula have been developed to educate volunteer managers, and, in larger long-term care settings or hospitals, the director of volunteer operations is a professional position demanding a specific background and training.

The intent here is not to describe in detail how to establish and manage a volunteer program. Detailed description is available in the leisure services literature (see Tedrick and Henderson, 1989) and in the growing work in the field of volunteer management. Journals such as *The Journal of Volunteer Administration* and *Volunteer Administrator* are excellent sources.

In brief form a number of elements are typically found in a well-run volunteer program (Tedrick and Henderson, 1989). A management system or scheme should consist of the minimum areas of planning, marketing, training and placement, supervision, and evaluation and recognition. Each area contains a number of elements which would be addressed (e.g., developing recruitment plans, writing job descriptions, identifying target markets with the broad category of marketing). At the outset the person given the responsibility of coordinating volunteers must understand that time, effort, financial and other staff resources must be devoted if significant results are to be achieved. Don't look at volunteers as free labor, or expect willing persons to descend from the heavens to do all the work staff can never get around to completing. Without constant attention the volunteer program will enter a downcycle, and once started it becomes difficult to halt.

Effective training with enrichment activities (life histories, writing projects and memory activities) was the centerpiece of a program in Michigan which involved 55 volunteers (Ozminkowski, Supiano, and Campbell, 1991). Eighty percent of the volunteers underwent training which included sensitization to aging, skills development in preparing life histories, working with memory groups, and creative writing. The training and experiences were most positive on the part of volunteers—nearly half stated their impression of nursing homes residents had changed for the better and nearly all said they would recommend such service to others and that visits with residents had been satisfying. The program concluded that appropriate training for volunteers is essential; those who participated in the training were significantly more satisfied as compared with those who did not.

Another approach to volunteerism on the west coast centered upon teams linking with a specific long-term care facility and a consortium of churches to do the bulk of recruiting for volunteers (Yeaney, 1986). A survey of area nursing homes revealed that half of residents had no family or friends. Teams of volunteers were then assigned to a specific facility, and relationships with residents began. Three types of volunteers were found: the regulars who visited weekly with a special friend-resident, the special volunteers who were less regular in their visits than the first group and who at times filled-in for regular volunteers, and the last group who were supportive (helped with feeding, gifts, or perhaps a special event) but did not want a one-to-one relationship with a resident. The team aspect was seen as an effective method of producing commitment in his program.

Based on a study of volunteers in Minnesota over the age of 60, three categories of service were discovered pertaining to those who offer their time and talents to formal volunteer organizations (Fischer, Mueller, and Cooper, 1991). The first, person-to-community, would be the type of volunteer to edit a newsletter or hold an office in a charitable organization. The second group, person-to-object, the volunteer enjoys performing a specific task which does not require direct contact with an individual recipient. Maintenance duties or office tasks might be desired by this volunteer. The third group person-to-person volunteers consist of those who thrive on human contact; they want to be interacting with others. This survey also highlighted the demographics of older adults who are more likely to volunteer their time. Volunteers were married, had higher income and education levels, good health, and the ability to drive.

The brief accounts given in this section emphasize that volunteering is a very broad concept—the intent and benefits of service will vary with the individual. The literature dealing with volunteers in long-term care settings, while lacking in empirical studies, is generally positive regarding the experiences of both those providing service and those receiving the service. If the activity department oversees volunteer services, a carefully planned, supervised, and managed effort will bring benefits to all concerned. The contact between volunteer and resident is one more method of enhancing personal and personnel relationships.

OLDER RESIDENT VOLUNTEERS

A primary group of potential volunteers as yet undiscussed are the residents themselves with their unique backgrounds, abilities, and talents. Remember that volunteers receive something in return for their endeavors. Feelings of usefulness, the ability to help another, having and sensing a purpose, sharing a talent or skill with another—these are the kinds of positive rewards expressed by volunteers, and residents, like the others, can share in these feelings if staff will take the time to include them as providers of service. Many probably occupy such roles in the home or facility without, perhaps, being formally classified as a volunteer. Those active in resident councils or planning committees, the helper in the reading room, or a resident providing informal assistance such as checking in daily with a weakened neighbor are all examples of unclassified volunteerism.

Residents do bring special concerns, and staff may need to exert a bit more effort in coordinating their volunteer pursuits—perhaps a team of volunteers from the outside could coordinate the residents of a volunteer program. Assessments should reveal information useful in planning what tasks could be performed. Assessments of residents' backgrounds should seek out prior volunteer activities and talents which could be useful in a volunteer capacity. Life experiences of elders have been put to good use in a number of communities by way of living history projects. In written or oral form the history of an area or era can be heard in first person. Students are able to witness history come to life.

If formal job descriptions for volunteers don't exist, staff should at a minimum create a file of duties which could be performed by residents. Categories discussed earlier might be helpful (separating jobs into those requiring personal contact and those which don't; doing some type of task in one's room). Tasks which could be done within the long-term care setting will most likely come to mind first, but do not confine thinking to only the residence itself.

There are many tasks which can aid individuals or organizations outside of the nursing home. Local churches, temples, or schools are excellent sources for ascertaining needs. A history teacher might be seeking a first hand account of an event, local or international, which a resident had experienced. Residents might be needed to help generate support for an issue. Mailings or certain office duties might be suitable for a group of residents. This link to local events can be stimulating to those interested.

Intergenerational programs have grown in number, operating in community settings and within long-term facilities. Reports have supported the notion that both groups, younger and older, benefit through these relationships. For teens or younger children residents can become a type of surrogate grandparent or older family member. Experiences can be shared and true friendships can be developed with adequate time and preparation for this type of program.

Many roles for resident volunteers have yet to be conceived. A lack of planning time on the part of staff is probably the greatest hindrance. Looked upon as a type of leisure programming, however, volunteerism by residents should receive the same effort that would be devoted to any activity available.

COMMUNITY RESOURCES AND PROGRAMMING

Community resources and programs represent an avenue extending to the doorway of the nursing home. Elders may leave their residence and seek those experiences not possible in the nursing home, or groups may bring the resources of neighborhood areas with them as they enter and spend time with residents. In Chapter 1 it was also noted that the OBRA guidelines concerning quality of life emphasize the need for residents to interact with members of the community both inside and outside of their long-term care facility. Whatever the direction of the flow, contact must be maintained with local citizens. An activity therapist at Bethany Manor (O'Brien, 1989) spoke of community involvement with residents as follows:

> When I got here there were hardly any trips out, maybe just to the (shopping) plaza on Fridays, but I really feel that's a big, important part of recreation because its getting the residents back out into the community. When people become institutionalized there are a lot of things that they feel are not available to them any more, and one of those things is the community trips and the community itself. I really try to get more residents out on these trips."

Such a sentiment stresses the need for continued involvement in matters beyond the walls of the nursing home. One of the most obvious benefits of community programming is varying the routine of daily life which becomes monotonous in any institutional environment.

Schools, religious institutions, government agencies, service groups, and private sector facilities such as theaters, malls, and other leisure-related services should be considered as potential programming opportunities (Greenblatt, 1988). Some organizations have active public service divisions and are eager to visit or arrange a tour or outing at their site. Obviously care must be taken in choosing which residents are taken on selected trips. Interest level, health, mobility/ambulation and staff resources must be given attention. Colleges and universities should be contacted; a nursing department or a gerontology program or a therapeutic recreation department might be interested in establishing a connection. Both students and residents might benefit from shared time either in the long-term care facility or on the campus. A recreation activity jointly engaged in by older adults and younger students is a way of breaking down inhibitions and barriers.

An excellent community-wide event which has been replicated in differing forms across the country is the senior Olympics for nursing home residents. Modeled after the Olympic events which culminate in state competition for those over 55 or 60, the events for nursing home residents are appropriately modified—wheelchairs or walkers are used in races, softballs or Nerf™ balls are tossed, portable games are set up. Many include mental activities, as well; trivia-type games, or Scrabble™ or spelling bees are held. Craft activities can be on display or judged in a competition—the best recipe or quilt square might garner a ribbon. The aspect to be stressed here is the excellent opportunity for community groups to play a role. Volunteers can range from youth to adults in service organizations; family members can assist activity staff. Such events typically receive media attention. In summary, the Olympics for nursing home residents can pull various community constituencies together in a fun-filled atmosphere.

General guidelines for establishing community programs or visiting resources beyond the long-term care setting begin with an information gathering phase. Find out what sites or organizations match the interests and abilities of the resident population. Community service directories are a starting point as are the yellow or blue pages of the phone book. Local activity directors are most often willing to share in any successes; they should be queried for suggestions. Locate the contact person and have a list of questions ready—accessibility, best times, recommended length of stay, and emergency plans all should be considered.

Unless absolutely impossible, visit the site for an initial inspection. While time is a consideration, it is worth the effort to know first-hand about environmental factors such as seating, distances to be traveled, types of slopes or surfaces to be negotiated, number and location of restrooms. Experience has shown that a telephone description may differ from what confronts a visitor at the site.

When beginning a community program, be particularly aware of staff-to-resident ratios and allow for the possibility of a minor or major crisis. Community programming may not involve all older adults, but it is a component of the total activity department which provides a change of pace to residents and staff. The most important aspect of these efforts may not be attendance figures. Most activity directors are able to gauge what events and degrees of exertion are suitable for specific participants and make the match accordingly.

Maintain an ongoing evaluation of events and programs. Correct minor flaws or make adjustments as necessary. Vary settings if staleness occurs. Residents can be rotated for different programs. Many sites will change with the seasons and offer new experiences on a quarterly basis. A final note is to thank all groups or individuals involved. As with any venture, once personal contact has been established with key resource personnel, continued efforts result in fewer snags.

PERSONNEL RELATIONSHIPS: STAFF-TO-STAFF

Job duties require interaction of another sort—staff interacting with other staff either inside the activity department or outside of it through meetings, inquiries, communications, and tasks shared with coworkers employed in long-term care facilities. While examined here in the last section of this chapter, these relationships are not to be construed as secondary or unimportant. Personnel relationships fraught with turf battles, condescension, or personality clashes may negatively effect the service delivered to residents or clients and thus must be carefully considered in a unit dealing with the variety of human interactions in long-term care settings.

The reader is referred to Figure 6.1, A Model of Exploring Leisure Activity and Older Adults in Chapter 6, (page 76) consisting of three pyramids or levels. The process of leisure programming begins appropriately with consideration (e.g., individual needs, conditions, perceived control) of the person receiving the activity service—an older adult within a long-term care site such as a nursing home. Next the model focuses on the deliverer of the service, the activity specialist or director, therapeutic recreator, or other activity therapist who designs and implements leisure experiences. The last pyramid entails the system or environment within which staff are working and part of that system involves the relationships, both formal and informal, of members of the activity department with other staff at the hospital, center, or residence. Viewed from a table of organization, activity staff are placed within a hierarchy indicating formal lines of authority. Many staff relationships, however, are horizontal and entail the cooperative efforts of various departments or employees (social work, nursing, occupational or physical therapy, for example) working as a team. Settings dealing primarily with rehabilitation or those with a strong medical focus will emphasize such a team process and in nearly all nursing homes the activity department must operate effectively with many staff if the goals

are to be accomplished. Thus, attention to these day-to-day relationships is necessary in order to maintain them in a positive fashion so that residents may benefit.

A major theme of this book is the role and image of the activity director/department as a part of what occurs in long-term care. In discussing quality of life in nursing homes the significant role of activities and those who provide them is stressed. Chapter 10, "Professionalism Issues," discusses the strides being made to bring activity specialists in line with other allied professionals. It is also noted that through helping dying clients and using the activity medium in a manner to assist individuals and family during this difficult time, the activity department can be perceived positively by other unit staff. Activity specialists are dependent upon other staff to program leisure experiences effectively, and additionally they must feel competent and confident to participate in team gatherings, interdepartmental planning sessions, or meetings with administrators.

How is the activity department perceived by other units in long-term care facilities? Obviously the answer varies according to each site, taking into account a host of factors such as department resources, the degree of residential care versus medical care provided, and the qualifications and performance of staff comprising the activity department. A recent survey activity directors in Midwestern nursing homes (Pieper and Gray, 1992) revealed that 84 percent of them felt that their relationships with other staff members or units were positive and that they were accepted as members of the care-giving team. Two-thirds of directors said their work was well-received and that other units could see the benefits provided to residents through leisure activities. While not a national sample, the perceptions expressed were positive.

Pagell (1993) analyzed the informal team process involving therapeutic recreators and other allied health professionals using a case study approach at two rehabilitation hospitals. The findings raised provocative questions about the role of therapeutic recreation and those who provide it as related to team membership in rehabilitation. Differences were found in the two sites. At the first rehabilitation hospital the therapeutic recreation staff rated the functioning of the team process the lowest of the seven different groups. Task roles within the group (giving and seeking information and opinions) and maintenance roles (encouraging others, keeping others focused on the task, and relieving tension) were explored, and the therapeutic recreation staff was perceived by others as playing more task than maintenance roles. Most often therapeutic recreators sought opinions or information rather than giving it. Psychologists were viewed by others as the most active in group meetings.

Findings at the second rehabilitation site revealed a more active, dynamic role played by the therapeutic recreation staff (Pagell, 1993). Recreation staff members were more often noted as giving information and opinions, and, while psychology was perceived as the most active in the team process, therapeutic recreation staff were in the midrange of involvement, ahead of social work and nursing. The therapeutic recreation department was noted four times (tied for the lead) as being the closest ally in team meetings. These results cannot be generalized to activity departments within nursing homes, but active team membership by therapeutic recreation staff accompanied by positive feelings from other units occurs in selected settings. Similar methodology should be used to explore team involvement by activity staff in a variety of long-term care settings and to determine if perceptions of allied healthcare staff toward activity specialists match the positive feelings found in the Pieper and Gray (1992) survey.

Concerning personnel relationships within the activity unit, recognition must be made of the variety of situations which exist in long-term care settings. The range of staffing patterns begins with the one-person department (perhaps a full-time activity director with a part-time aide and a few volunteers) and extends to a full-blown department of director,

assistants, and specialists such as music, art, or horticultural therapists, involving perhaps seven or eight full-time staff. This latter situation is seen more frequently in large rehabilitation hospitals and government-sponsored residences (e.g., Veterans Administration Hospitals). The ways in which positive staff morale is maintained might vary according to size, but the basis is respect for others while creating an environment where challenges match abilities.

Enlightened management today broadcast under the forms of T.Q.M. (Total Quality Management), such as shared goal-setting and decision-making, quality circles, emphasizes the group process and consensus-building. It would appear that strong group process skills would be expected of activity personnel, yet some department administrators may treat staff in a fashion far different from residents or clients. Three principles focused on building positive staff morale are offered: (1) Be democratic rather than authoritarian; when staff feel invested and a part of something, they will perform out of a sense of pride and accomplishment; (2) Allow activity specialists to grow on the job; burnout and turnover are serious problems in the field. Someone must give consideration to a structure which permits job growth—this could include expanded responsibilities, new training, or a shift to a different wing or programming for a new clientele at the facility; (3) Understand that staff on the "front line," those leading activities during the bulk of their time at work, possess valuable information. Seek their input. Encourage them to be problem analysts and solvers.

A final note pertaining to intradepartment matters is to caution directors or heads of the activity unit to not overlook department morale. Busy schedules and routine occurrences may lead one to the inappropriate conclusion that everything is running smoothly. Matters involving personnel are sometimes out in the open and apparent; other annoyances may be below the surface, yet nagging to staff. The suggestion is to monitor the quality of department life as a regular part of evaluation.

As to relations with administrative staff, particularly those in the higher levels such as chief executive officers, don't underestimate the power of information and promotion. At every opportunity capitalize on positive publicity/occurrences within the department. Some, perhaps many, high-level managers are aware of the importance of activity programming within the residence and within the lives of older residents. Others need to be educated of the personal value or therapeutic purpose of what goes on in the activity unit. Efficacy research is discussed in Chapter 9; whether through published research studies or, better still, evaluative research projects in-house, activity staff should share positive findings with administrators concerning the value of leisure activities. The cost-benefit environment of long-term care demands careful attention to output measures, and activity directors able to document the effects of their service are in a stronger position than those unable to do so. The trends stressing documentation and evaluation skills are strong and will likely continue to remain so.

Personnel relationships with other employees in the long-term care setting to include nursing, social work, medical doctors, psychologists, and occupational and physical therapists should be characterized by trust, respect, and a spirit of cooperation. Such is not always the case, but reference was made earlier about the opinions of activity directors who feel they are perceived positively by other care staff (Pieper and Gray, 1992). Pagell's (1993) findings that therapeutic recreators play differing roles within the team process should signal the need for activity departments to assert themselves in giving, seeking, and sharing client/resident information with caregiving team members. During leisure one is able to observe many of the behaviors or processes which are linked to specific resident goals. Careful observance and note taking will result in the accumulation of much data which can be shared in team meetings. This situation is a strength and should be an image-builder for the activity department.

One element of activity programming, scheduling, demands cooperation from a variety of units, but encouraging the good will of the nursing staff is apparent to all who have worked in a nursing home or hospital. Scheduling can involve a variety of variables, and at times it becomes difficult to coordinate all of the factors. Adequate publicity and use of the activity calendar will promote an awareness of upcoming events. Use of interpersonal skills make the relationship with the nursing department one built on professional respect accompanied by mutual helping.

Summary

Explored in this chapter was the variety of human interactions/behaviors which occur in a long-term care setting. Many groups or types of relationships exist—residents developing friendships with other residents, family and resident interactions, staff helping residents, and persons outside of the residence (community volunteers, for example) who meet and develop relationships with residents. Because of its role and function, the activity department helps to shape these relationships. Explored, also, were personnel interactions both within the activity unit and outside of it when activity specialists team with other allied staff.

Resident friendships are an important part of quality of life in a nursing home, and most older adults are able to identify a special friend at their site. These friendships and interactions are shaped by many factors, (e.g., how long one has been a resident, physical and mental conditions, whether one is an extrovert). Activity staff can be a positive force in meeting social goals and in assisting residents to share in group activities.

While many residents in long-term care settings are without family or community friends, those who are fortunate do experience the opportunity of sharing time with persons living in nearby communities. Circumstances of placement into the long-term care setting are responsible for positive or negative feelings regarding family members. Length of stay is a crucial factor as well, with the newly admitted viewing their former lifestyle in a manner different from those who have resided in a nursing home for a number of years. Research has shown that perceptions about the willingness of one's family to play a continued caregiving role are directly related to attitudes about entering a nursing home. Staff are involved in family-resident relationships and use activities such as parties, socials, or special occasions to encourage positive feelings during visits.

Resident and staff interactions involve formal (tasks and duties assigned) and informal (stopping to talk with a resident) components, and investigations have indicated that a sense of caring displayed by employees toward residents is the key criterion in evaluating this type of relationship. Residents will overlook shortcomings if they believe staff care about them. Job-related factors such as burnout, turnover, and lack of career paths affect these contacts. Staff act in an "underground" where frequently the formal aspects of their relationships with older clients are supplemented by opportunities for caring and special attention to one needing it. Specific recommendations are given to bolster resident-staff relations.

Volunteers in an extended care facility are significant for a number of reasons—they bring special talents, they often develop a one-on-one relationship with a resident, and they are in a different situation from either staff or family members. The value of ombudspersons is noted. Numerous examples exist as to how to develop strong volunteer programs; they must be managed properly like any other type of program or endeavor. Volunteers also represent the link to former communities. Community programming and resources can bring new life to tired activity offerings. Certain residents will benefit greatly through exploring interesting sights and sounds away from the long-term care setting. Suggestions are given on how to develop this type of program.

Residents themselves should, if possible, be considered as volunteers; they will benefit through feelings of doing something positive for others and being needed. The potential roles

are numerous; life or living history efforts where residents bring alive earlier times have been used in schools and with other community groups. Residents can also offer their service within the nursing home to assist the activity department or to help individuals with special needs.

Personnel relationships, considering the activity department as a unit working together and cooperating with staff such as nursing or occupational therapy, are another aspect of behavior in long-term care settings. The activity department as a whole must work together if effectiveness is to be achieved. The director should set the tone by encouraging all to be a part of a group effort. Group goal setting and problem solving are to be encouraged. One survey showed that most activity directors feel they were perceived positively by coworkers in other units. Activity specialists should feel comfortable in working with staff at all levels within the organizational hierarchy and use every opportunity to inform others of the value of their contribution to quality of life through meaningful leisure experiences.

PRACTICAL EXERCISES

1. Place yourself in the role of a newly admitted resident of a nursing home. How do you think you would feel about maintaining contacts with friends from your previous residence? Make a list of the ways that activity departments can encourage positive interactions (social) on the part of residents. How would you deal with an introverted resident who displays no interest in meeting others?

2. The notion of an ombudsperson was discussed. Describe in your own words what an ombudsperson is and the role they might play in a long-term stay residence. What qualities should an ombudsperson possess?

3. Residents as volunteers is a concept worth considering. What tasks within a nursing home could be appropriate for

resident volunteers? What tasks or duties beyond the residence might be considered? What benefits might older volunteers receive from their service?

4. Community resources and programming are an avenue to extend leisure participation beyond the residence. What are the positives of taking residents off-campus? Are there any negatives involved? If you are an activity director, what is the position of your facility on off-campus visits? If you are a student, conduct a survey to find out what local nursing homes are involved in community programming. Identify local sites which might be considered for visitations by residents in a nursing home.

5. One study discussed in this chapter looked at the roles played by activity department members in team meetings. What kinds of information do you think the activity department could provide about residents which would be helpful at team meetings? What information would activity staff seek about residents from the perspective of other allied health departments—nursing, occupational therapy, psychology, physical therapy, social work?

References

Adams, R. (1986). Secondary friendship networks and psychological well-being among older women. *Activities, Adaptation & Aging, 8*(2), 59-72.

Biedenharn, P. and Normoyle, J. (1991). Elderly community residents' reactions to the nursing home: An analysis of nursing home-related beliefs. *The Gerontologist, 31*(1), 107-114.

Cherry, R. (1991). Agents of nursing home quality of care: Ombudsperson and staff ratios revisited. *The Gerontologist, 31*(3), 302-308.

Clagett, M. and Schillis, P. (1990, May/June). May is volunteer month. *Creative Forecasting, 2*(3), 1-2.

Fischer, L. Mueller, D., and Cooper, P. (1991). Older volunteers: A discussion of the Minnesota senior study. *The Gerontologist, 31*(2), 183-194.

Fisk, V. (1984). When nurses' aides care. *Journal of Gerontological Nursing, 10*(3), 118-127.

Gallup, G. (1982, Winter). Gallup survey on volunteering. *Voluntary Action Leadership,* 26-29.

Grau, L. (1984). What older adults expect from the nurse. *Geriatric Nursing, 5*(1), 14-17.

Greenblatt, F. (1988). *Therapeutic recreation for long-term care facilities.* New York, NY: Human Sciences Press, Inc., pp. 116-126.

Moss, M., and Pfohl, D. (1988). New friendships: Staff as visitors of nursing home residents. *The Gerontologist, 28*(2), 263-265.

O'Brien, M. E. (1989). *Anatomy of a nursing home: A new view of resident life.* Owings Mills, MD: National Health Publishing.

Oliver, D. and Tureman, S. (1987/88). The human factor in nursing home care. *Activities, Adaptation & Aging, 10*(3/4), 1-202.

Ozminkowski, R., Supiano, K., and Campbell, R. (1991). Volunteers in nursing home enrichment: A survey to evaluate training and satisfaction. *Activities, Adaptation & Aging, 15*(3), 13-43.

Pagell, F. (1993). "A comparative case study of two therapeutic recreation definitions in rehabilitation hospitals: A look at organizational mission, informal team process, task characteristics, and selected personality variables." Unpublished doctorial dissertation, Temple University, Philadelphia, PA.

Pieper, H. and Gray, S. (1992). Perceptions of activity directors concerning their roles and their work. *Activities, Adaptation & Aging, 17*(2), 65-73.

Pietrukowicz, M., and Johnson, M. (1991). Using life histories to individualize nursing staff attitudes toward residents. *The Gerontologist, 31*(1), 102-106.

Shield, R. (1988). *Uneasy endings: Daily life in an American nursing home.* Ithaca, NY: Cornell University Press.

Tedrick, T., and Henderson, K. (1989). *Volunteers in leisure: A management perspective.* Reston, VA: American Alliance for Health, Physical Education, Recreation, and Dance.

Yeaney, S. (1986). I—you venture: Volunteers as creative partners with care facility residents and staff. *Activities, Adaptation & Aging, 8*(2), 73-79.

Therapeutic Recreation Research and Older, Geriatric Clients

A conference held in Philadelphia in September, 1991 brought together specialists in five areas of therapeutic recreation—chemical dependency, developmental disabilities, gerontology, pediatrics, physical medicine, and psychiatry (Coyle, Kinney, Riley, and Shank, 1991). Sponsored by the National Institute on Disability and Rehabilitation Research, the symposium sought to explore the benefits of therapeutic recreation for groups in the above categories. A related goal was to evaluate the status of efficacy research and to reach a consensus on future directions for empirical study.

Ten experts in leisure and aging focused on the benefits of therapeutic programming for older, frail adults (Riddick and Keller, 1991). A meta-analysis of the research literature yielded 38 studies published between 1980 and 1991 having a therapeutic recreation program as an intervention (Note: the 38 studies are included in a special reference section at the end of this chapter).

The review was broken into five major areas where therapeutic recreation programs had been tried as interventions: in the physical area, cardiovascular and related, and orthopedic; and in the psychological area, senile dementia, depression, and loneliness. Therapeutic recreation programs were found to be effective with geriatric clients in assisting with cardiovascular improvements. Similarly, orthopedic gains in strength and flexibility have been shown in programs utilizing fitness and water aerobics and even from the motion of stirring cookie batter! Nine studies were reviewed dealing with activities and senile dementia. Dance, music, visitations, and plush animal pets have been shown to assist with cognition. Contradictory results have been reported regarding improved cognitive function through reality orientation and reminiscence programs. In terms of depression (nine studies) such interventions as bibliotherapy, pet therapy, and reminiscence have been effective. Also, weekly visits, and dance/movement programs have assisted with loneliness, while an outdoor day camp experience did not significantly impact on the loneliness of older adults (Riddick and Keller, 1991).

As analyzed by Riddick and Keller, (1991), the status of therapeutic recreation studies with geriatric populations could be described as follows:

> There is a limited body of empirical research on the effects of therapeutic recreation on the health and well-being of various geriatric populations. For the most part, therapeutic out-comes of recreation programs have been projected on the basis on anecdotal evidence derived from case studies or from descriptive surveys that have taken place in clinical or community settings (p. 167).

Furthermore, greater scientific rigor in methodology and greater use of control procedures were needed. It was found that three-quarters of the studies were done by researchers outside the field of therapeutic recreation. The research literature was neither holistic nor multidisciplinary regarding the functioning of older clients. The research settings were also limited; Riddick and Keller (1991) urged the use of psychiatric hospitals, physical rehabilitation sites, extended care facilities, and adult care programs as settings for research. On the whole, the body of research was lacking in theory as it related to the problem studied. Thirty percent of the reviewed studies did not have a control group to compare with the treatment group, and, when experimental and control groups were present, statistical analysis failed to indicate both between and among group comparisons. Another area of weakness was the validity and reliability of test measures employed (Riddick and Keller, 1991). Using the previously mentioned meta-analysis as a

background, the group of experts met to consider the direction of research in aging and therapeutic recreation in the future (see Riddick and Keller, 1991). A number of themes were mentioned frequently throughout the conference. These suggestions provide an excellent background to consider the research (leisure and therapeutic recreation) needs related to long-term care settings.

Multidisciplinary approaches and collaborative efforts were noted quite often. Since teams—healthcare, nursing, social work, activities—are all a part of the functioning within long-term care, it would seem wise to utilize a variety of resources in research efforts as well as in daily direct service. From a theoretical perspective the knowledge from disciplines such as gerontology, human development, sociology, social work, and psychology are essential in providing a framework to study leisure of older adults. Research teams comprised of those with varied perspectives should help to alleviate the situation of very narrow studies with limited theoretical perspectives. In addition, collaboration needs to proceed on many fronts—academic researchers and practitioners; students, undergraduate and graduate, from many disciplines, and staff in gerontological settings; even collaborative arrangements as to sites, perhaps jointly-sponsored adult centers or labs staffed by long-term care facilities and academic institutions. With greater research funding in therapeutic program efficacy an obvious recommendation, a corollary suggestion, was to fund, specifically, collaborative efforts that bring teams of experts together to investigate need areas (Troyer, 1991).

Recommended, also, were ways to enhance the skills of researchers—traditional academic researchers, faculty and graduate students, and those in the field who primarily are charged with delivering services, but who may also have the desire to conduct empirical investigations. Greater attention should be given to research skills, particularly at the graduate level; knowing a variety of methodologies and understanding (awareness of and practice in administration, and experience with reliability processes) instruments were seen as keys. It was noted that practitioners have a difficult time in gaining access to measurement tools—where they are found and actually obtained. Grant writing should be a topic dealt with at the graduate level to include practical exercises such as the completion of a proposal. Sabbaticals and research leaves of absence should be established where researchers collaborate with other university faculty interested in leisure and aging, or with those who work directly in long-term care settings, daycare, or rehabilitation sites. Also suggested was the completion of at least one course in research methodology as a prerequisite to sit for the national certification exam (Certified Therapeutic Recreation Specialist through the National Council on Therapeutic Recreation Certification). Research internships were discussed: graduate students might work an entire semester in a jointly sponsored research project, perhaps an adult day program coadministered by an academic institution and a healthcare provider (Troyer, 1991).

The effect of interventions, such as therapeutic recreation upon clients' long-term health and as a factor in controlling healthcare costs, was recognized by experts as an area needing documentation as the nation continues to grapple with escalating health costs (Troyer, 1991). It would be extremely beneficial if therapeutic leisure programs aimed at health promotion or wellness, for example, could be shown to impact positively on healthcare costs of older individuals. Third-party payers could expect to be encouraged by any type of documentation showing a therapeutic intervention being associated with cost containment. This might be another area where collaboration would pay dividends; those who study healthcare costs could be a part of a research team from the formative stages as the specialists with therapeutic programs consider which activities might lead to lower healthcare costs and sustained levels of personal health.

Other recommendations were aimed at broadening therapeutic recreation—geriatric research (Troyer, 1991). As previously noted, it was thought that greater variety should be explored in terms of settings (e.g., rehabilitation sites, extended care facilities) and impact areas (cancer or substance abuse patients). Concern was expressed for knowledge about minority group members. A lack of uniform terminology of key concepts and conditions was perceived as problematic both internal to therapeutic recreation and external to include allied health and medical professionals. Another interesting theoretical issue surfaced via the call to explore life satisfaction, well-being and leisure participation by changing each from dependent to independent variables. Most often, studies have used leisure participation to gauge the dependent variable of life satisfaction, social interaction, and so forth. Might our efforts be improved with greater understanding of the variety and complexity of factors which predict successful leisure involvement in later life? Efforts such as Howe's (1988) in describing the process of participating in an exercise class by older women are noteworthy, and lines of investigation similar to this should be continued with older frail adults in various settings.

The Teaching Nursing Home as a Research Model

Researchers, as noted in the previous section, have emphasized new collaborative efforts, a model which holds promise is that of the teaching nursing home (Eisdorfer, 1985; Maddox, 1985; Ostfeld, 1985; and Rowe, 1985). Encouraged through grants from the National Institute on Aging (NIA) (Maddox, 1985) the teaching nursing home concept is one where service provision, teaching and professional preparation, and research should coexist with the ultimate goal being an improved quality of life for residents. The perspective is multidisciplinary.

Applied to research strategies the formation of teams bringing together and sharing specialized knowledge would encourage an holistic perspective. While this model appears to be in concert with many of the recommendations from the previous section, e.g., the theme of collaboration and the coalescing of allied health professions, there are obvious concerns, as well, in considering geriatric research linked to activity as an intervention. Perhaps it is best to view the model as an opportunity, while recognizing that research limitations exist and should be considered.

A nursing home or other long-term care facility designed to enhance professional education while providing exemplary service offers potential benefits to the researcher (Eisdorfer, 1985; Maddox, 1985; and Ostfeld, 1985). Ostfeld (1985) notes that a nursing home where teaching is instrumental is an enclosed system or environment. Nursing homes are most often slow changing; the resident or patient population is stable, and many will live there for a long time. Thus, in terms of internal validity, the researcher has the opportunity to manipulate certain variables while the rest of the environment stays relatively unchanged. While informed consent and ethical considerations will be reviewed later, the resident population is in most cases accessible and can be seen for repeated visits. Longitudinal studies can be conducted without many of the problems experienced in community settings. Controlled clinical trials (Ostfeld, 1985) involving training, drug therapies (or model therapeutic recreation programs) are possible in the teaching nursing home. As suggested by Maddox (1985) another area which bears investigation is the physical environment in nursing homes. Following the discussion in Chapter 7 of this book, it would seem imperative that researchers should begin investigating how modifications/adaptations to the activity room in addition to other parts of the total nursing home environment may create a more suitable match for residents.

Length of stay and necessary strategies to accommodate the new as opposed to the veteran resident should be addressed through research (Eisdorfer, 1985). The teaching nursing home offers the chance to explore the needs (social, medical, utilization of staff, and environmental) of groups having varied degrees of residential tenure. Extended to leisure/activity needs, what does one know—or should one know—about the progression of free-time opportunities in nursing homes? Does one assume that long tenure results in decline leading to fewer social interactions and ultimately room-bound programming? Would different or more intensive activities be needed for long-term residents? And who receives the lion's share of what meager programming resources are available? Is it the most able who are the haves? Related to activity programs in nursing homes and those who participate, it would seem that survey research; case studies of departments, facilities, and residents; and innovative therapeutic programs analyzed over time would be avenues for exploration.

In the framework of research considerations, nursing homes, teaching and otherwise, also present challenges which must be overcome. Generalization is an issue of concern (Maddox, 1985; and Ostfeld, 1985). The misconception that "all nursing homes are alike" can be refuted when one considers the impact of size, organizational structure, for profit or nonprofit status, religious affiliation, etc., as factors which often make for a population or setting where generalization of findings would be questioned. Other considerations would include (Eisdorfer, 1985; Maddox, 1985; Ostfeld, 1985; and Rowe, 1985) the "halo" effect where everyone might want to be included in a treatment group (where an innovative recreation program is being tried) and the attendant ethical considerations of who is placed in a control group; the situation of research overload where staff and residents feel probed and prodded to the extreme, results might very well be questioned when multiple effects become intermingled; and the "turf" wars that do happen when investigators see their project as central to everything happening in the home to the exclusion of other groups, most conspicuously, those who live there.

Rowe (1985) identified a number of problems focusing on those who conduct or approve research efforts. The geriatric specialty of medicine is not alluring enough to attract the numbers of medical doctors and research specialists needed to address existing questions, and not enough research is focused on long-term care issues and in nursing homes as settings. Administrators in long-term care facilities frequently lack appreciation of the value of empirical investigation, or they are leery of "experimentation" with older residents. He suggested greater efforts on behalf of schools of medicine, allied health programs, and university-wide departments dealing with the process of aging so that a new cadre of researchers grounded in gerontological theory as well as their own specialties would be prepared to move the research agenda forward. These comments are similar to the thrust of upgrading research skills of the experts in therapeutic recreation for geriatric clientele which was mentioned earlier.

Indeed, according to a recent survey (McNeil, Hawkins, Barber, and Winslow, 1990) there may well exist a strong bias of therapeutic recreation students, i.e., future professionals, against the elderly as a population group to be served. Their findings from 95 therapeutic recreation majors showed that no matter what the disability of interest (e.g., physical or mental impairment, chemical dependency, etc.) the strong preference was to work with younger, not older, clients. If such feelings are widespread among faculty and graduate students in leisure studies/therapeutic recreation programs across the nation, the negative implications for quality research and researchers is obvious. As ways to counteract the bias, the study authors suggested an improvement in the general ageism apparent in mass media, the introduction of aging material in undergraduate coursework, the projection of positive attitudes toward aging on behalf of professors, and the exposure of college students to older adults, thereby influencing attitudes positively.

Maddox (1985) critiqued the desired outcomes and priorities of the NIA Teaching Nursing Home (TNH) Project. Interestingly, three specific areas dealt with the impact of exercise, fitness activities and their relationship to cardiopulmonary fitness. Since movement would be considered within the domain of the activity department, collaboration on such research efforts would seem natural. While Maddox (1985) applauded the efforts of the TNH project to encourage collaboration, he expressed skepticism in generating broad-based attitudinal change (positive) on the part of the scientific community concerning aging. Since few medical doctors work full-time in nursing homes or other long-term care settings, he doubted their sustained involvement or interest in geriatric medicine, even if positive findings resulted from research. He also wondered about the ethical considerations (selection of treatment and control groups, withholding a beneficial or even enjoyable program or intervention for the sake of methodological requirements) when good science meshes with an older population in need. Perhaps these concerns when applied to therapeutic recreation interventions could be addressed through a methodology incorporating various innovative programs applied to random groups so that the control becomes the existing activity program normally operating in the facility. Denial or "withholding" of services/programs is de-emphasized in such a scheme. A model for research activities in teaching nursing homes developed by Rowe (1985) offers a sound strategy for any investigation in long-term care settings. A pilot study must be conducted before any long-range research is considered. It is imperative to educate administrators at the facility and to gain their trust and support. A research consortium or collaborative team should be established prior to any work, and the team must function at all steps of planning and while investigations are underway. Informed and complete consent must be obtained. It is necessary that all connected with the collaborative team (e.g.,boards, trustees, deans, administrative officials, human subject committees) be informed of all proposed and active elements of the investigation. This should result in mutual trust among all involved. Consideration must be given to the persons most affected by the research. Plans should be carefully developed to include residents, their families, and all staff levels, particularly nurses, so that the purpose of the study is clearly understood and practical suggestions as to how to minimize negative impact can be discussed and implemented during the pilot phase. Educational programs for patients or staff should be a natural part of the research. Attitudes might need to be changed in preparation for a new program or way of doing things. Finally, any positive public relations emanating from the effort should be shared. Acknowledge by name those groups and individuals who assisted with the completion of the research.

Ethical Considerations in Research

Within the far superseding issues such as instrument validation, collaborative committees, methodology decisions, or data analysis techniques lies the fundamental concern of ethics in all research focusing on leisure or recreation and its impact upon older adults. Just as therapeutic recreation or leisure activities in a long-term care setting has as its primary goal improvements in quality of life for residents, so, too, must investigators never lose sight of the ultimate goal of making individual lives better, whether the research be applied or basic. The tendency to become absorbed in methodological details and to be responsive to deadlines and other pressures can lead researchers to view older adults as "subjects" and sometimes to forget the human element in the scientific process. Researchers need to guard constantly against this tendency.

Cassel (1985, 1987, 1988) has developed an extensive body of work on the ethical issues of

research in long-term care. Based on general principles from the Belmont Report (see National Commission for the Protection of Human Subjects of Biomedical and Behavioral Research, 1978), Cassel (1988) identified thee major ethical concerns:

1. respectful treatment for all older adults involved in research;
2. beneficence, or the need to stress positives and not to permit harm to patients or subjects; and
3. justice, focusing on issues such as who does and does not get selected for treatments which may be enjoyable/beneficial.

She notes that many times positive benefits occur as research is ongoing; social interaction may be increased, residents feel better about themselves by virtue of being selected for a study (the "halo" effect), or interventions begin to show positive effects, mentally or physically, relatively rapidly as the research progresses. Often there is a balance which must be struck between protection and opportunity as the issue of subject selection is planned.

Using a Delphi technique in which 22 researchers with extensive experience in gerontological studies were queried, Cassel (1988) developed four major ethical areas:

1. consent;
2. competence;
3. confidentiality; and,
4. conflicts of interest.

Consent, as related to an older, frail population, raises obvious issues. Often older residents/patients will want to please caregivers and will be more than eager to be involved in anything which enhances their standing in the eyes of staff. Another factor related to consent is the positive or negative pressure applied from other residents in nursing homes. Previously cited, as well, is the status issue of being singled-out to participate in a study. The issue of consent is wrapped in more than a simple "yes" or "no."

One study (Cohen-Mansfield, Kerin, Paulson, Lipson, and Holdridge, 1988) specifically focused on the issue of informed consent with frail, aged adults. Consent was seen as including three elements: voluntariness, information, and competency. While conducting their study, a number of specific procedures were taken to address informed consent. Families of older relatives were notified about the study through a newsletter. It was clearly stated that residents could decide to participate or not. A research panel at the site reviewed the competency of each resident. For residents not competent to decide for themselves, family members were contacted, and if there were questions about the study, the family could call the research team. The purpose of the study was to compare consent rates of residents with their family members. There was a significant difference between family members (91 percent consent rate) and residents judged competent to decide (80 percent consent rate). The researchers explained that the difference could be attributed to the fact that family members saw any type of research as assisting their older relatives. It was also felt that family members did not use substitute judgment. In other words they expressed their own views and did not respond as they perceived their older relative in the home would have. Clearly, who decides eligibility and consent for a research project and what process is used in making that decision is a crucial and often a complex matter as related to the aged.

Another area which often presents problems due to the psychosocial environment in nursing homes is the area of confidentiality (Cassel, 1988). Many people intermingle, staff are curious, residents want to know what "these interviews are all about." Staff and administrators may have easy access to records and charts. It behooves the research team to consider carefully how confidentiality will be preserved, and this implies more than a statement on a form which study participants will sign. Where interviews will be held, how reports will be written, and what procedures are included in training of all researchers to guarantee confidentiality are pertinent considerations here.

A topic parallel to confidentiality is that of potential conflicts of interest. Interviewers can face the dilemma of wanting to disclose information when confidentiality has previously been ensured. What should one do, for example, if after making a pledge of confidentiality one discovers in the course of an interview with an older client that feelings of suicide were revealed? Or what if some type of abuse, verbal or otherwise, was suggested during a conversation with an elderly patient? Cassell (1988) indicates that while such examples are extreme, they are possibilities, and researchers must consider such probabilities before they occur. Dilemmas will not always be as critical as those above, yet problems can arise when certain staff or personnel or whole departments are noted as being less than dutiful, and these comments may not come from direct questioning but through the general nature of interviewing. If such information were shared, would it jeopardize any future research involvement? Could anything be inferred from a written report which might negatively affect a department or a facility? Such conflicts are possibilities and investigators should consider them during the planning and pilot phases of research.

Those actively involved in research with geriatric clients are referred to Cassell's (1988) guidelines of ethical conduct. Thirteen specific steps are given dealing with the broad categories of consent, deciding the capacity to consent, confidentiality, and conflicts of interest. The theme throughout the guidelines is careful planning. Research committees are recommended for review purposes. Pilot studies are essential. Selection of subjects should focus not only on exclusion, but also on inclusion with an eye toward the positive aspects of being involved in a study. Capacity for consent is a crucial area, and it is suggested that committees review cases where there may be doubts. Rules must be established and followed if surrogate decision makers are involved in the consent process. Conflicts of interest should be anticipated, and an ethics committee may be necessary. Honoraria or small stipends given to study participants should be examined as posing potential conflicts to older residents in need of money. The resulting summary is a message that research cannot be undertaken in a slipshod fashion. While the need to demonstrate that activity and therapeutic recreation programs efficacy with older, frail adults is great, the field will not be served by ill-conceived studies conducted under time pressures and without the goal of benefiting individual lives as the foundation for the scientific inquiry.

Consideration of Qualitative and Single-Subject Designs

The initial section of this chapter dealt with the use of experimental designs where a particular intervention (an activity or program) is assessed for effectiveness, generally using groups of persons as the subjects. While funders of research probably have a bias toward the use of experimental methods, recently there have been calls in the leisure studies and services literature for the use of multiple methodologies, particularly qualitative techniques, to explore issues of individuals involved in recreation or leisure activities (Henderson, 1991; Scott and Godbey, 1990; Howe, 1988; Riddick, DeSchriver, and Weissinger, 1984, 1991). Viewing the activity experience from the perspective of the "doer," a strength of qualitative studies seems appropriate when one considers older adults residing in long-term care settings. The ultimate goal of any activity is the benefit it provides to individuals, hence designs which incorporate an individualized perspective are to be valued.

At the core of these recent recommendations for greater use of qualitative studies is the recognition that leisure is an individual, subjective experience which doesn't easily translate into easily quantifiable numbers using scales or pre-established, forced-choice formats (Scott and

Godbey, 1990). Iso-Ahola (1986) noted that 90 percent of the studies published in one journal (*The Journal of Leisure Research*) were surveys suggesting that more qualitative studies were needed, especially those where the unit of exploration was one person. In similar fashion, Riddick, DeScriver, and Weissinger (1984, 1991) assessed the quality of studies published in the same journal during the periods of 1978 to 1982 and 1983 to 1987. They noted the overall quality of studies had improved markedly from the first to the second period, yet most studies still continued to use the survey as the data collection method. They argued for the use of alternative methods, including more experimental designs and qualitative pieces using case studies. Also recommended were studies which collected longitudinal data and those which focused on social group processes and structures. These last two points are highly pertinent to the study of leisure and older adults in long-term care settings. Studies which observe change over time from individual and group perspectives would be most useful to activity managers. In addition, a better understanding of group interactions in the activity setting and elsewhere could lead to different ways of teaching, conducting, or selecting activities.

Focusing on therapeutic recreation studies, a group of researchers (Voelkl, Austin, and Morris, 1991) analyzed studies published during the 1980s in the *Therapeutic Recreation Journal*. For the 95 empirical investigations in print over that time the methodologies were as follows: 54 percent experimental studies, 32 percent surveys, 10 percent field or case studies, 4 percent secondary analysis of existing data sets, and 1 percent other types. They urged greater female participation as researchers and called for collaboration between university departments/investigators and agencies/practitioners in the field. The collaboration theme has been a frequent one in this chapter.

Scott and Godbey (1990), in discussing greater use of qualitative methods, raised two issues applicable to older adults and leisure. They indicated that leisure behavior should be considered a formative process, and, as such, a life span perspective is needed. Most of the research conducted views leisure participation as a static experience; data are collected at one point and reported as such. Yet, they claim, leisure experiences and interpretations change as time progresses, even, perhaps, from moment to moment. Thus, if longitudinal studies were to be conducted in nursing homes, for example, we might be able to gain insight on how the activity experiences change for individuals over time. Does institutionalized behavior describe leisure/social activities as it might other areas? How about those judged most successful? If data were collected focusing on individuals, we might be able to translate the successes of some to others. The authors (Scott and Godbey, 1990) further argue for exploration of the social forces present which help to shape individual behavior in group settings—a topic of study well-suited to activity programming in long-term care.

Howe (1988) reported success with qualitative interviews to explore the process used by older women in deciding to engage in an aerobics class (Nicholson, 1985). A model of the decision process was tested with the older women. Key factors in the theoretical model were interests, receptiveness, a significant event leading to the activity, the social milieu, and knowledge of the program or activity. Using observations and interviews with the older women, the researcher documented how the decision was made to participate in the program. Howe (1988) offers detailed discussion as to the steps taken in conducting interviews and observations in the field. The application of this methodology to the study of activities in nursing homes and other settings is as follows: the activity adoption process needs to be studied in long-term care settings—would the theoretical model used above apply to other settings? Could oral life histories be focused on activities and recreation over the lifespan? Oral histories (Peterson, 1990; Harel, McKinney, and Williams, 1990) have been undertaken with aged adults for a variety of purposes. If the focus could be shifted to leisure based on a client's his-

tory, the activity director would have direction in planning specific, individualized activities. With continuity theory (Davis, 1982) suggesting that similar interests endure (even if the form of the participation might change—from a more active to a more passive form of engagement in some activities such as sports), a history of leisure pursuits during one's lifetime should give direction to program planning. A further use of qualitative techniques, specifically case studies, would be analyses of departments which offer activities to older adults in long-term care. What are the characteristics of those recognized as successful? Are there different ways that success is achieved? An observer/researcher using qualitative methods could begin to answer some of the questions above in a manner similar to O'Brien (1989) whose unit of observation was the entire nursing home.

An additional approach to research applicable to older, frail adults is that of single subject designs (Dattilo, 1989). Here the focus is the effect of some intervention (a novel program or activity) on one person with the results charted over a period of time. Often an undesired or desired behavior is observed relative to the treatment given. Dattilo (1989) notes the strengths of single subject designs as flexibility (treatments can be modified and noted), control (with one person the treatment is focused and other influencing factors can be tracked), accountability (if the treatment proves effective, such evidence is documented), and external validity (successful programs/activities can be replicated with other, similar individuals). This design would allow the exploration of two issues raised earlier: what degree of intensity and duration levels of activity are needed to afford benefit? The single subject approach would permit the adjustment of how much and for how long the intervention activity is used with a participant. Corresponding behavioral or other benefits are then recorded. While this methodology has been frequently used in psychology and the behavioral sciences, and, to a lesser degree, in therapeutic recreation, its use in the area of leisure with older adults has been infrequent.

The intent of this section has been to review alternative methodologies, qualitative techniques and single subject designs, as ways to broaden the research base centered upon activities and older, frail adults. The issue is not one of advocating these methodologies simply because too many surveys have been conducted. The method should always follow the question/issue of consideration. If leisure is a singular/subjective phenomenon and if the goal of activity programming is benefit received by individual consumers, then exploring issues through the eyes and words of those who matter most might have significant consequences.

Interviewing Older Adults

For those research efforts where the methodology will include interviewing older adults, a number of considerations are offered. These are based upon experience of the authors from activity programming and from investigations where older subjects discussed life events, attitudes, or feelings.

- Interviewers should approach older subjects with an attitude of respect. Older interviewees have agreed to share their thoughts and words, and without their cooperation the investigation would not be possible.
- If formal instruments or involved questions are to be used, a pilot study is essential to detect language or wording difficulties. The average length of interviews should be determined. There are a number of questionnaires, indexes, etc., designed specifically for use with older adults. Some are compiled and arranged by category in texts (George and Bearon, 1980; and Kane and Kane, 1981). When developing a new interview tool, simple, understandable language is necessary,

and the piloting process will reveal any changes necessary due to confusion.

- The order of questions should also be determined and a sequence established based on logic or flow. If it has been a length of time since the older subjects have been interviewed, some sample or trial questions may be useful in establishing rapport and continuity. Because of possible patient fatigue, it is generally recommend starting with easier questions, then placing the most difficult or probing questions in the middle followed by tapering to the less taxing items at the close of the interview.
- Investigators should be cautious not to speak for or "help" elderly respondents by putting words into their mouths. Read statements or instructions in a deliberate manner, stopping to reread, if needed. If no response is given due to confusion of terms, do not (unless instructed specifically to do so) get involved in lengthy, interpretive discourse. In most cases wording has been carefully established, and the perception should be that of the older adult, not some interpretation of meaning on the part of the interviewer. No response (after a careful restatement of the item/question) is preferable to a suspect answer clouded by levels of (mis)interpretation.
- The use of multiple interviewers requires training to promote consistency and reliability. Pilot tests, checking for reliability, are a must in this regard. How to deal with confusion or misunderstanding on the part of those being questioned is a topic of which all investigators must be aware. Specific follow-up procedures in such cases must be put into effect by each interviewer. If resources allow, teams of two interviewers may be beneficial, one person concentrating on reading items and guiding the interview while the other investigator writes responses. Unless audio taping presents a problem (unfamiliarity or consent issues), its use can serve as an excellent reliability check with gathered, written information.

- Interviewers should look for signs of fatigue evidenced by older adults and be prepared to stop the interview. An average time for completion will not apply to all of those interviewed. If agitation or physical signs of tiredness are present, it is much better to call a halt to the discussion and return later. Again, the researcher's data collection time frame must be secondary to the comfort and desires of aged subjects.
- Finally, at the conclusion of the interview offer a sincere "thank you," and promote a feeling of shared assistance in something which was worthwhile and might lead to a better quality of life. A written note of thanks or the use of a certificate of participation might be appreciated. As research reports are concluded, give thought to a presentation aimed at the older adults interviewed. While a technical research synopsis will not be of interest, residents and staff at a nursing home used for interviewing might enjoy hearing themes or issues developed from the study and discussed with an air of informality.

Summary

This chapter began with a synthesis of a recent conference held to explore the benefits of therapeutic recreation. The focus here was therapeutic recreation programs with older, frail adults and nearly 40 studies have addressed the topic. Studies were grouped into two areas: physical and psychological. A variety of physical exercise/movement programs have demonstrated positive results—water aerobics, fitness activities, and even common movement such as stirring cookie batter have been attempted in improving physical measures.

Therapies such as bibliotherapy, pet therapy, and reminiscence have been linked to improvements in cognition or psychological areas in older adults. The conference stressed the need for more and improved research. Investi-

gations are needed to explore links between recreation/activities and impacts upon health costs. Other recommendations included multidisciplinary research—bringing those with expertise in activities or recreation together with health/medical professionals. New sites for research are needed; rehabilitation settings and adult daycare sites were noted here. The skills of those who conduct research should be upgraded, and it was suggested that pre-med undergraduates complete a course in research.

A model whereby service, teaching and professional preparation, and research are incorporated has been labeled "the teaching nursing home." Its goal is to produce improved service to residents, upgrade the education experience of health and service professionals who work with aged adults, and at the same time provide expanded research opportunities which will enhance the field of gerontology. Nursing homes, relative to research, offer pros and cons. On the positive side an accessible population exists, longitudinal designs can be accommodated, and interventions, such as novel activity programs, can be included within the daily or weekly routine. Nursing homes also present negatives for purposes of research. Homes are not all alike as might be assumed, and generalization becomes a concern. Ethical problems—who receives and does not receive an innovative program—must be considered. Administrators may or may not encourage efforts by researchers. The teaching nursing home, however, does appear to be a model where activity specialists could collaborate in a team concept to assist with needed research.

Ethical questions frequently arise in the research process, and it was stressed that researchers must never jeopardize human participants in any study. Three goals: (1) respectful treatment, (2) beneficence (seeing that no harm comes to elderly subjects), and (3) justice, dealing with who is and is not selected, must be planned for and accomplished in investigations. Consent to participate is often not a simple issue with older adults who have varying capacities to understand the full impact of the proposed study. One survey found family members more willing to allow their loved ones to become subjects in studies than a group of capable older adults themselves living in a nursing home. Confidentiality must also be analyzed; issues such as access to records and how all information is to be used must be carefully reviewed. Conflicts of interest are potential problems also. Is it always possible to separate the areas of research and day-to-day operations which might be affected by some information gained in a study or survey?

Two research methodologies, qualitative studies and single-subject designs, were noted as having potential when older adults living in long-term care facilities are considered. A trend in the leisure studies literature has been the promotion of qualitative efforts. Here the object of concern is the nature of the leisure experience as perceived and interpreted by the older adult. Open-ended questions serve as prompts in an interview situation. Participant observation and analysis can be used as well. Exploration of a particular unit, an entire activity department or a nursing home (see O'Brien's, 1989, frequently cited analysis) gaining the meaning and interpretation through the variety of players, is another approach to qualitative work. Longitudinal studies where one elder is followed over a number of years are also compatible with qualitative designs. Single-subject research is well-suited to exploring the effects of an activity intervention on one client and observing key outcomes such as depression, social interaction, or improved flexibility. Questions dealing with optimal levels of activity intensity and duration can be answered in single-subject investigations. Interviewing suggestions concluded the chapter. Respect should be displayed toward all study participants. Wording, order of items, fatigue, reliability of interviewers, and situations involving misinterpretation of questionnaire statements are areas to be resolved before initiating any project.

PRACTICAL EXERCISES

1. Obtain a copy of one of the studies listed in the following bibliography and report to staff or classmates on the major findings of the investigation. Cover the following areas:
   a. What was the sample?
   b. What type of program or intervention was used?
   c. What were the findings?
   d. Could the results be generalized to other groups or situations?
   e. Note some of the study strengths and weaknesses.
2. Make a list of the questions you feel need to be answered regarding activities, those who conduct them, and older clients who participate in the activities. Suggest a research design (e.g., research questions, sample, treatment, measurement of results) which might be used with these questions.
3. How would you see the concept of a teaching nursing home fitting with what the activity department does? What contributions could the activity department make in terms of teaching and preparing future professionals, better serving older residents, and being involved in multidisciplinary research projects?
4. Ethical considerations involving older residents or clients and their participation in research projects were noted. Develop guidelines which could be implemented for research with adults in long-term care sites. Cover areas such as consent, who is selected and how, treatment of study participants by researchers, how information will be handled, and confidentiality.
5. Participate in a qualitative study. Decide on a topic and develop a series of questions which could be answered by a given respondent—an older adult or a staff member working in the activities

department. Conduct the interview and report findings to fellow staff or classmates. How could this information be used to improve the quality of leisure experiences offered?

Bibliography

The following studies were cited in the review by Riddick and Keller noted in the beginning of the chapter. They all involve therapeutic programs or interventions with older adults. Readers may wish to refer to them as background for discussions on research methodology or for potential inclusion in programmatic efforts.

Banziger, G. and Rousch, S. (1983). Nursing homes for the birds: A control-relevant intervention with bird feeders. *The Gerontologist, 23*, 527-531.

Beck, P. (1982). The successful interventions in nursing homes: The therapeutic effects of cognitive activity. *The Gerontologist, 22*, 379-383.

Bell, P. (1984). "The effects of supportive touch on depression and anxiety among female residents of a nursing home." Unpublished doctoral dissertation, University of Missouri, Columbia, MO.

Berryman-Miller, S. (1988). Dance movement: Effects on elderly self concepts. *Journal of Physical Education, Recreation & Dance, 59*, 42-46.

Buettner, L. (1988). Utilizing development theory and adaptive equipment with regressed geriatric patients in therapeutic recreation. *Therapeutic Recreation Journal, 22*(3), 72-79.

Bumanis, A. and Yoder, J. (1987). Music and dance: Tools for reality orientation. *Activities, Adaptation & Aging, 10*, 23-35.

Conroy, M., Fincham, F., and Agard-Evans, C. (1988). Can they do anything? Ten single-subject studies of the engagement level of hospitalized demented patients. *British Journal of Occupational Therapy, 51*, 129-132.

Cutler Riddick, C. (1985). Health, aquariums, and the noninstitutionalized elderly. In M. Sussman (Ed.), *Pets and the family* (pp. 63-173). New York, NY: Haworth Press.

Cutler Riddick, C. and Dugan-Jendzejec, M. (1988). Health related impacts of a music program on nursing home residents. In F. Humphrey and J. Humphrey (Eds.), *Recreation: Current selected research* (pp. 155-166). New York, NY: AMS Press.

Cutler Riddick, C., Spector, S., and Drogin, E. (1986). The effects of videogames play on the emotional states and affiliative behavior of nursing home residents. *Activities, Adaptation & Aging, 8*, 95-108.

DeSchriver, M. and Cutler Riddick, C. (1990). Effects of watching aquariums on elders' stress. *Anthrosoos, 9*(1), 44-48.

Ferguson, J. (1980). "Reminiscence counseling to increase psychological well being of elderly women in nursing home facilities." Unpublished doctoral dissertation. Columbia, SC: University of South Carolina.

Francis, G. and Baly, A. (1986). Plush animals: Do they make a difference? *Geriatric Nursing, 7*, 140-142.

Francis, G. and Munjas, B. (1988). Plush animals and the elderly. *Journal of Applied Gerontology, 7*, 161-172.

Fry, P. (1983). Structured and unstructured reminiscence training and depression among the elderly. *Clinical Gerontologist, 1*(3), 15-37.

Gowing, C. (1984). "The effects of minimal care pets on homebound elderly and their professional caregivers." Unpublished doctoral dissertation, University of Illinois at Urbana-Champaign.

Green, J. (1989). Effects of a water aerobics program on the blood pressure, percentage of body fat, weight, and resting pulse rate of senior citizens. *Journal of Applied Gerontology, 8*(1), 132-138.

Hughston, G. and Merriam, S. (1982). Reminiscence: A nonformal technique for improving cognitive functioning in the aged. *International Journal of Aging & Human Development, 2*, 139-140.

Keller, M. J. (1991). "The impact of a water aerobics program on older adults." Unpublished manuscript. Northern Texas State University, Reston, TX.

Malde, S. (1983). "Guided autobiography: A counseling and educational program for older adults." University of California, Unpublished doctoral dissertation, Santa Barbara, CA.

McGuire, F. (1984). Improving the quality of life for residents of long term care facilities through video games. *Activities, Adaptation & Aging, 6*, 1-8.

Morey, M., Cowper, P., Feussner, J., DiPasquale, R., Crowley, G., Kitzman, D., and Sullivan, R. (1989). Evaluation of a supervised exercise program in a geriatric population. *Journal of American Geriatrics Society, 37*, 348-354.

Munson, M. (1984). "Evaluation of the effectiveness of two visitation programs for isolated and lonely elderly persons: The impact on life satisfaction." Unpublished doctoral dissertation, University of Missouri-St. Louis.

Norberg, A., Melin, E., and Asplund, K. (1986). Reactions to music, touch and object presentation in the final stage of dementia: An exploratory study. *International Journal of Nursing Studies, 23*, 315-323.

Olderog Millard, K. and Smith, J. (1989). The influence of group singing therapy on the behavior of Alzheimer's disease patients. *Journal of Music Therapy, 26*, 58-70.

Osgood, N., Meyers, B., and Orchowsky, S. (1990). The impact of creative dance and movement training on the life satisfaction of older adults. *Journal of Applied Gerontology, 9*, 255-265.

Perotta, P. and Meacham, J. (1981-82). Can a reminiscence intervention alter depression and self-esteem? *International Journal of Aging and Human Development, 14*, 23-30.

Preston, E. (1987). "Factors affecting nursing home residents' loneliness, leisure satisfactions, and leisure activity." Unpublished doctoral dissertation, University of Maryland, College Park, MD.

Riegler, J. (1980). Comparison of a reality orientation program for geriatric patients with and without music. *Journal of Music Therapy, 17*, 26-33.

Robb, S., Boyd, M., and Pristash, C. (1980). A wine bottle, plant and puppy. *Journal of Gerontological Nursing, 6*, 721-728.

Schafer, D., Berghorn, F., Holmes, D., and Quadagno, J. (1986). The effects of reminiscing on the perceived control and social relations of institutionalized elderly. *Activities, Adaptation & Aging, 8*, 95-110.

Scogin, F., Hamblin, D., and Beutler, L. (1987). Bibliotherapy for depressed older adults: A self-help alternative. *The Gerontologist, 27*, 383-387.

Scogin, F., Jamison, C., and Davis, N. (1990). Two-year follow-up of bibliotherapy for depression in older adults. *Journal of Consulting and Clinical Psychology, 58*, 665-667.

Scogin, F., Jamison, C., and Gochneaur, K. (1989). Comparative efficacy of cognitive and behavioral bibliotherapy for mildly and moderately depressed older adults. *Journal of Consulting and Clinical Psychology, 57*, 403-407.

Shary, J. and Iso-Ahola, S. (1989). Effects of a control relevant intervention program on nursing home residents' perceived competence and self-esteem. *Therapeutic Recreation Journal, 23*, pp. 7-16.

Supiano, K., Ozminkowski, R., Campbell, R., and Lapidos, C. (1989). Effectiveness of writing groups in nursing homes. *Journal of Applied Gerontology, 8*, 382-400.

Wolfe, J. (1983). The use of music in a group sensory training program for regressed geriatric patients. *Activities, Adaptation & Aging, 4*(1), 49-62.

Yoder, R., Nelson, D., and Smith, D. (1989). Added purpose versus rote exercise in female nursing home residents. *American Journal of Occupational Therapy, 43*(9), 581-586.

References

Cassel, C. (1988). Ethical issues in the conduct of research in long term care. *The Gerontologist, 28 (Supplement)*, 90-96.

Cassel, C. (1987). Informed consent for research in geriatrics: History and concepts. *Journal of the American Geriatrics Society, 35*, 42-544.

Cassel, C. (1985). Research in nursing homes: Ethical issues. *Journal of the American Geriatrics Society, 33*, 795-799.

Cohen-Mansfield, J., Kerin, P., Paulson, G., Lipson, S., and Holdridge, K. (1988). Informed consent for research in a nursing home: Process and issues. *The Gerontologist, 28*(3), 355-358.

Coyle, C., Kinney, T., Riley, B., and Shank, J. (1991). *Benefits of therapeutic recreation: A consensus view*. Philadelphia, PA: Temple University.

Dattilo, J. (1989). Unique horizons in research: Single subject designs. In D. Compton (Ed.), *Issues in therapeutic recreation: A profession in transition* (pp. 445-461). Champaign, IL: Sagamore Publishing.

Davis, N. (1982). The role continuity approach to aging: Implications for leisure programming. In M. Teague, R. MacNeil, and G. Hitzhusen (Eds.) *Perspectives on Leisure and Aging in a Changing Society* (pp. 298-318). Columbia, MO: University Press Services.

Eisdorfer, C. (1985). Implications of research for public policy. In E. Schnieder, et al., (Eds.), *The teaching nursing home*, (pp. 293-303). New York, NY: Raven Press.

George, L. and Bearon, L. (1980). *Quality of life in older persons: Meaning and measurement*. New York, NY: Human Sciences Press.

Harel, Z. McKinney, E., and Williams, M. (1990). *Black aged: Understanding diversity and service needs*. Newbury Park, CA: Sage Publications.

Henderson, K. (1991). *Dimensions of choice: A qualitative approach to recreation, parks and leisure research*. State College, PA: Venture Publishing, Inc.

Howe, C. (1988). Using qualitative structured interviews in leisure research: Illustrations from one case study. *Journal of Leisure Research, 20*(4), 305-324.

Iso-Ahola, S. (1986). Concerns and thoughts about leisure research. *Journal of Leisure Research, 13*(3), pp. 5-10.

Kane, R. L. and Kane, R. A. (1981). *Assessing the elderly: A practical guide to measurement.* Lexington, MA: Lexington Books.

MacNeil, R., Hawkins, D., Barber, E., and Winslow, R. (1990). The effect of a client's age upon the employment preferences of therapeutic recreation majors. *Journal of Leisure Research, 22*(4), 329-340.

Maddox, G. (1985). The teaching nursing home and beyond: Research objectives for the 1980s. In E. Schnieder, et al., (Eds.), *The teaching nursing home,* (pp. 267-279). New York, NY: Raven Press.

National Commission for protection of human subjects of biomedical and behavioral research. (1987). *The Belmont report: Ethical principles and guidelines for the protection of human subjects of research.* DHEW Publication No. (OS). Bethesda, MD: U.S. Government Printing Office.

Nicholson, L. (1985). "The process of adapting exercise programs by older women." Unpublished master's thesis, University of Georgia, Athens, GA.

O'Brien, M. E. (1989). *Anatomy of a nursing home: A new view of resident life.* Owings Mill, MD: National Health Publishing.

Ostfeld, A. (1985). The teaching nursing home: Research strategies and issues. In E. Schnieder, et al., (Eds.), *The teaching nursing home* (pp. 281-285). New York, NY: Raven Press.

Peterson, J. (1990). Age of wisdom: Elderly black women in family and church. In J. Solokousky (Ed.), *The cultural context of aging: Worldwide perspectives,* (pp. 213-227). New York, NY: Bergin and Garvey Publishing.

Riddick, C., DeSchriver, M., and Weissinger, E. (1984). A methodological review of research in *Journal of Leisure Research* from 1978 to 1982. *Journal of Leisure Research, 16,* 311-321.

Riddick, C., DeSchriver, M., and Weissinger, E. (1991). A methodological review of research in *Journal of Leisure Research* from 1983 to 1987. Unpublished manuscript.

Riddick, C. and Keller, J. (1991). The benefits of therapeutic recreation in gerontology. In C. Coyle, T. Kinney, B. Riley, and J. Shank (Eds.), *Benefits of therapeutic recreation: A consensus view* (pp. 151-204). Philadelphia, PA: Temple University.

Rowe, J. (1985). Factors facilitating and impeding research in the teaching nursing home setting. In E. Schnieder, et al., (Eds.), *The teaching nursing home* (pp. 287-292). New York, NY: Raven Press.

Scott, D. and Godbey, G. (1990). Reorienting leisure research: The case for qualitative methods. *Society and Leisure, 13*(1), 189-205.

Troyer, L. (1991). Summary of gerontology consensus group. In C. Coyle, T. Kinney, B. Riley, & J. Shank (Eds.), *Benefits of therapeutic recreation: A consensus view* (pp. 394-397). Philadelphia, PA: Temple University.

Voelkl, J. E., Austin, D. R., and Morris, C. (1992) An analyses of articles published in the *Therapeutic Recreation Journal* during the 1980s. *Therapeutic Recreation Journal, 26*(2), 46-50.

Professional Issues

Professionals, Professionalism, and Activity Professionals

An issue which has generated much concern and debate among those who work in the activity area in long-term settings is that of "professionalism." It is a frequent topic when activity personnel gather at local or national forums. In a triangulated fashion the issue impacts on those striving toward professional status, those allied health team members and administrative staff who work with activity personnel on a daily basis, and most important, the residents or patients who should be the beneficiaries of improved service through the specialties associated with a profession. A question facing all emerging professions is "who benefits most?"

Phyllis Foster (1991) in her comments at the eighth annual NAAP Conference indicated that this striving toward professional status was an issue of great concern to her and to those in attendance. The term "activity professional" was used throughout her address and its meaning should be examined. Not too many years ago "diversional activities" was frequently used to describe what was offered by those seeking to add meaning and routine to the free hours of residents in nursing homes and other long-term care settings. Currently, words such as "therapist" or "professional" are more popular and reflect not only a change in philosophy and scope of the job, but also signal a desire on the part of those providing the service to achieve greater respect among coworkers. From the semantic perspective, we might also wonder if "professional" has taken on different meanings over the years, i.e., has it become devalued with nearly all groups of workers vying for their claim to the term? From dry cleaning service to termite protection, from those who service indoor plants to those who handle parking at the airport, we are bombarded with "professionals." It would seem there should/ought/must be differentiation between those eligible to practice medicine and the worker who clears clogged drainspouts. The typical reference groups for activity personnel appear to be the allied health areas of nursing, occupational therapy, physical therapy, etc., (Parker, 1991).

Perhaps the most accurate description of the current movement is "striving toward professionalism." Foster (1991) mentioned the comparisons with allied health members, the need to establish educational requirements for activity directors beginning with specific college level courses leading one day to specialized graduate training, and the ongoing demand for research to document how activity involvement impacts on quality of life for those in long-term care. Efforts in this area are essential as well if practice is to advance and a body of knowledge developed so that theory may be tested and modified.

Professional image is a concern for activity practitioners (Foster, 1991). Respect in the long-term care setting is one which has not been universally given to activity staff. Foster (1991) also evidenced the mixed emotions that the decision to seek professional status brings. Specifically, might the approach become too clinical and in the process the joy and spontaneity of delivering leisure services to residents be somewhat diminished? The following reflects philosophical considerations (Foster, 1991):

> I am committed to the notion that I can do more for residents of a facility by developing an environment that encourages continued participation in living than I can as a deliverer of independent therapy schemes of certain duration—undertaken by prescription.

While assessment, prescription, and evaluation are aligned with healthcare and are positively associated with improved image, the movement toward professional status will be accompanied by transitions, some requiring personnel to consider what is or who are most important.

Accounts have been given in the literature signifying that the job of the activity director is undergoing change. More is required than simply being an effective leader or programmer, and, similar to many administrative positions, the individual skills which were responsible for success initially within the organization are not necessarily the same talents needed when administrative responsibilities are assumed. Karras (1988) in reflecting on the duties of an activity director noted many tasks and responsibilities one would associate with managing—understanding and blending staff talents, a personal self-assessment to determine an awareness of strengths and weaknesses, proper time management, an understanding of politics within the work environment, and a consciousness of image to include dress and behaviors. The shift for some activity directors/department heads is often abrupt for those who have "come through the ranks," starting as an activity aide with special skills. Some might even feel that managers or administrative heads, as opposed to those who work directly with residents, most deserve professional status. Not all would agree that management duties immediately place one higher on the image hierarchy than those who work directly with residents or patients. Teaching is an example where calls have been made to confer professional status on those who do so successfully and remain in the classroom. Also, the concept of a master recreation therapist has been discussed. Here one would receive recognition and status based upon programming effectiveness, not by electing an administrative job route. To assume that programming and leadership skills are somehow less worthy in contributing to image or professionalism is deserving of careful review, yet the nature of the activity director's job has undergone change as added responsibilities accompanied by increased management skills are now the norm.

Among the duties performed by most activity directors are personnel management functions, and the groups being supervised are often vastly different in makeup. Full-time and part-time activities staff can vary greatly in age, background, educational preparation, and programming talents. In addition, most activity directors have the responsibility of coordinating volunteers who range in age, interests, commitment and primary motivations. Student volunteers doing sustained field work or practicum experiences may comprise another group of supervisees. It takes an astute administrator to blend the talents of such a diverse unit. Most important, the residents themselves must be considered as the primary recipients of supervisory or administrative talent.

Making the transition from group or individual resident activity programming to one leading and supervising a staff who can then successfully deliver a full leisure program is not always an easy one to make (Halberg and Waters, 1991). Reflective of the concern expressed by many activity directors or newly appointed (activity) department heads, Halberg and Waters (1991) indicate that a management perspective is essential if directors are to gain an improved status within the long-term care setting. Directors must not fear encounters with other administrators, and they must feel comfortable with delegating to others many of the direct contact aspects of leisure programming. Planning skills are necessary as are the typical personnel skill requirements of hiring, orienting, motivating, and evaluating the different groups of employees and volunteers.

The aspect of continuing education and staying current with new developments is associated with professionalism, and Maypole (1985) surveyed activity staff as to their priorities. Both a national and a state-level sample were drawn, and the demographics of participants are pertinent as the concept of a profession is considered.

About half of the national sample had not completed college, while for the state group the number was nearly two-thirds. The mean salary for the national sample was $12,700 and more than $3,000 less for the state group (Maypole, 1985). These figures are comparable to a 1989 survey (Parker, 1991) which described the profile of an activity director in Illinois as having a high school education with some college work and earning about $14,000 a year.

More recent figures supplied by the NAAP (Sifford, 1993) show educational levels to be improving. More than a third of those active in the NAAP have completed a four-year degree with another 20 percent having had some college. More than 7 percent have attained a graduate degree. Most members placed their salary between $15,000 and $24,000 a year (Sifford, 1993). Beyond demographics, however, the priorities of continuing education noted by Maypole (1985) were learning to deal with difficult patients, learning new activity techniques, dealing with death, and learning group work techniques. Administrative areas ranked highly were conflict resolution, program evaluation, and leadership techniques. Those of lesser importance were the more traditional management-oriented areas of delegating, budgeting, evaluating, and supervising. It would be interesting to see if results would differ currently given the greater awareness of the activity director's role as involving more than programming.

Defining Professionalism

A number of criteria are typically used in defining a "profession." Common elements would include an identifiable body of knowledge which guides practice, a code of ethics, a lengthy education and training (internship) period, credentialling using the stricter forms of certification or licensure, accreditation by institutions that provide the education and training, control over who enters the profession, and a socialization process for newly admitted practitioners (Witt, 1985). Others might view aspects such as monitoring (i.e., review boards to evaluate cases of suspect practices), the commitment one must make to undergo the process of entry, or, considering perquisites, large salaries and acknowledgment from the general public as representative of professionalism. A cursory glance of the aforementioned criteria matched with the statements in previous paragraphs would lead one to believe that the phrase, "striving toward professionalism" is an accurate assessment of the circumstance of those promoting leisure opportunities in long-term care facilities. Pay, perks, and prestige come in amounts less than abundant for many activity therapists, and, while existing educational backgrounds are far from desirable, although improving, strides are being made in other areas of professionalism. Certification is in place through bodies such as the NCCAP or the National Council for Therapeutic Recreation Certification. Many nursing homes, however, do not require such a certification for directors or assistants. Continuing education coursework is a requirement for certification, yet the quality of workshops and training sessions can vary, and, with the number of different agencies involved (professional associations, colleges at all levels, and in-house efforts) overall quality becomes nearly impossible to monitor. The goal of developing a two or four-year curriculum at community colleges or universities as noted by Foster (1991) is of immediate need, but developing the curriculum which might address "a unique body of knowledge" would be a major undertaking. The placement of such a program would vary greatly from campus to campus depending upon resources, reputation, and other internal factors. Thus, movement toward professional status through improved education and the creation of a body of knowledge to include empirical research, evaluation studies, and theory building will require much effort on many fronts. Noteworthy are publication outlets in the form of specialized houses focusing on aids to improve programming and journals such as

Activities, Adaptations & Aging or *The Therapeutic Recreation Journal* which offer research studies, often of an applied nature, with implications for practitioners.

Another pertinent issue related to how quickly professional recognition might be attained is the source of the impetus to move activity personnel in that direction. If it remains inside, i.e., within groups of activity directors or organizations such as the National Association of Activity Directors who lobby or cajole industry (long-term care) administrators, lawmakers, or regulatory bodies (HICFA), the speed of action would differ from the situation resulting when outside forces interact to bring about response from within the activities field. If administrators could agree that a baccalaureate degree and certification (NCCAP) were necessary criteria for one to hold the position of activities specialist, reaction would occur. If state legislatures or regulatory agencies established such requirements, those seeking job eligibility would respond. If activity involvement (defined as therapeutic) were eligible for third-party reimbursement, one could easily speculate that a series of events would follow leading to greater prestige, more pay and stiffer requirements for staff. History in the short and long term has not shown a clamoring on the part of "outside" forces to upgrade the requirements and pay of activity directors. The push most likely will come from those active in leisure service provision in long-term care environments, and progress will be experienced as a result of cooperative efforts.

Professionalism— Who Benefits?

At the core of the issue of increased "professionalism" is the matter of benefit, e.g., who is likely to benefit the most? The need for higher salaries and improved status for activity personnel is apparent and has been actively voiced, yet the aging resident or client must remain the focal point of professionalism. However, not all are in agreement that the professional approach, particularly in regard to leisure activities, best serves the needs of recipients (Lord, Hutchison, and Van Derbeck, 1985). Because of their background emphasizing a logical, analytical, detached perspective, activity professionals may create a dependency on the part of clients, and the very essence of leisure—a carefree, spontaneous, and internally motivated approach—may run counter to what the leisure "professional" offers (Lord, Hutchison, and Van Derbeck, 1985). We tend to trust professionals, and through that trust comes a power relationship not always to the advantage of the older client. Among professional practices a narrow focus may also bring negatives as far as the client is concerned. Because professionals are typically specialized, would the therapeutic aspect overshadow all else, and would there be a place for spontaneous leisure? A particular standard of service, perhaps too inflexible, is associated with professionalism; how that standard of service functions is a key when the unending demands of the activity director are considered along with the varied demands of residents. Equity and impartiality of services are hallmarks of professionalism as well, yet reality might dictate disproportionate amounts of time being spent with certain residents (Lord, Hutchison and Van Derbeck, 1985). Philosophical tenets may clash with day-to-day reality—how these elements of professionalism are translated into practice to best serve all clients is the fundamental consideration.

The authors (Lord, Hutchison, and Van Derbeck, 1985) present a dichotomy of the characteristics of a professional: self-restrained, cautious, stability-seeking, logical, conventional, and wary of the unstructured contrasted with those qualities associated with children (this applies to leisure or play behavior)—spontaneous, unrestrained, risk-taking, intuitive, exploratory, and at ease with chaos. Are there not a number of qualities in this latter group which might serve as goals or benefits of leisure for those in long-term care residences? It probably is not accurate to label all activity directors as profes-

sionals using the first group of descriptors—unconventional, unstructured, and less than self-constrained might describe more than a few activity directors. The major issue, it seems, is not to let those qualities associated with the scientific method overshadow all else so that programming becomes routine, boring, and anything but challenging for residents. Similar thoughts may be reflected in Foster's (1991) address to NAAP conventioneers—use the positive aspects of professionalism to upgrade the service and the image of activity directors, but preserve the fun and spontaneity that is so much a part of what programming is all about. The necessary vision of professionalism according to Lord, Hutchison, and Van Derbeck (1985) is one anchored in a new equality where all individuals, inclusive of older, frail persons, are valued by nonprofessionals and professionals alike. It is also signified by a change in the client-professional relationship where control is shared. Finally, deprofessionalization must occur at any time when the movement begins to tilt in favor of advantages only to those within the profession to the detriment of those served. Although possible, such action appears unlikely for those in the activity arena, but it serves as a reminder of who should benefit most through professionalism.

Another model of professionalism (Witt, 1985; and Cullen, 1978) sees two distinct approaches in answering the question of who benefits most. One, the cultural-exchange view, is characterized by a shared bargain between the professional and the client. Professionals must endure a great deal simply to enter their field, e.g., long training, advanced and continuing education, and licensure by the state. They must monitor themselves, and this all works to protect the client. Prestige and high pay are typically seen as part of the bargain, but there is recognition on the part of the layperson that a vital service is provided by someone who has sacrificed a great deal while maintaining high performance standards in the conduct of their job.

The counter view, one much more negative in evaluating those within the field, views professionalism from the orientation of power. Professionalism is seen as no more than a power grab by those within the group. Self-interest rules; the interests of those served are secondary. Traditional elements such as a code of ethics (only a public relations tool here) or licensure (only used to restrict who gets in and to keep fees high) are negatives, not positives. Witt (1985) contends that the cultural-exchange model and the power orientation model often work together, typically in situations where both task complexity and intellectual sophistication are inherent in the service provided. In cases where the task is less complex and learning requirements are not stringent, the tendency is for occupational groups to seek professionalism through power orientation.

The above point is worthy of reflection considering the status of activity specialists. While it's far from true, many feel that anyone can assist with activities for older, frail adults. After all, fun is the focus, and games are the tools. How hard can it be? These attitudes on the part of coworkers are frequently experienced by activity staff. Based upon current levels of training and formal education, it is doubtful that professionalism through the exchange method would be feasible for activity personnel. Yet the movement toward continually upgrading education and promoting certification is a positive force. The dangers of the "power grab" approach are apparent, and those within the field must balance legitimate gain on their part with improved service to clients. Every step taken toward delivering a better leisure experience to residents/patients must be documented. The perceived negative image as related to task complexity and intellectual sophistication in the exchange model is one which activity specialists must counteract through communication. Research can address efficacy and cost effectiveness and will need to be part of the strategy. Client benefit is a message to be broadcast. In the near future a variety of forces— increased certification, continuing education, teamwork with allied health staff and others likely to impact from outside (e.g., regulatory activity, pub-

lic opinion)—will affect the striving for professionalism on the part of activity directors/specialists. The high road of exchange bringing better pay and status for improving the lives of the elderly through leisure should be the route taken.

CERTIFICATION

When one considers credentialling as an important criterion related to professionalism, it should be noted that there are three levels in the process based upon stringency of requirements. The least rigorous credentialling path which could be loosely associated with the term "professional" is that of registration. Some combination of education, experience, and continuing education is typically represented in the backgrounds of those workers who choose to register. It is thought that a level of protection is offered the recipient of the service, yet qualifications of those who register can vary greatly, and nobody assumes the responsibility of establishing a minimum level of performance based upon registration. Acceptance criteria are usually broadly defined, and for some groups registration may represent the first step toward professional status.

The second level applicable to activity personnel is that of certification. Requirements for certification are more rigorous than for registration, although not as demanding as for licensure. Formal education, experience, and continuing education requirements are spelled out and accepted by a governing body. These requirements are used in evaluating the backgrounds of applicants, and typically a certification board is established to review all applications. Certification boards operate independently from state authority or other regulatory bodies. Continuing education credits are generally needed to maintain certification status. Although an examination (standardized test) may be required, frequently the assessment includes a careful evaluation of the application based upon meeting established criteria.

The most rigorous credentialling path is that of licensure which implies strict adherence to educational attainment from institutional programs having undergone review (i.e., some form of accreditation from bodies associated with the professional area). Components of the body of knowledge are spelled out, and competencies must be met. Supervision of practice through internships, residencies, etc., is a method of insuring an acceptable level of performance. Knowledge and practical performance are measured by a comprehensive examination (e.g., state medical board exams) taken upon completion of all educational requirements. Admittance to the profession is strictly controlled through the process; those not meeting the requirements are denied the right to practice.

Currently the certification process applicable in the broadest perspective to those working in activity/ leisure programming with older, frail adults is the National Certification Council for Activity Professionals (NCCAP). Other plans exist such as the National Council for Therapeutic Recreation Certification for any practitioner working in therapeutic recreation. The NCCAP notes that its target market is activity personnel working in a variety of long-term care settings including skilled nursing, intermediate care, senior centers, or other adult daycare settings. The NCCAP plan, modeled after that for therapeutic recreators, offers certification in three areas for four groups: activity assistant certified, activity director certified, activity director provisional certified, and activity consultant certified, (see Appendix A for the NCCAP Standards according to the three areas). All levels include a combination of attainment based on formal post-secondary education, continuing education through approved workshops, and experience in the field. Specific coursework in topical areas is spelled out as is the nature of practical experience. Applicants submit a detailed resumé of education and experience which is judged by those sitting on the council.

Activity assistants, those who lead activities with aging adults under the supervision of a director, may qualify under two tracks: Track 1 having 30 college semester credits plus 2,000

hours of experience and 20 clock hours of continuing education from body of knowledge or Track 2 through having a high school diploma plus the NAAP/NCCAP 90 hour basic education course or six college credits and 4,000 hours of experience and 20 clock hours of continuing education from body of knowledge. Three tracks and an activity director provisional certified are available to activity directors having supervisory responsibilities with other staff. Completion of an appropriate bachelor's degree with a combination of work experience and continuing education units will qualify one at this level. Certain coursework areas (e.g., gerontology, sociology, activity skills, biology) must be present in the activity assistant's academic transcript. The activity director provisional certified is a provisional five year certification for one who is working to meet the NCCAP requirements for activity director certified.

Consultants face the most demanding academic requirements. Track 1 requires either a master's degree plus 2,000 hours activity experience, 40 clock hours of continuing education body of knowledge, and 200 hours consulting experience, or Track 2 requires a bachelor's degree plus 4,000 hours of activity experience, 40 clock hours of continuing education body of knowledge, and 200 hours of consulting; these are the routes to certification here. Initially all levels had a "grandfathering" mechanism which expired in 1992.

Earlier the phrase "striving toward professionalism" was used, and reflection upon the criteria under the NCCAP plan would indicate that activity personnel have made a concerted attempt to become truly professional. The requirement of continuing education is appropriate and encouraging; further advancement might be undertaken in agreeing on what the critical topics for workshop sessions should be and if performances of those attending such workshops should be expected and measured. Should assignments, tests, or other performance measures be a part of continuing education activities? Careful thought has also been given to formal education topics deemed essential for activity personnel. As spelled out in the NCCAP guidelines, six broad areas have been identified within the appropriate body of knowledge: working with residents (e.g., biology, psychology, basic health); communications (e.g., public speaking, public relations, motivation); evaluating residents (e.g., assessment, charting), regulations (those at different levels, state surveys); programming (e.g., planning and exposure to areas such as exercise, arts, room-bound persons); and management/personnel (e.g., leadership, finances, professional associations). The goal must be to expose more activity specialists to those areas through degree or nondegree experiences. As previously discussed, the backgrounds of typical activity directors would not be equal to those in selected medical areas, yet positive movement is present in terms of increased rigor. If demands to make certification a requirement for employment can become reality, the pace will likely quicken in the journey toward professionalism.

Consultants, Computers, and Time Management

Tools to assist the activity supervisor include outside help from a paid consultant, the use of computers in a variety of ways, and understanding principles of time management. One of the ways in developing an effective relationship with a consultant is to have a clear understanding (on the part of administrators, activity directors and their staff, the consultant, and the residents who should benefit most) of why they are being employed and how they are to operate within the activity department. An experienced consultant (Cunninghis, 1985) has analyzed the dynamics of an effective relationship within the framework of initial understanding, what they [consultants] can and cannot do, and the responsibilities of the activity director in maximizing this form of outside talent.

The decision to hire an activities consultant and how that decision is communicated can set the stage for a successful or an unsuccessful venture (Cunninghis, 1985). If the agreement comes as a result of a request on the part of the staff activity director, thought will have been given as to why the assistance is needed. If administration makes the decision, care needs to be taken to assure all concerned that the consultant's role is not to snoop around with the intention of exposing weaknesses of the activity department, particularly those stemming from the director. A positive foundation is laid if administration, the activity staff, and the consultant are in agreement as to why and how this service is to be used. It makes sense if all parties draw up an agreement as to what is to be accomplished and what the key areas of exploration or investigation will be. Some areas might eventually be expanded, but such an agreement may ease the fears of activity staff who may be suspicious of purpose or intent. These guidelines will also assist the consultant in establishing parameters for the job. In short, in the early stages of effective consulting, all parties share a consensus view as to the roles, authority, and assistive nature of everyone involved in the team.

A number of skills are particularly relevant and should be found in any consultant; these talents then are tapped by directors and staff. At the top of this list is communication and problem solving skills. Communication is the primary tool at the disposal of the consultant, and the nature of the job is that of problem formulation and analysis, reflecting on possible solutions, and relaying these suggestions to staff. Consultants should be up to date on all regulations applicable to the activity program, and they should understand how state surveyors think and operate in regards to activity requirements. They must know and be able to teach the how and why of activities; activity analysis—the ability to breakdown any leisure task or experience on the basis of intended goals, conduct, materials required with adaptations if necessary—and the specific motor and cognitive skills needed. Successful consultants also have the ability to involve department members in the process. They seek input and information from the activity director and generate a feeling of teamwork (Cunninghis, 1985).

A few "don'ts" also apply to staff expectations of the activities consultant. Don't expect the consultant to do an acceptable job if resentment by staff is the rule and any suggestion to change the status quo is greeted with obstinate resistance. Withholding information, minimizing major problems, and avoiding personnel issues such as personality conflicts or other areas causing dissatisfaction are sure to undermine the effectiveness of consultants. Consultants don't know everything about the department and how it interacts with the residents, and it is impossible to gain this information in the limited time they visit. Yet staff can greatly assist the process by providing a well-organized orientation and providing background in areas under investigation. Consultants don't wave magic wands and change strained relationships with other departments (e.g., nursing, physical therapy), and they don't have the power to change attitudes on the part of administrators. Consultants can inform, enlighten, suggest and recommend, but in the end their effectiveness is only seen when the investigation ends and staff are left to implement recommendations (Cunninghis, 1985). On the positive side, however, a useful role often played by consultants is that of an intermediary. If all parties are open, the go-between role can impact upon strained relationships which may have existed simply because no party was willing to come forward and honestly discuss sources of dissatisfaction.

To maximize the activity consultant's role Cunninghis (1985) has suggested a number of tactics on the part of staff. For maximum effectiveness schedule meetings with the consultant. Some days this might mean meeting during activity programming, and on other days quiet, undisturbed periods will be required. Have an agenda for all meetings; write down questions or issues and bring them to the consultant's attention. If information or documentation is requested, have it ready for the meeting. Mentioned earlier was the necessity of a solid orientation; schedule it carefully in order for the consultant to gain a "feel" for the operation. Don't bring the consultant in initially on an atypical day—the day when everything or nothing works perfectly is probably not the best day for the consultant's first introduction. Directors should be honest with their feelings making their expectations clear. If this is the first time a consultant has been used, any fears of a hidden agenda must be expressed along with possible doubts and questions. Finally, have a clear idea of what will occur when the consultant's services are terminated. Discuss this with staff. How will recommendations be considered? Will there be a timeline for implementation? Will formal evaluation of suggestions be part of the plan? With planning, honesty, and a desire to improve services to residents or clients, a consultant can be an asset to activity departments in long-term care facilities.

Computers

The computer has greatly affected communication in the business and leisure worlds. For some staff it creates an immediate phobia, and the thought of older residents wanting to learn to operate a computer is a notion hard for many to imagine. Yet evidence exists that this modern time-saving device is affecting activity professionals and the residents they serve. Sortais (1992) details the impact of computer use on both staff and residents. Initially her feeling toward the department's new computer was one of trepidation. With practice and a plan of gradual, incremental steps and built-in success, Sortais was able to overcome her fears and view the device as an indispensable part of her daily routine. Using activity calendars, Sortais dramatically reduced production time and greatly improved quality using color graphics effectively. It was shown that activity directors can also put the computer to good use in care plans, charting and progress notes, and in tabulating participants' records. Letters, thank-you notes, and other routine forms of correspondence, posters and banners, and standard word-processing capabilities are additional uses. Obviously any task involving the completion and maintenance of lists is well-suited to the computer.

Beyond staff use, however, residents gained in many ways from the computer (Sortais, 1992). In her study care was taken to locate a portable model (not a laptop because of poor representation on the screen) which was sturdy and had excellent screen visibility. A multipurpose printing program and a card game were the first programs purchased. Three residents showed initial interest, and Sortais (1992) detailed the personal benefits of computer use with them: improved communication (e.g., a stroke victim could type messages), greater confidence as new skills were demonstrated, creativity, and an elevation of self-worth. Eventually volunteers were asked to educate residents about the computer's many uses.

The use of computers as a therapeutic tool for older adults with specific rehabilitative needs or cognitive deficits is currently in an early, yet exciting stage. The potential to assist those with such disorders as brain injury or communication or memory loss appears to be very positive (Fisher, 1986a, 1986b; Ryan and Heaven, 1986). Fisher (1986b) noted that computer programs exist and are being tested with adults who face rehabilitation after brain injuries. Perceptual problems can be addressed using games that require the user to scan a visual field and to activate a response by pressing the keyboard. Activities and programs are available to stimulate conceptual thinking, attention, or memory losses although motivation of the patient or client remains a difficult problem. Rehabilitation is most often a lengthy process. The pluses of computer programs for cognitive therapy are many (Fisher, 1986b): the objective manner in which information is presented, the immediate feedback, that control is held by the user to operate at his or her pace, and to repeat tasks as desired, and to move to

increasing levels of difficulty. As far as long-term care facilities are concerned, the ease of portability is a definite plus.

At an adult daycare setting, a program involving computer literacy through hands-on manipulation found that some of the older adults were more eager to participate and that a process of involvement usually progressed in stages (Fisher, 1986a). Half of the attendees had experienced brain damage and many suffered from physical disabilities. Males were more likely than females to resist the computer, a factor attributed to higher levels of depression among men. It was speculated that men were more sensitive about performance and did not want to display their ignorance with this new technology. When staff tried to add a competitive spirit by using poker chips, some men were enticed. Many who were apprehensive at first eventually became converts.

The issue of computer anxiety or apprehension was explored (Temple and Gavillet, 1990) in a group of senior center members who were exposed to a twelve-hour course in computer awareness and applications. The seniors who enrolled in the course were found to have low levels of computer anxiety initially (perhaps the self-selection factor), and posttesting revealed no significant drop in apprehension. Computer anxiety was not related to either age or previous exposure to computers. Posttesting also found significant improvements in computer knowledge, but not in application. The authors urged instructors to analyze teaching styles carefully, and they indicated the greatest problem may not be reluctant seniors, but, rather, too few resources in terms of willing teachers, and available hardware and software.

In order for staff to promote innovative programming with computers in long-term care facilities, personal anxieties or phobias about computers must be put aside. There must be an awareness of the types of software available which can be used successfully with different older groups. The articles reviewed in this section touched upon these concerns; some programs were evaluated as having too fast a pace;

others were found by older adults as being too childish. More experimental efforts need to be attempted in nursing homes with reports made available to activity directors. Computer uses as an integral part of activity programming should become a regular topic in the professional literature and at conferences where activity specialists gather.

Time Management

While the computer has proved itself as a time-saving device, there are numerous factors, many under the direct control of the activity specialist or department head, which result in more productive days or, if left unattended, reduce greatly what can be accomplished in a given eight or nine hour period. The study of time management has revealed that time wasters are, on the whole, generic; each job is somewhat unique, but workers with similar levels of responsibility report common problems when it comes to managing time (McKenzie, 1972, 1989). As discussed earlier in the chapter, the jobs of the activity specialist and certainly that of the director or department head have expanded. Direct face-to-face time spent with residents is not the only task for directors. In fact their time might be better spent thinking of ways to assist all others who work directly with residents in leisure activities.

As in many areas of life the first step in improving time management skills in a residential care facility begins with a personal recognition of the problem and a desire to address it. Analyze how daily time is spent; for example, what percentage of work time is spent in meetings with others? How much time could be accounted for in direct contact with residents or their family members? If serving as a director, what percentage of the time is allocated to supervising staff? Documentation and paperwork are a reality; do they take a disproportionate amount of time? Could the process be improved? And perhaps most important, how often do directors spend time on the "big picture" or "future" issues? Management literature indicates that someone,

arguably here the department head or director, must be concerned with issues affecting the future—what will the department look like in five years? Is there a philosophy that is being implemented? Could existing resources (or fewer) be used any more effectively? If not considered, these issues may lead an adequate department to its demise.

Examination should also reveal a personal style of time management. Does the director attack issues head-on? Where does he or she fall on the organization-disorganization continuum? Is he or she a procrastinator? Could crisis management describe his or her leadership or supervisory style? Recognition of the methods used to deal with and structure work time is necessary for positive change.

Two types of time wasters exist: one external and the other resting squarely within the activity specialist, internal. External time wasters include legitimate, unplanned crises—something goes wrong which was nearly impossible to predict. These occurrences are most difficult to anticipate, but must be dealt with and will affect one's planned work schedule. Other problems outside the individual worker's control may be personal interruptions, meetings attended which are poorly planned or run; tardiness on the part of others; others' socialization desires; and any other unscheduled happenings in which the director plays no part other than to be involved at a moment's notice. Although more difficult to manage than internal time wasters, some action is possible in fighting these external sources by notifying others that the matter presents a problem in achieving stated goals. A mutual agreement of the amount of time to spend on the issue can sometimes be reached between the director and the source of the problem.

Internal time wasters, on the other hand, can be personally controlled, if recognized. Poor organization is a frequent one: files are in random order or easily misplaced; the tools of the job can never be easily located; the desk is a mess, or the general appearance of the work area cries, "Disaster." All of these negatively

affect the ability to do the job as quickly and efficiently as possible. How does the director rate
on the sociability scale? We would expect activity directors to be friendly extroverts, but does
this hamper productivity? For some, establishing priorities is a most difficult task. These
types may appear to be considerably busy yet
the tasks they're engaged in may not be the
most important ones. Some workers are also
comfortable with a crisis management style
which uses procrastination as the preferred approach until the deadline cannot be avoided. A
moderate success can be achieved by this route,
yet maximum effectiveness will never be
reached. Finally, time is frequently wasted
through a lack of delegation. Some directors are
perfectionists and must have every task under
their control. Instead of developing the talents
of others, they typically frustrate themselves doing tasks at a level which is below them in the
organizational hierarchy.

So, what to do? Internal deficiencies should
be approached in a straightforward manner.
The following are our recommendations to a director or administrator for improved time management.

1. Analyze your job and identify the most
   critical job tasks (would your list agree
   with your boss's perception of the job?).
   Detail in categories or areas how your
   time is spent. Do you find time wasters?
   Are some internal while others are external?
2. How do you rate as a delegator? Are
   there tasks from the above list which
   could be done by other staff or volunteers? Do you nurture the talent of others? If those you supervise are allowed
   to grow, will it benefit you in the long-
   run?
3. Organize if needed. Where and in what
   condition are the tools of your job? Carefully review your filing system—do the
   words "purge" or "reorder" apply? Are
   reference materials—e.g., dictionary, applicable regulations, procedure manual—

handy? Time spent cleaning-up and ordering will pay future dividends.

4. Evaluate your social and personal interactions on the job. Estimate the time
   spent with residents, and with staff. Is
   the amount of time spent and the nature of the interaction in line with the
   total job responsibilities? Perhaps you
   even come up short here. This analysis
   requires some philosophical consideration and a fixed amount of time applicable in all areas does not exist. Certainly personal contact (staff and residents) must be a priority and must be
   reviewed in terms of total job demands.
5. If your position is that of a supervisor or
   department head, take a careful look at
   meetings you plan and communication
   methods used with staff. Are meetings
   most often productive, or do they end up
   being periods of information sharing but
   without the consensus needed or direction spelled out to move on the big issues? Is an agenda established prior to
   the meeting and direction given as to
   how each member should prepare for
   the meeting? Review work or necessary
   reading for the meeting should be required for all attending. Could other
   forms of communication better serve
   some to the purposes of the meeting?
   Prioritize the topics of the meeting so
   that the crucial issues receive the most
   time. Some managers set time limits for
   each segment of the meeting so that
   ample time is devoted to key issues. If
   follow-up is required, be sure to delin-
   eate responsibilities with time lines so
   that each member is clear as to what
   they will do and when. Frustration will
   build if everyone feels that discussion
   never reaches a point to precipitate action.
6. A "To-Do" list is a good starting point in
   visualizing the variety of tasks which
   need to be accomplished, but go one step
   further after completing the list. Go
   back and prioritize so that the most im-

portant jobs will be tackled first. It is better to do a thorough job with the immediate or most important concerns than it is to complete all items on the list with varying degrees of attention. Most activity directors do become successful in this area so that their schedule involves a series of short-, mid-, and long-term projects in order for each to attain its goals. The situation is analogous to juggling three different balls at the same time—the accomplished juggler knows the speed of all the balls and is able to take the appropriate action as each begins to drop at different times. Long- and medium-range events require specific attention weeks before their resolution. Thus, the list of duties should reflect immediate and future deadlines with appropriate work time allocated to each.

7. Understand your biorhythms or peaks of energy. Each person differs as to the time of day when he or she is most efficient. Compounding the problem are the regularly scheduled events and duties which may not be adjusted to fit one's personal schedule. It makes sense, however, to take on the most demanding tasks when you are most efficient leaving the more menial jobs for times when you are lower on energy reserves.

8. Is contingency planning part of your regular scheme? It should be. Continually ask the "what if" questions. The typical activity specialist has faced situations where carefully planned programs went astray. It's far better to invest a bit more time here, and instead of collapsing an entire event, have a back-up plan.

9. Over a period of weeks evaluate and modify, if necessary, your approaches to time management. Some of the skills mentioned will become second nature if awareness is maintained. A number of

the suggestions require an initial investment of time, but they will result in a greater efficiency over the long haul. Don't be afraid to challenge entrenched habits. Ask others to provide feedback—they may appreciate the way your improved performance assists them.

Assisting the Dying Resident

While the goals of activity programming—fun, happiness, socialization with others—are in direct contrast to the notion of death and dying, the reality of the long-term care environment is that death is a part of the picture. Some who provide the fun and social opportunities find the thought of terminal illness inconsonant with leisure activities. Yet, we strongly feel that a case can be presented that activity professionals, because of their role with residents, are in a position to assist elderly persons who are dying.

Kastenbaum (1987) emphasizes the point that while only about 5 percent of the older population is living in nursing homes or other extended-care facilities at any given time, the odds of dying in such an environment are about one in five. As has been frequently noted throughout this book, the institutional environment often creates roadblocks to individuality and positive self-esteem and these barriers have particular effects upon those who are dying. It is not difficult, for example, for staff to devalue residents with terminal conditions because their time is limited. Once designated as "dying," one can become merged even further into the mass of residents with an accompanying loss of individuality.

A number of attitudes about the dying elderly are addressed by Kastenbaum (1987). Some falsely believe that most elderly adults are "ready" and "willing" to die; others see death as being "natural" for older persons. A certain percentage of terminal clients may be ready to die, yet others will try to extract the fullness of each new day. Another improper attitude is that there is no need to memorialize those who have died; doing so is simply morbid, and it is better to move on. Another possible attitude is that little can be done for older residents who are dying—especially by staff who are not trained to do so. All of these notions can prohibit long-term care personnel from effectively serving the dying at a time when their assistance is most needed.

The manner in which most nursing homes deal with death has improved greatly over the years. An institutional approach of denying death was not uncommon in past years. It was felt that residents and staff would be upset by thinking about a friend who had died. The correct approach was to become absorbed in the daily routine and concentrate only on the living. Currently there is recognition that grief and bereavement are experienced by staff and residents, and allowing for those processes to occur is a healthy, positive approach. Attention has also focused on the needs of individual residents with terminal illnesses. Aid in funeral planning and organizing memorial services are common activities within long-term care facilities (Weiner, 1986). Many terminally ill find it comforting to have funeral arrangements made and to know that friends will recognize them in a memorial service. Staff, resident friends, and family are able to share in this.

STAFF CONCERNS

As part of a training workshop conducted by Tedrick, (1989) 34 activity specialists were queried as to needs and actions in working with aging terminal residents or patients. With such a small, self-selected sample no claims for broad generalization are made, yet the opinions of the group offer a background in considering the role of activity specialists in dealing with dying residents. Clearly, death was a topic of concern for the group ranking fourth out of 16 potential topics for future training sessions. Two-thirds of the participants indicated they had never experienced training to assist them in working

with the dying, and of those who had been exposed to the topic, the format had been workshop or conference sessions or simply talking with other staff members. When asked if any activities were helpful in working with dying residents, only one-quarter responded. Methods noted were being available to talk and listen, music, social activities, life review groups, and involving the older person with a terminal disease in volunteer activities.

The concept of helping family members to cope with the impending death was also touched upon in the survey. Slightly more than half (53 percent) of the activity specialists felt it was someone else's responsibility to help families in this way. The above findings are probably not surprising given the various duties and time constraints imposed upon activity personnel; dying becomes one more issue for them to deal with. For those who indicated they did lend support, the specific ways were being assistive and involved with the grief process, including family members in activities with the older loved one, exploring the process or stages of dying with family through conversation, and also keeping family members apprised of the condition of the dying loved ones on a regular basis.

It should be remembered that staff are just as vulnerable to the negative attitudes surrounding death as anyone. As noted by Leviton and Campenelli (1982), caregiving professionals may avoid the dying because they are reminded of their own mortality, and that may not be easy for them. Personnel may also shun those with a terminal status because the final outcome is known, and making a personal investment will not change that result. Others may object to the loss of control; in a fashion similar to some in the medical community the older dying adult is spurned because whatever is offered is temporary and will not change the course of the disease. Another avoidance technique centers on a type of investment-loss ratio; some feel that the more they become actively involved in helping the dying adult, the greater the loss experienced when death comes. It simply becomes easier to divest oneself earlier. Whatever the reasons may be, it is imperative for staff to recognize these potential rationalizations and view the situation from the perspective of the older adult who is greatly in need of support at this time.

Why is it that activity professionals may be well-suited (even considering their lack of specific training in most instances) to aid the dying? First, the role of the activity professional is not markedly altered with diagnosis of a terminal condition. Immediate needs of the resident may change, and daily conditions may necessitate activity adaptations, but the primary role of the activity department—to provide meaningful experiences which assist each participant—remains the same. Indeed, activity staff may have a real advantage here when compared with other allied professionals; a program of activity or leisure experiences exists which has been used throughout the resident's stay and can be continued with modifications until the time of death. Activities, then, become a natural device around which the relationship between the activity director and terminal resident may continue. Certain activities such as music, writing, life review discussions or simply talking can aid in overcoming some of the discomfort which may be felt by all involved when it becomes known that a terminal illness exists.

Second, the knowledge that activity specialists are providing a needed service can sustain all parties. Activities help to maintain normal routines; they provide something to look forward to. Short-term goals can be approached; activities can be modified as needed. A particularly enjoyable pursuit can provide comfort during difficult periods, and activity specialists having seen the effects of continued participation will be able to refer to past involvement as future situations arise.

Two advantages in working with the dying are presented to activity staff. The process usually helps staff to become more comfortable regarding their own thoughts about death and dying. With experience, fears may be overcome, and it may be seen that dying becomes another stage of the life cycle. Also, activity professionals are offered another opportunity to gain pro-

fessional respect. Peers at work can witness the effective use of activities in helping the terminally ill and their families cope with dying. Again, activity staff may be in a better position here than other allied professionals because of the nature of their relationship with the resident facing death.

Among the general principles staff should utilize is the awareness that personal defense mechanisms can be triggered when thoughts of the dying are present. "I'm too busy," or "I'll stop by later" may be ways of avoidance. The avoidance may stem from the staff person's general reluctance to deal honestly with the idea of death. Also, understanding one's own mortality—death is a reality for all—is an essential step in becoming an effective professional. In-service training for staff allowing personal reflection is a wise starting point. Being aware of the stages of dying (Kubler-Ross, 1969) is essential, yet Kastenbaum (1987) noted that the application of the model to practice has probably gone beyond what Kubler-Ross's (1969) intentions were. True, reactions labeled as denial, anger, bargaining, depression, and acceptance may be seen, but the course of one's illness, one's ethnic or religious background, and the environment lived in may all affect the progression of dying and coping (Kastenbaum, 1987). Staff may rush, for example, to move toward acceptance on the part of those dying. The model (Kubler-Ross, 1969) is best used as a general framework noting individual variation; certainly reactions at the various stages should be noted as staff consider the needs of the dying and the types of activities which might be appropriate.

Specific suggestions regarding activity techniques include the continuation or use of life review projects. Many long-term care settings use these as a regular part of the total leisure program. Oral or written autobiographies, collections, photos, and other hobby pursuits can be useful in gaining insight to lifetime events. Recording pleasant memories and remembering personal contributions can be very comforting. Staff must continue to maximize opportunities for personal choice; personal control may be waning as a disease progresses, but the astute activity director will find ways to allow decision making to occur. Be alert to emotions and the daily personal condition of the patient as affected by medication and other factors; plan to adapt and modify as needed. Have two or three ideas ready as a backup. Continue the regular, favored activities as long as possible. These will provide routine and orientation and offer a future, however short. Consider the resident with a terminal illness as some type of a volunteer. Can a project be developed (a craft or piece of artwork) which will provide permanence and/or remembrance of its creator after death? Any type of volunteer activity which allows the participant to feel a sense of contributing will be meaningful. One of the most effective "programs" may simply be listening and being available to talk. The activity specialist may not be a trained counselor or therapist, but good listening skills combined with empathy can be a comfort to those needing a willing ear. Activity staff, as a regular part of departmental meetings, should review the dying process of residents and how activities were used. Through such review staff may see their contribution in this area and develop approaches for future use.

Summary

A variety of concerns or issues affecting activity specialists were presented in this chapter. Professionalism is a central issue to those working in the activity area in long-term care settings. The question of what constitutes a profession was addressed, and characteristics of professionalism were noted and discussed relative to those serving as activity personnel. The issue of who benefits by professionalism—those served or those within the profession—was examined. One movement seen currently is the certification of activity specialists. The requirements of educational background, experience, and continuing education of the National Certification Council for Activity Professionals were noted. The term "striving toward professionalism" was used to describe the process underway to upgrade the image and level of service provided by those who assist frail, older adults through planned and appropriate activities.

Consultants, computers, and time management are tools at the disposal of the activity director to accomplish more efficiently and creatively the variety of tasks faced daily. Establishing a working relationship with consultants begins with a mutual understanding of the nature of their service and the needs of the residence. A clear understanding must exist on the part of all parties as to the role of the consultant. The "dos" and "don'ts" of utilizing consultant services were noted.

For some the computer brings a real fear, but given the variety of tasks which the activity director must perform, it is tool well-suited to efficiency. Not only was the computer examined as a job tool, but its use in a programming context with older residents was also noted.

Time management begins with an assessment of how hours and minutes are used on the job. With activity directors having to assume more management and supervisory responsibilities, along with increased documentation demands, the effective use of work time becomes crucial. Styles of time management were discussed, and time wasters were described in two categories, internal and external. Specific techniques were given ranging from analyzing job tasks to organization and delegation.

Activity staff are called upon to work with dying residents. It is a sensitive area where personal reactions and views must intermingle with the needs of those to be served. The role of activity personnel in this area was examined, and a point was made about the advantaged position, when compared with other staff, held by activities specialists. Specific activity techniques were presented as ways to assist terminal residents. Simply being available to listen to and to comfort them is invaluable.

PRACTICAL EXERCISES

1. What does professionalism mean to you? What are the characteristics of a "professional" activity director?

2. What is your assessment of how other allied professionals view activity specialists/directors? In your situation how would nursing, other medical staff, doctors, physical therapists, occupational therapists, etc., view the activity department or personnel within?

3. If you were to develop a code of ethical behavior for activity professionals, what elements would be in that code? When you are finished check Appendix A (page 183) for the code of ethics applicable to activity directors.

4. It was noted that the job of activity director has changed over the past few years. In your opinion (or if you are a student, interview an activity director), how has the job of activity director changed? What must you do now that wasn't requested in years past? Has the job changed for the better? What job tasks must you spend more time on as compared with the past?

5. If you are unfamiliar with the requirements for certification through the NAAP, turn to the Appendix A (pages 171-182) and review the appropriate criteria. Do you feel these requirements are appropriate? What areas would you rank as priority topics for continuing education workshops?

6. If you are working in an activity department and have used a consultant's service, how would you evaluate your relationship with the consultant and the assistance provided by that consultant? Make a list of the areas or topics pertinent to your setting which could be analyzed by a consultant. Would having an "outside" view or perspective be helpful? If you were to serve as a consultant to other departments how would you define your job and the value of your service to agencies seeking your assistance?

7. Obtain copies of computer software (educational and/or entertainment) which could be used in an activity department serving older adults, and evaluate the different programs or activities. What are their strengths and weaknesses? Are different levels of involvement possible? What are the requirements in terms of speed and response, dexterity required, or short-term memory needed for activities?

8. How would you rate yourself as a time manager? What is your style of managing time? Make a list of time wasters. Which items would be external as opposed to internal (items over which you have control)? Make a list of suggestions or recommendations to improve your management of time.

9. What role do your think the activity specialist should play in helping the client with a terminal illness? It was noted in the chapter that the activity department may be better-suited than others to assist dying. How is this so? What qualities do you possess which could be helpful with those dying? List the ways that the activity department can aid family members of residents who are facing death.

References

Cullen, J. (1978). *The structure of professionalism: A quantitative examination.* New York, NY: Petrocelli Books, Inc.

Cunninghis, R. (1985). Working with an activities consultant. *Activities, Adaptations & Aging, 7*(2), 123-130.

Fisher, S. (1986a). Increasing participation with a computer in an adult daycare setting. *Activities, Adaptations & Aging, 8*(1), 31-36.

Fisher, S. (1986b). Use of computers following brain injury. *Activities, Adaptations & Aging, 8*(1), 81-93.

Foster, P. (1991). NAAP (1980) Keynote address. *Activities, Adaptations & Aging, 15*(4), 5-20.

Halberg, K. and Waters, E. (1991). Functioning as a department head and supervisor: A new role for the activity coordinator. *Activities, Adaptation & Aging, 15*(4), 61-85.

Karras, B. (1988). A first job as an activities director. *Activities, Adaptation & Aging, 11*(1), 95-105.

Kastenbaum, R. (1987). Death, Dying, and Bereavement in Old Age. In H. Cox (Ed.) *Aging* (5th ed.), (pp. 163-170). Guilford, CT: Duskin Publishing, Inc.

Kubler-Ross, E. (1969). *On death and dying.* New York, NY: Macmillan Publishing Company, Inc.

Leviton, D. and Campenelli, L. (1982). HPERD for two forgotten populations—"The Frail Aged" and "Dying Aged": Challenge and Response. *The Easterner, 7*(1), 1, 3, 5, 6.

Lord, J., Hutchison, P., and Van Derbeck, F. (1985). Narrowing the options: The power of professionalism in daily life and leisure. In T. Goodale and P. Witt (Eds.), *Recreation and leisure: Issues in an era of change,* (pp. 302-319). State College, PA: Venture Publishing, Inc.

Mackenzie, A. (1972). *The time trap: How to get more done in less time.* New York, NY: McGraw-Hill Book Co.

Mackenzie, A. (1989). *Time for success: A good getter's strategy.* New York, NY: McGraw-Hill Publishing Co.

Maypole, D. (1985). Activity Therapist continuing education needs assessment. *Activities, Adaptation & Aging, 7*(2), 15-24.

Parker, S. (1991). A new perspective on the value of activity directors. *Activities, Adaptation & Aging, 16*(2), 81-85.

Ryan, E. B. and Heaven, R. K. (1986). Promoting vitality among older adults with computers. *Activities, Adaptation & Aging, 8*(1), 15-30.

Sifford, P. (1993, May). Personal Communication with Ted Tedrick.

Sortais, C. (1992). Computers and the activity department. *Activities, Adaptation & Aging, 16*(3), 73-80.

Tedrick, T. (1989). Continuing education and activity directors. Poster session at the American Therapeutic Recreation Association, Seattle, WA.

Temple, L. L. and Gavillet, M. (1990). The development of computer confidence in seniors: An assessment of changes in computer anxiety and computer literacy. *Activities, Adaptations & Aging, 14*(3), 63-76.

Weiner, A. (1986). Living with dying: A model for helping nursing home residents and staff deal with death. *Activities, Adaptation & Aging, 8*(3/4), 133-142.

Witt, P. (1985). Gaining professional status: Who benefits? In T. Goodale and P. Witt (Eds.), *Recreation and leisure: Issues in an era of change,* (pp. 289-301). State College, PA: Venture Publishing, Inc.

Activity Professional Certification Standards (Abridged)

January 1, 1995

Dear Activity Professional:

Welcome to the process of becoming a certified activity professional. The National Certification Council for Activity Professionals (NCCAP) has granted certification to well over 8,000 activity professionals internationally. NCCAP exists to:

1) *establish national standards* for professional competency in the activity profession;
2) *grant certification* to individuals who meet the standards and apply for certification;
3) *provide*, for those who adhere to the standards, *a means of renewing or upgrading* their activity professional certification.

These standards require academic education, experience, and continuing education keeping professionals current in the activity field.

The information on the following pages will assist you to accurately complete the enclosed NCCAP certification application form.

Please feel free to contact the NCCAP office with any questions.

Sincerely,
The NCCAP Board and Administrators

Step-by-Step Instructions
for Completing Your Application for Certification

1. Check that the application you are about to complete is for the current year. If not write or call to get current certification materials: NCCAP OFFICE, 520 Stewart, Park Ridge, IL 60068. Office phone 708-698-4263, Monday-Friday 9 a.m.-12 and 1-4 p.m. Central Time.
2. Read the instructions thoroughly *before* completing the application.
3. Make a copy of the form to use as a work sheet.
4. Study *all* levels for certification that are offered to determine the highest level for which you are qualified.
5. Refer to page 6 "**Number and Area of Course Work**" to determine if your course work meets standards for the level of certification for which you are applying.
6. Make copies of documentation regarding workshops, conferences, in-services (keep the originals of CE documentation for your files). Originals may be requested. Make sure the documentation for continuing education includes *all* criteria (see page 9 for criteria). Make copies of letters of verification of employment, **but send originals with application**. Without this verification, your certification will be delayed or denied. If your transcripts are coming directly from the school, indicate that information on the application form.
7. Print or type information on the original application form. Other than the documentation required, all other information **must be placed directly on the application form**.
8. Make a copy of the completed application form for your file.
9. Have application notarized by a notary public. This seal attests that information presented is true, complete and accurate. Any inaccurate representation may result in NCCAP's permanent refusal of future applications.
10. Sign declaration.
11. Mail **Original Application Form**, the necessary documentation requested, and your check for the required fee to the NCCAP office, 520 Stewart, Park Ridge, IL 60068.
12. Keep this instruction book in your file for future use for coursework or **Body of Knowledge information**.
13. Please, feel to contact Marilyn Lamken, NCCAP Administrator for any assistance you may need. We want you to succeed at your first application.

Certification Standards and Illustrated Tracks

Levels of Certification

NCCAP has three levels of certification:
1. Activity Assistant Certified-AAC
2. Activity Director Certified-ADC
   Activity Director Provisional Certified-ADPC
3. Activity Consultant Certified-ACC

Each of these three levels has more than one track which may be used to become certified. Requirements within the levels vary according to the track used for requesting certification. Each track has a minimum of three components:

A. Academic Education

B. Activity Experience

C. Continuing Education

D. Consulting Experience, if applicable

Activity Assistant Certified

The Activity Assistant Certified (AAC) is one who meets NCCAP standards to assist in carrying out, with supervision, an activity program.

Track 1
A) ACADEMIC EDUCATION
   30 college semester credits including 4 required coursework areas (see page 6).
   Complete page A2.

   and
B) ACTIVITY EXPERIENCE
   2,000 hours within past 5 years.
   Complete page A3.
   and
C) CONTINUING EDUCATION
   20 clock hours from Body of Knowledge, pages 10-12.
   Complete page A4.

Track 2
A) ACADEMIC EDUCATION high school diploma or GED, plus the NAAP/NCCAP 90-hour Basic Education Course, or 6 college credits.
   Complete page A2.

   and
B) ACTIVITY EXPERIENCE
   4,000 hours within past 5 years.
   Complete page A3.
   and
C) CONTINUING EDUCATION
   20 clock hours from Body of Knowledge, pages 10-12.
   Complete page A4.

Activity Director Certified

The Activity Director Certified (ADC) is one who meets NCCAP standards to direct/coordinate/supervise an activity program, staff and department primarily in a geriatric setting.

Track 1
- A) ACADEMIC EDUCATION
  Bachelors Degree (must include 8 required coursework areas, see page 6).
  Complete page A2.
  and
- B) ACTIVITY EXPERIENCE
  2,000 hours within past 5 years.
  Complete page A3.
  and
- C) CONTINUING EDUCATION
  20 clock hours from Body of Knowledge, pages 10-12.
  Complete page A4.

Track 2
- A) ACADEMIC EDUCATION
  60 College semester credits (must include 6 required coursework areas-see page 6)
  Complete page A2.
  and
- B) ACTIVITY EXPERIENCE
  6,000 hours within past 5 years.
  Complete page A3.
  and
- C) CONTINUING EDUCATION
  30 clock hours (Body of Knowledge, pages 10-12.)
  Complete page A4.

Track 3
- A) ACADEMIC EDUCATION
  30 college semester credits (must include 4 required coursework areas, see page 6) or NAAP/NCCAP Basic Education Course plus NAAP/NCCAP Advanced Management Course plus 12 semester or 18 quarter credits.
  Complete page A2.
  and
- B) ACTIVITY EXPERIENCE
  10,000 hours within past 5 years.
  Complete page A3.
  and
- C) CONTINUING EDUCATION
  30 clock hours (Body of Knowledge, pages 10-12)
  Complete page A4.

Activity Director Provisional Certified

The Activity Director Provisional Certified is one who is working towards requirements to meet NCCAP standards for ADC certification. It is provisional for five years, and nonrenewable after that time. To maintain provisional certification it must be renewed every two years during the five years with 30 CE hours. by the end of the five-year period all five components must have been met to be ADC. Valid January 1, 1995 through December 31, 1999.

The ADPC must meet three of the following five standards
- A) ACADEMIC EDUCATION
  1. NAAP/NCCAP Basic Education Course
  2. NAAP/NCCAP Advanced Management
  3. 12 semester college credits (including 2 coursework areas)
     and
- B) ACTIVITY EXPERIENCE
  4. 10,000 hours within past 5 years.
     and
- C) CONTINUING EDUCATION
  5. 30 clock hours (Body of Knowledge, pages 10-12.)

3

Activity Consultant Certified

The Activity Consultant Certified (ACC) is one who meets NCCAP requirements to be a consultant, trainer, or instructor for an activity program, staff, department, or course work.

Track 1
A) ACADEMIC EDUCATION
Masters Degree (must include 8 required coursework areas, page 6).
Complete page A2.
and
B) ACTIVITY EXPERIENCE
2,000 hours activities experience
Complete page A3.
and
C) CONTINUING EDUCATION
40 clock hours (Body of Knowledge, pages 10-12)
Complete page A4.
and
D) CONSULTING EXPERIENCE
200 hours of activity consulting experience within past three years
Complete page A5.

Track 2
A) ACADEMIC EDUCATION
Bachelor's Degree (must include 8 required coursework areas, page 6).
Complete page A2.
and
B) ACTIVITY EXPERIENCE
4,000 hours activities experience
Complete page A3.
and
C) CONTINUING EDUCATION
40 clock hours (Body of Knowledge, pages 10-12)
Complete page A4.
and
D) CONSULTING EXPERIENCE
200 hours of activity consulting experience within past three years
Complete page A5.

The Certification Review Process

When an application is received at the NCCAP office, the staff immediately:
- determines if the application and documentation is complete;
- requests further material if documentation is missing or incomplete (the application will be kept on file six months awaiting completion), or
- sends a postcard indicating all appears in order; sends application file to the Certification Review Committee (CRC). The (CRC) is a team of volunteers who: carefully look at every aspect of the application, grant or deny certification based upon NCCAP standards, then return the application file to the NCCAP office with their decision (within three to six weeks).

The NCCAP office sends out the certification.

If certification is denied, a letter is sent stating the reason for denial. There are then three recourses for the applicant:
1. Get the additional:
   a. academic education, or
   b. more activity and/or consulting experience, or
   c. more continuing education. Then reapply; or
2. Prepare an appeal; or
3. Accept the denial.

4

Renewal Process

As activity professionals we need to keep up with new trends in our profession. Therefore, certification is renewed every two years.

- Three months before the expiration date, a renewal letter and form are sent to members due for renewal.
- A second notice is sent one month before the expiration date.
- Members are expected to submit the form listing the required number of Continuing Education (CE) hours and attach documentation showing all the information required (refer to page 8, number 6, "Continuing Education Standards for all levels"). Documentation of CE must be from within the last two years with a one-month leniency, to qualify for renewal. A renewal fee of $30.00 is required.

Standards for renewal CE are the same as for original application

Activity Assistant Certified (AAC)—20 clock hours
Activity Director Certified (ADC)—30 clock hours
Activity Director Provisional Certified (ADPC)—30 clock hours
Activity Consultant Certified (ACC)—40 clock hours

Members have a two-month grace period after expiration to send in renewal. Files are destroyed one year after expiration date if certification is not renewed. After the grace period, a member may be reinstated up to a year from expiration by submitting CE documentation and $45.00. After a year a new application must be made based upon current standards. Please keep the NCCAP office informed of any change of your address or name.

The Appeal Process

To appeal the decision of the Certification Review Committee, the applicant may send a typed letter within 60 days of the denial to NCCAP stating the reason for appeal. The application file is then held until the Appeals Committee meets. They meet in the spring and fall. The appeal Committee reviews the applicant's file and the appeal letter to make a decision. The decision of the Appeals Committee is final.

Level Changes

To move to a higher certification level, the current standards for that level must be met. Submit a new application and an additional $10.00 . The original expiration date will remain the same. If renewal standards cannot be met, a person may request a level change (at a lower level). However to upgrade to the former level at a later time, current standards for that level must be met. To move from ADPC to ADC submit a new application and the full ADC fee.

General Standards for Certification on all Levels

1) **High School Diploma or GED**. This is a requirement for certification application as an AAC on Track 2

2) **Academic Degrees**—Many degrees form a good background for qualifying a person to be an activity professional. **There is no time limit on how long ago this kind of education may have taken place**. Academic education must be taken at an accredited college or university. Degrees from outside the USA will be evaluated by the Certification Review Committee.

5

3) **Required Content Coursework Area**—Content courses are generally interpreted as having theoretical and/or philosophical focus of study. Regardless of an applicant's years of education or area of degree, the following content courses are required to be taken as part of the qualification for certification. If these courses were not included in degree work, they must be taken additionally.

   If an applicant is using **one year of academic education** to qualify for certification, at least **four** of the following coursework areas must be included. If an applicant is using **two years of academic education** to qualify for certification, at least **six** of the following coursework areas must be included. If an applicant is using a **bachelors degree or more** to qualify for certification, **eight** areas of coursework from bachelors, masters and/or doctorate may be included.

4) **Number and Areas of Applicable Coursework**

   1. Gerontology or Aging
   2. Overview of the Activity Profession
   3. Communication Arts, Graphics
   4. English, Journalism Writing
   5. Leadership Skills, Group Dynamics
   6. Psychology, Human Development
   7. Sociology, Sociology of Aging, Death and Dying
   8. Standards of Practice: Practitioner Behavior
   9. Activity Care Planning for Quality of Life
   10. Methods of Service Delivery in the Activity Profession
   11. Activity Department Responsibilities
   12. The System of Activity Program Development
   13. Administrative Practices in the Activity Profession
   14. Community Relations
   15. Speech, Drama or Theater
   16. Art Appreciation, History or Theory
   17. Music Appreciation, History or Theory
   18. Physical Education, Fitness, Movement or Dance Appreciation or Theory
   19. Health Sciences (e.g., Public Health, Nursing, Pharmacology, Medical Technician, Wholistic Health, Nutrition)
   20. Management or Administration (Business, Computer, Math)
   21. Education Theory
   22. Therapy (Art, Dance, Music, Drama, Recreation, Occupational, Physical)
   23. Biological Sciences (Biology of Aging, Perceptual Motor Development, Adapted Physical Education, Recreation for the Disabled, Anatomy, Physiology, etc.)
   24. Human Services (Drugs and Alcohol Rehabilitation, Counseling, Biofeedback, Compulsive Disorders, Stress Management, Journal Writing, Family Services)
   25. NAAP/NCCAP Basic Education Course and practicum—counts for **two** coursework areas equals nine semester hours or 13.5 quarter hours.
   26. NAAP/NCCAP advanced Management Course and practicum-counts for **two** coursework areas, equals **nine** semester or 13.5 quarter hours.

5) **College Coursework Hours or Units**
   Some schools use the term "hours," others use the term "units"—the important word is the one preceding it. One year of coursework equals 30 **semester** hours/units or 45 **quarter** hours/units; two years of coursework equals 60 **semester** units or 90 **quarter** units, etc. (one **semester** unit equals 1.5 **quarter** units).

6

6) Documentation of Academic Education
Documentation is required to verify all academic degrees and/or courses:
  a. For AAC applicants, Track 2, submit proof of high school diploma or GED—name, city and state of school or GED program must be included.
  b. For those using NAAP/NCCAP Basic Education or Advanced Management Courses, submit certificate of satisfactory completion of course and practicum.
  c. An official transcript must be submitted to verify and receive credit for education beyond high school.
  d. Transcript must indicate dates of education and date of graduation, if any.
  e. Transcript must accompany the application unless the college is sending transcripts directly to NCCAP. In the latter case, include a copy of your dated letter to the college requesting they send your transcripts to NCCAP.

B. General Activity Experience Standards for All Levels

1) "Activity Program" or "Activity Professional" refers to a program or person providing the activity program in skilled nursing, intermediate care, board and care, community care, retirement, senior center or day care facility, which provides services or care primarily for the elderly.

2) Activity Experience Guidelines
  a. Activity experience shall be specifically in delivering direct activities program services (i.e., hands-on programming, documentation).
  b. Volunteer experience in an activity department may be used. This cannot exceed 20 percent of the experience time needed.
  c. Activity experience must be from within past five years for ADC, AAC and ADPC tracks. There is no time limit on how long ago activity experience for ACC occurred.
  d. For programs with mixed populations (MI, DD, etc.) more than 50 percent of the population served must be elderly (ages 55 and over).

3) Documentation of Experience
  a. Experience must be verified by original letters signed by the employer on facility or program letterhead. The letter must state employee title, dates of activity employment, and total hours of activity employment.
  b. For programs with mixed populations, a letter from the administrator must verify that the population served is more than 50 percent elderly (over 55).
  c. When activity professionals are employed in additional roles outside of activities (i.e., Social Services), the administrator's letter must indicate total number of hours spent directly in the delivery of activity services.

4. Activity Consultant Experience Guidelines
  a. An activity consultant has a high degree of expertise and is called upon to advise, counsel and express opinion for activity and other staff persons on providing activities.
  b. Consulting in activities may include: one-to-one, advising a group, teaching a class, conducting a workshop or inservice of at least one contact hour, publishing professional articles, direct on-site practicum supervision (maximum of 40 hours credit per applicant), and/or managing five or more activity staff persons.
  c. Published state or national professional material counts one hour of consulting per 1,000 words. A copy of the material must be submitted with the application.
  d. At least 20 percent of consulting experience must occur outside of the current place of employment (such as conducting workshops, teaching a class, publishing professional articles, consulting at another facility).

7

e. The actual presentation time may count each time it is presented, for consulting experience.

f. At least 20 percent of the consulting experience must be direct activity consultation in a setting serving an elderly population.

5) Documentation

a. Consulting experience to a facility or program must be documented on the employer's facility or program letterhead and signed by the administrator or administrative supervisor.

b. Teaching used for consulting experience must be verified by a brochure with the information NCCAP requires for CE (see page 7).

d. For programs with mixed populations (MI, DD, etc.) a letter from the administrator must verify that the population served is more than 50 percent elderly (over 55).

C. General Continuing Education (CE) Standards for All Levels

1) Continuing Education Time Guidelines

When applying for certification, **CE must be completed within the previous five years before application**. This includes college coursework used to fulfill the CE requirement. For certification renewal, CE must be completed within **two years** previous to application for **renewal**, with a one-month leniency.

2) Qualifying Continuing Education

a. Qualifying CE is: Adult education classes, workshops, seminars, college courses, educational sessions at professional meetings of activity professionals and allied associations, articles published in state or national professional publications, and speeches and workshops presented on professional issues.

b. Credit will be given only once for articles and speeches or workshops presented.

c. Articles count one CE hour per 1,000 words. Copy of material (e.g., state newsletter, book, journal) must be included.

d. For speeches and workshop presented by applicant, double the actual time of presentation may be counted for CE credit.

e. CE (contact) hours must be spent in a group or educational setting with a leader. The participants must have the opportunity to discuss content with the leader during the class.

f. A CE hour must be at least 60 minutes in length to be consistent with IACET standards.

g. Entertainment, reading, travel, and business and committee meetings may not be used to meet CE standards.

h. Inservices may be used if the content is applicable. No more than 20 percent of CE may be comprised of inservice.

i. No more than 20 percent of CE may come from personal enrichment education or growth, and no more than 20 percent may come from ancillary (CNA, medications, paramedic, transport) courses.

j. The Body of Knowledge should be used to determine whether content of any CE is applicable. If there is any question of CE submitted being applicable, submit a written explanation of how it may apply to activities programming.

k. A Basic course can be used for CE only once. However, the NAAP/NCCAP Basic Education Course of 90 hours with 90-hour practicum may be use if past basic course was of shorter time length.

l. Independent Study Courses may be used to meet certification or renewal requirements. They must be topics from the Body of Knowledge or Required Content Coursework Areas. An official transcript, course outline/syllabus, course title and a general overview of the course must accompany the application.

m. Correspondence Study Course may be used to meet certification or renewal requirements, if topics are from the Body of Knowledge or Required Content Coursework Areas.

n. Self-taught courses will not be considered for certification or renewal.

o. Facility tours can be used for CE when held in conjunction with state and national activity professional conventions and having NCCAP preapproval.

3) Course Approval

NCCAP approves individual CE courses and grants two-year provider approval. Instructors or providers may obtain application forms from the NCCAP office. Approval is not mandatory but is security for the participant.

4) Using Accredited College Coursework for CE

When translating accredited college coursework from semester and quarter hours/units into contact/clock hours for continuing education, use the following equivalencies: one semester hour equals 15 clock hours; one quarter hour equals ten clock hours (the terms "contact" and "clock" are used interchangeably when referring to CE hours.) When using college courses for CE, only the transcript is necessary for documentation. The college coursework for CE must be within the past five years. Correspondence courses may be used. If they are for college credit, use the above equivalency. If the correspondence course offers "CEUs," in this case one CEU will be considered 10 hours of CE. Only college courses not included in Academic Education standards can be used to fulfill CE standards.

5) Topics for Continuing Education

Found in Body of Knowledge (see pages 10-12).

6) Documentation of Continuing Education must indicate:

a. name of attendee

b. topic of CE that is found within Body of Knowledge or Required Coursework.

c. dates of the CE

d. place of CE (city and state)

e. clock hours spent in CE

f. instructor's name and qualifying credentials

g. signature of sponsor or instructor

h. for inservice CE, a copy of the sign-in sheet is required with all of the above information

7) Original CE documentation may be requested

Certification Fees

Activity Assistant Certified (AAC) .... $35.00   Discount for NAAP members ......– $5.00
Activity Director Certified (ADC) .... $45.00   Renewal $30.00
Activity Director Provisional Certified (ADPC) .... $40.00   Replacement of certificate .... $ 5.00
Activity Consultant Certified (ACC) .... $55.00   Reinstatement $45.00

- A nonrefundable service charge of $15.00 is included in all fees.
- A certified check, money order or personal check must be submitted with application, payable to **NCCAP**. Do not send cash, and do not staple check to application.
- NCCAP encourages membership in the National Association of Activity Professionals (NAAP). To be come a member, contact NAAP at 1225 Eye St. NW, Suite 300, Washington, DC 20005 or call 202-289-0722.

Body of Knowledge

Topics for Continuing Education

CURRICULUM CONTENT FOR ACTIVITY PROFESSIONALS

WORKING WITH PATIENTS/RESIDENTS

1) **Human Development and Late Adult Years**
   - Life Span Potential
   - Theories of Aging

2) **Human Development and Aging**
   - Human Behavior and Aging
   - Potential and Creativity
   - Wellness and Self-Esteem

3) **Spirituality of Aging**
   - Reminiscing
   - Tasks of Life Review
   - Ego Integrity
   - Worship—Religion
   - Death—Dying
   - Ethics

4) **Biology of Aging**
   - Changes—Physical and Sensory
   - Sexuality
   - Medications
   - Nutrition
   - Healthy Aging
   - Illness and Dysfunction

5) **Sociology of Aging**
   - Involvement—Isolation
   - Dependence/Independence
   - Living Alone—Social Networks
   - Cultural Attitudes
   - Social Histories
   - Long-Term Care Social Needs
   - Living Arrangements—Retirement Housing, Older Communities, Long-Term Care
   - language

6) **Psychology of Aging**
   - Leisure and Aging
   - Psychological Choices—Depression, Anxiety, Fears
   - Drugs and Alcohol
   - Security
   - Successful Adaptations
   - Hospice
   - Counseling Techniques
   - Stereotypes—Myths
   - Confusion/Disorientation
   - Institutionalization

7) **Leisure and Aging**
   - Recreation—Definition, Types, Philosophy
   - Life Styles
   - Retirement Living
   - Attitudes—Motivation
   - Analysis of Leisure Time
   - Client Interests
   - Client Rights—Different Categories
   - Volunteerism

8) **Basic Health**
   - First Aid (Certificate)
   - Health Precautions
   - Personal Health Issues

9) **Group Instruction/Leadership**
   - Adult Learning Modes
   - Instruction Methods—Lecture, Handouts, Demonstrations, Samples, Slides, Participation Games, Discussion, Survey
   - Teaching Materials—Tools, Resources
   - Group Dynamics/Leadership
   - In-Service

10) **Therapy for the Disabled Aging**
    - Overview of P.T., O.T., Speech, Recreation, Art, Dance, Music, Drama, Horticulture and Poetry Therapy, Validation, Reality Orientation, Remotivation, etc.
    - Restorative Programs—Feeding Training, ADL Skills, etc.
    - Patient Physical Transfer Techniques
    - Therapeutic Approach—Meaningful, Purposeful, How it Helps

11) **With Residents & Staff**
    - Types of Communication
    - Listening Skills
    - Responding Skills
    - Communication with Frail
    - Communication with Confused
    - Intercultural Concerns

12) **Public Speaking**
    - Professional Image
    - Leading Meetings
    - Business Etiquette

Abridged version Reprinted by permission from NCCAP and Marilyn Jaeger.

Body of Knowledge (continued)

13) **Public Relations**
  - The Written Message
  - Media Use—Press Releases, P.S.A., T.V., Radio
  - In-House Publicity—Newsletter, Bulletin Boards, Posters, Graphic Techniques
  - Letters of Appreciation
  - Volunteers Programs
  - Fund Raising
  - Computer Skills

14) **Interpersonal Relationships**
  - Staff Team Approach—Working Together
  - Coordination of Services—Staff, Families, Volunteers, etc.
  - Peer Relationships—Staff, Residents
  - Family Relationships—Various Age Needs and Attitudes
  - Hierarchy of Management Relationships/ Personality Evaluation
  - Staff/Client Relationships
  - Consultant Relationships
  - Organizational Relationships
  - Organization Structures in Different Levels of Care

15) **Motivation**
  - Of Clients, Families, Staff, Volunteers
  - Professional Improvement

16) **Community Services/Support/Relations**
  - Recreation Resources
  - Service Clubs
  - Religious Resources
  - Mainstreaming
  - Adult Health Services—Alzheimer's, Ostomy Clubs
  - Business—Chamber of Commerce
  - Family Open Houses

17) **Regulations**
  - State and Federal Activities, Regulations
  - Survey Process
  - Legislative Updating

PROGRAMMING

18) **Individualized Care Planning**
  - Assessment
  - Interdisciplinary Team
  - Activity Goals, Approach, Progress Notes
  - Professional Standards
  - Legal—Ethical Issues
  - Medical Terms

  - Charting—Confidentiality
  - Patient—Resident Involvement

19) **Program Management**
  - Philosophy of Operation
  - Program Scope—Physical, Mental, Social, Emotional, Community, Spiritual
  - Program Planning—Resident Centered
  - Organization—Calendar
  - Program Implementation—Conducting Activities
  - Evaluation Techniques
  - Operating Audio-Visual Equipment
  - Equipment and Supplies—Control, Safety Precautions, Resource Materials, Ordering

20) **Program Types—Theory and Practice**
  - Supportive
  - Maintenance
  - Empowerment
  - Exercise—General, Volleyball, e.g., Wheelchair
  - Social—e.g., Parties
  - Outdoor—e.g., Barbecues, Games, Walks
  - Away from the facility—e.g., Visits to Community Places of interest
  - Religious—e.g., Bible Study, Services
  - Creative—e.g., Crafts, Drama, Writing
  - Educational—e.g., Current Events, Alzheimer's Group
  - Residents with special needs—e.g., AIDS, DDs, MRs, MS et al.
  - Resident Planned—e.g., Resident Council or any Activity
  - In-Room—e.g., Adapt Out-of-Room Activities
  - Sensory—e.g., Braille Materials, Any Sensory Stimulation, Pet, Food Related
  - Reality Awareness—e.g., With Other Programs
  - Entertainment—e.g., Games, Entertainer Resources
  - Self-Help—e.g., Nail Polish Group, Independent Activities
  - Music—Basic and Adaptive Techniques
    1. Accompaniment Instrument—Chord Structure, Ear Training
    2. Recreational—Rhythm Instruments, Musical Games, Movement, Literature for the Aged
  - Community Oriented—e.g., Intergenerational, Community Groups in the Facility

11

Abridged version Reprinted by permission from NCCAP and Marilyn Jaeger.

Body of Knowledge (continued)

MANAGEMENT/PERSONNEL LEGAL AND ETHICAL ISSUES

21) Personnel Employment
   - Recruitment, Interviewing, Hiring, Development, Recognition, Evaluation, Termination—Staff and Volunteers
   - Job Search—Resume Writing, etc.

22) Management Leadership
   - Interdisciplinary Care Plan Team
   - Leadership Styles
   - Program Management
   - Program Evaluation
   - Supervision Philosophies and Techniques
   - Delegating—Enabling Staff Ability
   - Self-Analysis
   - Time Management
   - Activity Staff In-Service
   - Conducting Meetings—Staff, Association
   - Problem Solving
   - Resident Council
   - Record Keeping

23) Management Writing Skills
   - Documentation—Chart Auditing
   - Job Descriptions
   - Policies and Procedures Manuals
   - Incident Records/Reports
   - Letters of Request—Direct Mail

24) Financial Management
   - Reimbursement
   - Budget Writing
   - Record Keeping
   - Expense Control
   - Establishing Nonprofit Status
   - Fund raising

25) Professionalism
   - Certification
   - Professional Attitude Toward Residents
   - Professional Associations
   - Business Expectations
   - Professional Standards—Ethics

26) Consulting
   - Consultant's Role, Goals, Knowledge

27) Resources
   - Working with Volunteers
   - Working with Supervisors
   - Working with Consultants

NCCAP Code of Ethics

Please keep this Code of Ethics in your life.

All NCCAP-certified persons are expected to adhere to these standards in their professional practice and in maintaining their certification. If it is found that a member is not adhering to the NCCAP Code of Ethics—through reports, through "doctored" documents, etc.—the member's certification will be rescinded or denied. The mechanism for review in such instances will be through the Certification Review Committee, the administrator, and finally the NCCAP Board.

Code of Ethics

National Certification Council for Activity Professionals

Purpose

The purpose of the National Certification Council for Activity Professionals is to establish credentialing standards for activity professionals and credential those individuals who apply and meet those standards.

In order to develop and maintain high standards of preparation and performance in activity programming, NCCAP sets forth the following Code of Ethics:

Educational Standards:

1. To enroll in academic and continuing educational sessions in order to more thoroughly understand the residents and the role activities play in their lives.
2. To report accurately and fairly what educational sessions have been attended and credit received.
3. To refuse to participate in falsification of any educational documents.
4. To seek competence rather than fulfill minimum requirements.
5. To continue to enroll in educational sessions in order to keep abreast of quality activity programming.
6. To maintain professional skills by reading and studying professional journals and newsletters.
7. To obtain and review catalogues and brochures on the resources available in the field.

Experiential Standards

1. To learn activity programming through supervised experience in conduction activities in the various gerontological settings.
2. To spend supervised time in a long-term care facility before marketing oneself as a professional in that area.
3. To be a high quality provider of activities that enhance the lives of the residents.
4. To avoid any falsification or misrepresentation of one's employment record.
5. To respect the agency offering quality of life by supporting administration and being an effective team member.
6. To function at the highest practical level of one's ability and skills to the benefit of the residents.
7. To adhere to the appropriate state and federal regulations for the benefit of the residents.

Adopted by NCCAP Board—Date: September 22, 1990

Certification Review Committee

Helen Dickey ACC (1987-)
3209 Thunder Road
Alamongordo, NM 88310
505-434-7344

Donna Esmay ACC (1988-) Chairman
1642 11th Avenue, North
Fort Dodge, IA 50501
Work: 515-573-2121
Home: 515-955-5891

Jayna Glemby ACC (1986)
Box 633
Charlton, MA 01507
Work: 617-248-7344
Home: 617-248-6905

Sandra Greet ACC (1990-)
2326 Broadmeade Road
Louisville, KY 40205
502-459-8750

Resident Rights

As a resident of this facility, you have the right to a dignified existence and to communicate with individuals and representatives of choice. The facility will protect and promote your rights as designated below.

Exercise of Rights
- You have the right and freedom to exercise your rights as a resident of this facility and as a citizen or resident of the United States without fear of discrimination, restraint, interference, coercion or reprisal.
- If you are unable to act in your own behalf, your rights are exercised by the person appointed under state law to act in your behalf.

Notice of Rights and Services
- You will be informed of your rights and of all rules and regulations governing resident conduct and responsibilities both orally and in writing.
- You have the right to inspect and purchase photocopies of your records.
- You have the right to be fully informed of your total health status.
- You have the right to refuse treatment, to participate in experimental research and to formulate an advance directive in accordance with facility policy.
- You will be informed of Medicare and Medicaid benefits. This information will be posted.
- You will be informed of facility services and charges.
- The facility will inform you of procedures for protecting personal funds. If you deem necessary, you may file a complaint with the state survey and certification agency.
- You will be informed of your physician, his or her speciality, and ways of contacting him or her.
- The facility must consult with you and notify your physician and interested family member of any significant change in your condition or treatment, or of any decision to transfer or discharge.
- The facility will notify you and interested family member(s) of a room or roommate change.
- The facility will periodically update the address and telephone number of your legal representative or interested family member.

Protection of Funds
- You may manage your own financial affairs. You are not required to deposit personal funds with the facility.
- The facility must manage your deposited funds with your best interest in mind. Your money will not be commingled with facility funds.
- The facility will provide you with an individualized financial report quarterly and upon your request.
- Any remaining estates will be conveyed to your named successor.
- All funds held by the facility will be protected by a security bond.

Free Choice
- You may choose your own personal physician.
- You will be informed of and may participate in your care and treatment and any resulting changes.

Privacy
- You have the right of privacy over your personal and clinical records.
- Your privacy will include personal care, medical treatments, telephone use, visits, letters, and meetings of family and resident groups.

❏ **CONTINUED ON REVERSE SIDE**

Adapted from and reprinted with permission from Briggs: CFS 1-3 © 1992 Briggs Corporation, Des Moines, IA 50306 (800) 247-2343
Printed in U.S.A.

Resident Rights (continued)

- You may approve or refuse the release of your records except in the event of a transfer or legal situation.

Grievances
- You may voice grievances concerning your care without fear of discrimination or reprisal.
- You may expect prompt efforts for the resolution of grievances.

Examination of Survey Results
- You may examine survey results and the plan of correction. These, or notice of their location, will be posted in a readily accessible place.
- You may contact client advocate agencies and receive information from them.

Work
- You may perform or refuse to perform services for the facility.
- All services performed must be well documented in the care plan to include nature of the work and compensation.

Mail
- You may promptly send and receive your mail unopened and have access to writing supplies.

Access and Visitation Rights
- You have the right to receive visitors at any reasonable time in the facility.
- You have the right and the facility must provide access to visit with any relevant agency of the state or any entity providing health, social, legal or other services.

Telephone
- You have the right to use the telephone in private.

Personal Property
- You can retain and use personal possessions as space permits.

Married Couples
- A married couple may share a room.

Self-Administration of Drugs
- You may self-administer drugs unless determined unsafe by the interdisciplinary team.

ADMISSION, TRANSFER AND DISCHARGE RIGHTS

Transfer and Discharge
- You may not be transferred or discharged unless your needs cannot be met, safety is endangered, services are no longer required, or payment has not been made.
- Notice of and reason(s) for transfer or discharge must be provided to you in an understandable manner.
- Notice of transfer or discharge must be given 30 days prior, except in cases of health and safety needs.
- The transfer or discharge notice must include the name, address and telephone number of the appropriate, responsible protective agency.
- A facility must provide sufficient preparation to ensure a safe transfer or discharge.

❏ **CONTINUED ON NEXT PAGE**

Adapted from and reprinted with permission from Briggs: CFS 1-3 © 1992 Briggs Corporation, Des Moines, IA 50306 (800) 247-2343
Printed in U.S.A

Resident Rights (continued)

Notice of Bed-Hold Policy and Readmission
- You and a family member must receive written notice of state and facility bed-hold policies before and at the time of a transfer.
- The facility must follow a written policy for readmittance if the bed-hold period is exceeded.

Equal Access to Quality Care
- The facility must use identical policies regarding transfer, discharge and services for all residents.
- The facility may determine charges for a nonmedicaid resident as long as written notice was provided at the time of admission.

Admission Policy
- The facility must not require a third party guarantee of payment or accept any gifts as a condition of admission or continued stay.
- The facility cannot require you to waive your right to Medicare or Medicaid benefits.
- The facility may obtain legal financial access for payment without incurring your personal liability.
- The facility may charge a Medicaid-eligible resident for items and services requested.
- The facility may only accept contributions if they are not a condition of admittance or continued stay.

RESIDENT BEHAVIOR AND FACILITY PRACTICES

Restraints
- The facility may not use physical restraints or psychoactive drugs for discipline or convenience or when they are not required to treat medical symptoms.

Abuse
- You have the right to be free from verbal, sexual, physical or mental abuse, corporal punishment and involuntary seclusion.

Staff Treatment
- The facility must implement procedures that protect you from abuse, neglect or mistreatment, and misappropriation of your property.
- In the event of an alleged violation involving your treatment, the facility is required to report it to the appropriate officials.
- All alleged violations must be thoroughly investigated and the results reported.

Quality of Life
- The facility must care for you in a manner that enhances your quality of life.

Dignity
- The facility will treat you with dignity and respect in full recognition of your individuality.

Self-Determination
- You may choose your own activities, schedules and health care and any other aspect affecting your life within the facility.
- You may interact with visitors of your choice.

❏ CONTINUED ON REVERSE SIDE

Adapted from and reprinted with permission from Briggs: CFS 1-3 © 1992 Briggs Corporation, Des Moines, IA 50306 (800) 247-2343
Printed in U.S.A

Resident Rights (continued)

Participation in Resident and Family Groups
- You may organize or participate in groups of choice.
- Families have the right to visit with other families.
- The facility must provide a private space for group meetings.
- Staff or visitors may attend meetings at the group's invitation.
- The facility will provide a staff person to assist and follow up with the group's requests.
- The facility must listen to and act upon requests or concerns of the group.

Participation in Other Activities
- You have the right to participate in activities of choice that do not interfere with the rights of other residents.

Accommodation of Needs
- You have the right as a resident to receive services with reasonable accommodations to individual needs and preferences.
- You will be notified of room or roommate changes.
- You have the right to make choices about aspects of your life in the facility that are important to you.

Activities
- The facility will provide a program of activities designed to meet your needs and interests.

Social Services
- The facility will provide social services to attain or maintain your highest level of well-being.

Environment
- The facility must provide a safe, clean, comfortable, home-like environment, allowing you the opportunity to use your personal belongings to the extent possible.
- The facility will provide housekeeping and maintenance services.
- The facility will assure you have clean bath and bed linens and that they are in good repair.
- The facility will provide you with private closet space as space permits.
- The facility will provide you with adequate and comfortable lighting and sound levels.
- The facility will provide you with comfortable and safe temperature levels.

END

Adapted from and reprinted with permission from Briggs: CFS 1-3 © 1992 Briggs Corporation, Des Moines, IA 50306 (800) 247-2343
Printed in U.S.A.

Daily Schedule of Activities

7:30   • Breakfast

9:00   • AM Care and Grooming—Maintain self-care skill
        • Reality Orientation
        • Program Announcements

10:00   • One-to-One and Small Group Activities—Meaningful programs that provide mental and
          sensory stimulation

11:00   • Exercise—Maintain strength, range of motion, and body awareness
        • Current Events—Provides mental stimulation and encourages group discussion

12:30   • Lunch—Meal-time activities are ideal for nonparticipants and provide opportunities for
          sensory stimulation and socialization

1:30   • Group Activity—To promote socialization and group interaction

2:30   • Small Group Activity—To encourage physical, mental, social, emotional, and/or spiritual
          expression

3:30   • One-to-One Activities—To provide interaction with residents who are unwilling or unable to
          participate in group activities

4:30   • Unit Activities—A variety of activities offered in the dining areas for lower-functioning residents

5:30   • Dinner

6:30   • Group Activity—(listening to music, games, or reminiscing) depending on the residents' level of
          functioning and interests

Minimum Data Set for Nursing Home Resident Assessment and Care/Screening (MDS)
(Background Information/Intake at Admission)

I. IDENTIFICATION INFORMATION

| 1. | RESIDENT NAME | _____ |
| | | (First)   (Middle Initial)   (Last) |

| 2. | DATE OF CURRENT ADMISSION | ▢▢ ▢▢ ▢▢▢▢ |
| | | Month   Day   Year |

| 3. | MEDICARE NO. (SOC. SEC. OR COMPARABLE NO. IF NO MEDICARE NO.) | ▢▢▢▢▢▢▢▢▢▢▢▢ |

| 4. | FACILITY PROVIDER NUMBER | Federal Number ▢▢▢▢▢▢▢▢▢▢ |

| 5. | GENDER | 1. Male   2. Female |

| 6. | RACE/ ETHNICITY | 1. American Indian/ Alaska Native   4. Hispanic
2. Asian/Pacific Islander   5. White, not of Hispanic origin
3. Black, not of Hispanic origin |

| 7. | BIRTHDATE | ▢▢ ▢▢ ▢▢▢▢
Month   Day   Year |

| 8. | LIFETIME OCCUPATION | _____ |

| 9. | PRIMARY LANGUAGE | Resident's primary language is a language other than English
0. No   1. Yes _____
(Specify) |

10.	RESIDENTIAL HISTORY PAST 5 YEARS	(*Check all settings* resident lived in during 5 years prior to admission)
		Prior stay at this nursing home	a.
		Other nursing home/residential facility	b.
		MH/psychiatric setting	c.
		MR/DD setting	d.
		NONE OF ABOVE	e.

| 11. | MENTAL HEALTH HISTORY | Does resident's RECORD indicate any history of mental retardation, mental illness, or any other mental health problem?
0. No   1. Yes |

12.	CONDITIONS RELATED TO MR/ DD STATUS	(*Check all conditions* that are related to MR/DD status, that were manifested before age 22, and are likely to continue indefinitely)
		Not applicable–no MR/DD (Skip to item 13)	a.
		MR/DD with organic condition	
		Cerebral palsy	b.
		Down's syndrome	c.
		Autism	d.
		Epilepsy	e.
		Other organic condition related to MR/DD	f.
		MR/DD with no organic condition	g.
		Unknown	h.

| 13. | MARITAL STATUS | 1. Never Married   4. Separated
2. Married   5. Divorced
3. Widowed |

| 14. | ADMITTED FROM | 1. Private home or apt.   3. Acute care hospital
2. Nursing home   4. Other |

| 15. | LIVED ALONE | 0. No   1. Yes   2. In other facility |

16.	ADMISSION INFORMATION AMENDED	(*Check all that apply*)
		Accurate information unavailable earlier	a.
		Observation revealed additional information	b.
		Resident unstable at admission	c.

II. BACKGROUND INFORMATION AT RETURN/READMISSION

| 1. | DATE OF CURRENT READMISSION | ▢▢ ▢▢ ▢▢▢▢
Month   Day   Year |

| 2. | MARITAL STATUS | 1. Never Married   4. Separated
2. Married   5. Divorced
3. Widowed |

| 3. | ADMITTED FROM | 1. Private home or apt.   3. Acute care hospital
2. Nursing home   4. Other |

| 4. | LIVED ALONE | 0. No   1. Yes   2. In other facility |

5.	ADMISSION INFORMATION AMENDED	(*Check all that apply*)
		Accurate information unavailable earlier	a.
		Observation revealed additional information	b.
		Resident unstable at admission	c.

Signature of RN Assessment Coordinator: _____

Signatures of Others Who Completed Part of the Assessment:

_____

_____

_____

_____

_____

_____

(Continued on Reverse Side)

Adapted from and reprinted with permission from Briggs: Form 1807HF © Briggs Corporation, Des Moines, IA 50306 (800) 247-2343
Printed in U.S.A.

Minimum Data Set for Nursing Home Resident Assessment and Care Screening (MDS)
(continued)

III. CUSTOMARY ROUTINE (ONLY AT FIRST ADMISSION)

1. CUSTOMARY ROUTINE (YEAR PRIOR TO FIRST ADMISSION TO A NURSING HOME)	(***Check all that apply.*** *If all information UNKNOWN, check last box only*)	
	CYCLE OF DAILY EVENTS	
	Stays up late at night (e.g., after 9 p.m.)	a.
	Naps regularly during day (at least 1 hour)	b.
	Goes out 1 + days a week	c.
	Stays busy with hobbies, reading, or fixed daily routine	d.
	Spends most time alone or watching TV	e.
	Moves independently indoors (with appliances, if used)	f.
	NONE OF ABOVE	g.
	EATING PATTERNS	
	Distinct food preferences	h.
	Eats between meals all or most days	i.
	Use of alcoholic beverages(s) at least weekly	j.
	NONE OF ABOVE	k.
	ADL PATTERNS	
	In bedclothes much of day	l.
	Wakens to toilet all or most nights	m.
	Has irregular bowel movement pattern	n.
	Prefers showers for bathing	o.
	NONE OF ABOVE	p.
	INVOLVEMENT PATTERNS	
	Daily contact with relatives/close friends	q.
	Usually attends church, temple, synagogue (etc.)	r.
	Finds strength in faith	s.
	Daily animal companion/presence	t.
	Involved in group activities	u.
	NONE OF ABOVE	v.
	Unknown—Resident/family unable to provide information	w.

END

Adapted from and reprinted with permission from Briggs: Form 1807HF © Briggs Corporation, Des Moines, IA 50306 (800) 247-2343
Printed in U.S.A.

Minimum Data Set for Nursing Home Resident Assessment and Care Screening (MDS)

(Status in last seven days, unless other time frame indicated)

SECTION A. IDENTIFICATION AND BACKGROUND INFORMATION

1.	ASSESSMENT DATE	Month Day Year
2.	RESIDENT NAME	(First) (Middle Initial) (Last)
3.	SOCIAL SECURITY No.	
4.	MEDICAID No. (IF APPLICABLE)	
5.	MEDICAL RECORD No.	
6.	REASON FOR ASSESSMENT	1. Initial admission assessment 2. Hosp/Medicare reassessment 3. Readmission assessment 4. Annual assessment 5. Significant change in status 6. Other (e.g., UR)
7.	CURRENT PAYMENT SOURCE(S) FOR N.H. STAY	*(Billing office to indicate; check all that apply)* Medicaid a. VA d. Medicare b. Self pay/ private insurance e. CHAMPUS c. Other f.
8.	RESPONSIBILITY/ LEGAL GUARDIAN	*(Check all that apply)* Legal guardian a. Other legal oversight b. Durable power of attorney/health care proxy c. Family member responsible d. Resident responsible e. NONE OF ABOVE f.
9.	ADVANCED DIRECTIVES	*(For those items with supporting documentation in the medical record, check all that apply)* Living will a. Do not resuscitate b. Do not hospitalize c. Organ donation d. Autopsy request e. Feeding restrictions f. Medication restrictions g. Other treatment restrictions h. NONE OF ABOVE i.
10.	DISCHARGE PLANNED WITHIN 3 MOS.	*(Does not include discharge due to death)* 0. No 1. Yes 2. Unknown/uncertain
11.	PARTICIPATE IN ASSESSMENT	a. Resident 0. No 1. Yes b. Family 0. No 1. Yes 2. No family a. b.
12.	SIGNATURES	Signature of RN Assessment Coordinator

Signatures of others who completed part of the assessment

_____   _____

_____   _____

_____   _____

SECTION B. COGNITIVE PATTERNS

1.	COMATOSE	*(Persistent vegetative state/no discernible consciousness)* 0. No 1. Yes **(Skip to Section E)**
2.	MEMORY	*(Recall of what was learned or known)* a. Short-term memory OK— seems/appears to recall after 5 minutes 0. Memory OK 1. Memory problem a. b. Long-term memory OK— seems/appears to recall long past 0. Memory OK 1. Memory problem b.
3.	MEMORY/RECALL ABILITY	*(Check all that resident normally is able to recall during last 7 days)* Current season a. Location of own room b. Staff names/faces c. That he/she is in a nursing home d. None of Above are recalled e.
4.	COGNITIVE SKILLS FOR DAILY DECISION MAKING	*(Made decisions regarding tasks of daily life)* 0. Independent— decisions consistent/reasonable 1. Modified independence— some difficulty in new situations only 2. Moderately impaired— decisions poor; cues/supervision required 3. Severely impaired— never/rarely made decisions
5.	INDICATORS OF DELIRIUM—PERIODIC DISORDERED THINKING/AWARENESS	*(Check if condition over last 7 days appears different from usual functioning)* Less alert, easily distracted a. Changing awareness of environment b. Episodes of incoherent speech c. Periods of motor restlessness or lethargy d. Cognitive ability varies over course of day e. NONE OF ABOVE f.
6.	CHANGE IN COGNITIVE STATUS	Change in resident's cognitive status, skills, or abilities in **last 90 days** 0. No change 1. Improved 2. Deteriorated

Code the appropriate response = ▢

Check all the responses that apply = ▢

(Continued on Reverse Side)

Minimum Data Set for Nursing Home Resident Assessment and Care Screening (MDS)

(Status in last seven days, unless other time frame indicated)

SECTION C. COMMUNICATION/HEARING PATTERNS

1.	Hearing	(*With hearing appliance, if used*) 0. Hears adequately—normal talk, TV, phone 1. Minimal difficulty when not in quiet setting 2. Hears in special situations only—speaker has to adjust tonal quality and speak distinctly 3. Highly impaired/absence of useful hearing	
2.	Communication Devices/ Techniques	(*Check all that apply during last 7 days*) Hearing aid, present and used a. Hearing aid, present and not used b. Other receptive comm. techniques used (e.g., lip read) c. NONE OF ABOVE d.	
3.	Modes of Expression	(*Check all used by resident to make needs known*) Speech a. Writing messages to express or clarify needs b. Signs/gestures/sounds c. Communication board d. Other e. NONE OF ABOVE f.	
4.	Making Self Understood	(*Express information content—however able*) 0 Understood 1. Usually understood—difficulty finding words or finishing thoughts 2. Sometimes understood—ability is limited to making concrete requests 3. Rarely/never understood	
5.	Ability to Understand Others	(*Understanding verbal information content—however able*) 0. Understands 1. Usually understands—may miss some part/intent of message 2. Sometimes understands—responds adequately to simple, direct communication 3. Rarely/never understands	
6.	Change in Communication/ Hearing	Resident's ability to express, understand, or hear information has changed over **last 90 days** 0. No change 1. Improved 2. Deteriorated	

SECTION D. VISION PATTERNS

1.	Vision	(*Ability to see in adequate light and with glasses, if used*) 0. Adequate—sees fine detail, including regular print in newspapers/books 1. Impaired—sees large print, but not regular print in newspapers/books 2. Highly Impaired—limited vision; not able to see newspaper headlines; appears to follow objects with eyes 3. Severely Impaired—no vision or appears to see only light, colors, or shapes	
2.	Visual Limitations/ Difficulties	Side vision problems—decreased peripheral vision (e.g., leaves food on one side of tray, difficulty traveling, bumps into people and objects, misjudges placement of chair when seating self) a. Experiences any of following: sees halos or rings around lights; sees flashes of light; sees "curtains" over eyes b. NONE OF ABOVE c.	
3.	Visual Appliances	Glasses; contact lenses; lens implant; magnifying glass 0. No 1. Yes	

Code the appropriate response = [ ]
Check all the responses that apply = [ ]

(Continued on next page)

Adapted from and reprinted with permission from Briggs: Form 1808HF © Briggs Corporation, Des Moines, IA 50306 (800) 247-2343
Printed in U.S.A.

Minimum Data Set for Nursing Home Resident Assessment and Care Screening (MDS)

(Status in last seven days, unless other time frame indicated)

SECTION E. PHYSICAL FUNCTIONING AND STRUCTURAL PROBLEMS

1. ADL Self-performance—(*Code* for resident's *PERFORMANCE OVER ALL SHIFTS During Last 7 Days—Not* including setup)

- **0. INDEPENDENT**—No help or oversight—OR—Help/oversight provided only 1 or 2 times during last 7 days
- **1. SUPERVISION**—Oversight, encouragement, or cueing provided 3+ times during last 7 days—OR—Supervision plus physical assistance provided only 1 or 2 times during last 7 days
- **2. LIMITED ASSISTANCE**—Resident highly involved in activity; received physical help in guided maneuvering of limbs or other nonweight bearing assistance 3+ times—OR—More help provided only 1 or 2 times during last 7 days
- **3. EXTENSIVE ASSISTANCE**—While resident performed part of activity, over last 7-day period, help of following type(s) provided 3 or more times:
  ____ Weight-bearing support
  ____ Full staff performance during part (but not all) of last 7 days
- **4. TOTAL DEPENDENCE**—Full staff performance of activity during entire 7 days

2. ADL Support Provided—(*Code* for MOST SUPPORT PROVIDED OVER ALL SHIFTS During Last 7 Days; CODE REGARDLESS of resident's self-performance classification)

- 0. No setup or physical help from staff
- 1. Setup help only
- 2. One-person physical assist
- 3. Two+ persons physical assist

			(1) Self-performance	(2) Support
a.	BED MOBILITY	How resident moves to and from lying position, turns side-to-side, and positions body while in bed		
b.	TRANSFER	How resident moves between surfaces—to/from: bed, chair, wheelchair, standing position (exclude to/from bath/toilet)		
c.	LOCOMOTION	How resident moves between locations in his/her room and adjacent corridor on same floor. If in wheelchair, self-sufficiency once in chair.		
d.	DRESSING	How resident puts on, fastens, and takes off all items of street clothing, including donning/removing prosthesis		
e.	EATING	How resident eats and drinks (regardless of skill)		
f.	TOILET USE	How resident uses the toilet room (or commode, bedpan, urinal); transfer on/off toilet, cleanses, changes pad, manages ostomy or catheter, adjusts clothes		
g.	PERSONAL HYGIENE	How resident maintains personal hygiene, including combing hair, brushing teeth, shaving, applying makeup, washing/drying face, hands, and perineum (EXCLUDE baths and showers)		

Code the appropriate response = ▨
Check all responses that apply = ☐

3. BATHING How resident takes full-body bath/shower, sponge bath and transfers in/out of tub/shower (**EXCLUDE** washing of back and hair. **CODE FOR MOST DEPENDENT** in self-performance and support. Bathing Self-performance codes appear below)

	(1) Self-performance a.	(2) Support b.
0. Independent—No help provided		
1. Supervision—Oversight help only		
2. Physical help limited to transfer only		
3. Physical help in part of bathing activity		
4. Total dependence		

4. BODY CONTROL PROBLEMS (***Check all that apply*** during last 7 days)

Balance—partial or total loss of ability to balance self while standing	a.
Bedfast all or most of the time	b.
Contracture to arms, legs, shoulders, or hands	c.
Hemiplegia/hemiparesis	d.
Quadriplegia	e.
Arm—partial or total loss of voluntary movement	f.
Hand—lack of dexterity (e.g., problem using toothbrush or adjusting hearing aid)	g.
Leg—partial or total loss of voluntary movement	h.
Leg—unsteady gait	i.
Trunk—partial or total loss of ability to position, balance, or turn body	j.
Amputation	k.
None of Above	l.

5. MOBILITY APPLIANCES/ DEVICES (***Check all that apply*** during last 7 days)

Cane/walker	a.	Other person wheeled	d.
Brace/prosthesis	b.	Lifted (manually/mechanically)	e.
Wheeled self	c.	NONE OF ABOVE	f.

6. TASK SEGMENTATION Resident requires that some or all of ADL activities be broken into a series of subtasks so that resident can perform them
0. No   1. Yes

7. ADL FUNCTIONAL REHABILITATION POTENTIAL

Resident believes he/she capable of increased independence in at least some ADLs	a.
Direct care staff believe resident capable of increased independence in at least some ADLs	b.
Resident able to perform tasks/activity but is very slow	c.
Major difference in ADL Self-Performance or ADL Support in mornings and evenings (at least a one category change in Self-Performance or Support in any ADL)	d.
NONE OF ABOVE	e.

8. CHANGE IN ADL FUNCTION Change in ADL self-performance in **last 90 days**
0. No change   1. Improved   2. Deteriorated

(Continued on Reverse Side)

Minimum Data Set for Nursing Home Resident Assessment and Care Screening (MDS)
(Status in last seven days, unless other time frame indicated)

SECTION F. CONTINENCE IN LAST 14 DAYS

1. Continence Self-Control Categories
(**Code** for resident performance over all shifts)
- 0. **CONTINENT**—Complete control
- 1. **USUALLY CONTINENT**—Bladder, incontinent episodes once a week or less; bowel, less than weekly
- 2. **OCCASIONALLY INCONTINENT**—Bladder, 2+ times a week but not daily; bowel, once a week
- 3. **FREQUENTLY INCONTINENT**—Bladder, tended to be incontinent daily, but some control present (e.g., on day shift); bowel, 2-3 times a week
- 4. **INCONTINENT**—Had inadequate control. Bladder, multiple daily episodes; bowel, all (or almost all) of the time

a. Bowel Continence	Control of bowel movement, with appliance or bowel continence programs, if employed	
b. Bladder Continence	Control of urinary bladder function (if dribbles, volume insufficient to soak through underpants), with appliances (e.g., foley) or continence programs, if employed	

2. INCONTINENCE RELATED TESTING (*Skip* if resident's bladder continence code equals 0 or 1 and no catheter is used)
- Resident has been tested for a urinary tract infection — a.
- Resident has been checked for presence of fecal impaction, or there is adequate bowel elimination — b.
- NONE OF ABOVE — c.

3. APPLIANCES AND PROGRAMS
- Any scheduled toileting plan — a.
- External (condom) catheter — b.
- Indwelling catheter — c.
- Intermittent catheter — d.
- Did not use toilet room/commode/urinal — e.
- Pads/briefs used — f.
- Enemas/irrigation — g.
- Ostomy — h.
- NONE OF ABOVE — i.

4. CHANGE IN URINARY CONTINENCE — Change in urinary continence/appliances and programs in **last 90 days**
- 0. No Change 1. Improved 2. Deteriorated

Code the appropriate response = ▨
Check all the responses that apply = ☐

SECTION G. PSYCHOSOCIAL WELL-BEING

1. SENSE OF INITIATIVE/INVOLVEMENT
- At ease interacting with others — a.
- At ease doing planned or structured activities — b.
- At ease doing self-initiated activities — c.
- Establishes own goals — d.
- Pursues involvement in life of facility (e.g., makes/keeps friends; involved in group activities; responds positively to new activities; assists at religious services) — e.
- Accepts invitations into most group activities — f.
- NONE OF ABOVE — g.

2. UNSETTLED RELATIONSHIPS
- Covert/open conflict with and/or repeated criticism of staff — a.
- Unhappy with roommate — b.
- Unhappy with residents other than roommate — c.
- Openly expresses conflict/anger with family or friends — d.
- Absence of personal contact with family/friends — e.
- Recent loss of close family member/friend — f.
- NONE OF ABOVE — g.

3. PAST ROLES
- Strong identification with past roles and life status — a.
- Expresses sadness/anger/empty feeling over lost roles/status — b.
- NONE OF ABOVE — c.

(Continued on next page)

Adapted from and reprinted with permission from Briggs: Form 1808HF © Briggs Corporation, Des Moines, IA 50306 (800) 247-2343
Printed in U.S.A.

Minimum Data Set for Nursing Home Resident Assessment and Care Screening (MDS)

(Status in last seven days, unless other time frame indicated)

SECTION H. MOOD AND BEHAVIOR PATTERNS

1.	SAD OR ANXIOUS MOOD	(*Check all that apply during last 30 days*)	
		Verbal Expressions of Distress by resident (sadness, sense that nothing matters, hopelessness, worthlessness, unrealistic fears, vocal expressions of anxiety or grief)	a.
		DEMONSTRATED (OBSERVABLE) SIGNS OF MENTAL DISTRESS Tearfulness, emotional groaning, sighing, breathlessness	b.
		Motor agitation such as pacing, handwringing, or picking	c.
		Failure to eat or take medications, withdrawal from self-care or leisure activities	d.
		Pervasive concern with health	e.
		Recurrent thoughts of death—e.g., believes he/she about to die, have a heart attack	f.
		Suicidal thoughts/actions	g.
		NONE OF ABOVE	h.
2.	MOOD PERSISTENCE	Sad or anxious mood intrudes on daily life over **last 7 days**—not easily altered, doesn't "cheer up" 0. No 1. Yes	
3.	PROBLEM BEHAVIOR	(*Code for behavior in last 7 days*) 0. Behavior not exhibited in last 7 days 1. Behavior of this type occurred less than daily 2. Behavior of this type occurred daily or more frequently	
		WANDERING (moved with no rational purpose, seemingly oblivious to needs or safety)	a.
		VERBALLY ABUSIVE (others were threatened, screamed at, cursed at)	b.
		PHYSICALLY ABUSIVE (others were hit, shoved, scratched, sexually abused)	c.
		SOCIALLY INAPPROPRIATE/DISRUPTIVE BEHAVIOR (made disrupting sounds, noisy, screams, self-abusive acts, sexual behavior or disrobing in public, smeared/threw food/feces, hoarding, rummaged through others' belongings)	d.
4.	RESIDENT RESISTS CARE	(*Check all types of resistance that occurred in the last 7 days*)	
		Resisted taking medications/injections	a.
		Resisted ADL assistance	b.
		NONE OF ABOVE	c.
5.	BEHAVIOR MANAGEMENT PROGRAM	Behavior problem has been addressed by clinically developed behavior management program. (Note: Do not include programs that involve only physical restraints or psychotropic medications in this category) 0. No behavior problem 1. Yes, addressed 2. No, not addressed	
6.	CHANGE IN MOOD	Change in mood in **last 90 days** 0. No change 1. Improved 2. Deteriorated	
7.	CHANGE IN PROBLEM BEHAVIOR	Change in problem behavioral signs in **last 90 days** 0. No change 1. Improved 2. Deteriorated	

SECTION I. ACTIVITY PURSUIT PATTERNS

1.	TIME AWAKE	(*Check appropriate time periods over last 7 days*) Resident awake all or most of time (i.e., naps no more than one hour per time period) in the:	
		Morning	a.
		Afternoon	b.
		Evening	c.
		None of Above	d.
2.	AVERAGE TIME INVOLVED IN ACTIVITIES	0. Most—more than 2/3 of time 1. Some—1/3 to 2/3 of time 2. Little—less than 1/3 of time 3. None	
3.	PREFERRED ACTIVITY SETTINGS	(*Check all settings in which activities are preferred*)	
		Own room	a.
		Day/activity room	b.
		Inside NH/off unit	c.
		Outside facility	d.
		NONE OF ABOVE	e.
4.	GENERAL ACTIVITY PREFERENCES (ADAPTED TO RESIDENT'S CURRENT ABILITIES)	(*Check all preferences whether or not activity is currently available to resident*)	
		Cards/other games	a.
		Crafts/arts	b.
		Exercise/sports	c.
		Music	d.
		Read/write	e.
		Spiritual/religious activities	f.
		Trips/shopping	g.
		Walking/wheeling outdoors	h.
		Watch TV	i.
		NONE OF ABOVE	j.
5.	PREFERS MORE OR DIFFERENT ACTIVITIES	Resident expresses/indicates preference for other activities/choices 0. No 1. Yes	

Code the appropriate response = ▨

Check all the responses that apply = ☐

(Continued on Reverse Side)

Minimum Data Set for Nursing Home Resident Assessment and Care Screening (MDS)
(Status in last seven days, unless other time frame indicated)

SECTION J. DISEASE DIAGNOSES

CHECK ONLY THOSE DISEASES PRESENT THAT HAVE A RELATIONSHIP to current ADL status, cognitive status, behavior status, medical treatments, or risk of death (Do not list old/inactive diagnoses)

1. Diseases (If none apply, check the None of Above box)

HEART/CIRCULATION

Arteriosclerotic heart disease (ASHD)	a.
Cardiac dysrhythmias	b.
Congestive heart failure	c.
Hypertension	d.
Hypotension	e.
Peripheral vascular disease	f.
Other cardiovascular disease	g.

NEUROLOGICAL

Alzheimer's	h.
Dementia other than Alzheimer's	i.
Aphasia	j.
Cerebrovascular accident (stroke)	k.
Multiple sclerosis	l.
Parkinson's disease	m.

PULMONARY

Emphysema/Asthma/COPD	n.
Pneumonia	o.

PSYCHIATRIC/MOOD

Anxiety disorder	p.
Depression	q.
Manic depressive (bipolar disease)	r.

SENSORY

Cataracts	s.
Glaucoma	t.

OTHER

Allergies	u.
Anemia	v.
Arthritis	w.
Cancer	x.
Diabetes mellitus	y.
Explicit terminal prognosis	z.
Hypothyroidism	aa.
Osteoporosis	bb.
Seizure disorder	cc.
Septicemia	dd.
Urinary tract infection **in last 30 days**	ee.
NONE OF ABOVE	ff.

2. OTHER CURRENT DIAGNOSES AND ICD-9 CODES

a. _____
b. _____
c. _____
d. _____
e. _____
f. _____

SECTION K. HEALTH CONDITIONS

1. PROBLEM CONDITIONS (*Check all problems* that are present in last 7 days unless other time frame indicated)

Constipation	a.
Diarrhea	b.
Dizziness/vertigo	c.
Edema	d.
Fecal impaction	e.
Fever	f.
Hallucinations/delusions	g.
Internal bleeding	h.
Joint pain	i.
Pain—resident complains or shows evidence of pain daily or almost daily	j.
Recurrent lung aspirations in **last 90 days**	k.
Shortness of breath	l.
Syncope (fainting)	m.
Vomiting	n.
NONE OF ABOVE	o.

2. ACCIDENTS

Fell in **past 30 days**	a.
Fell in **past 31-180 days**	b.
Hip fracture in **last 180 days**	c.
NONE OF ABOVE	d.

3. STABILITY OF CONDITIONS

Conditions/diseases make resident's cognitive, ADL or behavior status unstable—fluctuating, precarious, or deteriorating	a.
Resident experiencing an acute episode or a flare-up of a recurrent chronic problem	b.
NONE OF ABOVE	c.

(Continued on next page)

Minimum Data Set for Nursing Home Resident Assessment and Care Screening (MDS)

(Status in last seven days, unless other time frame indicated)

SECTION L. ORAL/NUTRITIONAL STATUS

1.	ORAL PROBLEMS	Chewing problem	a.
		Swallowing problem	b.
		Mouth pain	c.
		NONE OF ABOVE	d.

2.	HEIGHT AND WEIGHT	Record height (**a.**) in inches and weight (**b.**) in pounds. Weight based on most recent status in **last 30 days**; measure weight consistently in accord with standard facility practice—e.g., in a.m. after voiding, before meal, with shoes off, and in nightclothes.

	(a.)		(b.)	
	HT (in.)		WT (lbs.)	

c. Weight loss (i.e., 5% in **last 30 days**; or 10% in **last 180 days**)	
0. No 1. Yes	

3.	NUTRITIONAL PROBLEMS	Complains about the taste of many foods	a.
		Insufficient fluid; dehydrated	b.
		Did **NOT** consume all/almost all liquids provided **during last 3 days**	c.
		Regular complaint of hunger	d.
		Leaves 25%+ food uneaten at most meals	e.
		NONE OF ABOVE	f.

4.	NUTRITIONAL APPROACHES	Parenteral/IV	a.
		Feeding tube	b.
		Mechanically-altered diet	c.
		Syringe (oral feeding)	d.
		Therapeutic diet	e.
		Dietary supplement between meals	f.
		Plate guard, stabilized built-up utensil, etc	g.
		NONE OF ABOVE	h.

SECTION M. ORAL/DENTAL STATUS

1.	ORAL STATUS AND DISEASE PREVENTION	Debris (soft, easily movable substances) present in mouth prior to going to bed at night	a.
		Has dentures and/or removable bridge	b.
		Some/all natural teeth lost—does not have or does not use dentures (or partial plates)	c.
		Broken, loose or carious teeth	d.
		Inflamed gums (gingiva); swollen or bleeding gums; oral abscesses, ulcers, or rashes	e.
		Daily cleaning of teeth/dentures	f.
		NONE OF ABOVE	g.

SECTION N. SKIN CONDITION

1.	STASIS ULCER	Open lesion caused by poor venous circulation to lower extremities
		0. No 1. Yes

2.	PRESSURE ULCERS	(***Code for highest stage*** of pressure ulcer)
		0. No pressure ulcers
		1. Stage 1: A persistent area of skin redness (without a break in the skin) that does not disappear when pressure is relieved
		2. Stage 2: A partial thickness loss of skin layers that presents clinically as an abrasion, blister, or shallow crater
		3. Stage 3: A full thickness of skin is lost, exposing the subcutaneous tissues—presents as a deep crater with or without undermining adjacent tissue
		4. Stage 4: A full thickness of skin and subcutaneous tissue is lost, exposing muscle and/or bone

3.	HISTORY OF RESOLVED/CURED PRESSURE ULCERS	Resident has had a pressure ulcer that was resolved/cured in **last 90 days**
		0. No 1. Yes

4.	SKIN PROBLEMS/ CARE	Open lesions other than statis or pressure ulcers (e.g., cuts)	a.
		Skin desensitized to pain, pressure, discomfort	b.
		Protective/preventive skin care	c.
		Turning/repositioning program	d.
		Pressure relieving beds, bed/chair pads (e.g., egg crate pads)	e.
		Wound care/treatment (e.g., pressure ulcer care, surgical wound)	f.
		Other skin care/treatment	g.
		NONE OF ABOVE	h.

Code the appropriate response = ▢

Check all the responses that apply = ▢

(Continued on Reverse Side)

Adapted from and reprinted with permission from Briggs: Form 1808HF © Briggs Corporation, Des Moines, IA 50306 (800) 247-2343
Printed in U.S.A.

Minimum Data Set for Nursing Home Resident Assessment and Care Screening (MDS)
(Status in last seven days, unless other time frame indicated)

SECTION O. MEDICATION USE

1.	NUMBER OF MEDICATIONS	(*Record the number of different medications used in the last 7 days; enter "0" if none used*)
2.	NEW MEDICATIONS	Resident has received new medications during the **last 90 days** 0. No 1. Yes
3.	INJECTIONS	(*Record the number of days injections of any type received during the last 7 days*)
4.	DAYS RECEIVED THE FOLLOWING MEDICATIONS	(*Record the number of days during last 7 days; enter "0" if not used; enter "1" if long-acting medications used less than weekly*) Antipsychotics a. Antianxiety/hypnotics b. Antidepressants c.
5.	PREVIOUS MEDICATION RESULTS	(*Skip this question if resident currently receiving antipsychotics, antidepressants, or antianxiety/hypnotics—otherwise code correct response for last 90 days*) Resident has previously received psychoactive medications for a mood or behavior problem, and these medications were effective (without undue adverse consequences) 0. No, drugs not used 1. Drugs were effective 2. Drugs were not effective 3. Drug effectiveness unknown

Code the appropriate response = ☐
Check all the responses that apply = ☐

SECTION P. SPECIAL TREATMENT AND PROCEDURES

1.	SPECIAL TREATMENTS AND PROCEDURES	**SPECIAL CARE—Check** treatments received during the last 14 days Chemotherapy a. IV Medications f. Radiation b. Transfusions g. Dialysis c. O₂ h. Suctioning d. Other ___ i. Trach. care e. NONE OF ABOVE j. **THERAPIES—Record the number of days** each of the following therapies was administered (for at least 10 minutes during a day) in the last 7 days: Speech–language pathology and audiology services k. Occupational therapy l. Physical therapy m. Psychological therapy (any licensed professional) n. Respiratory therapy o.
2.	ABNORMAL LAB VALUES	Has the resident had any abnormal lab values during the **last 90 days**? 0. No 1. Yes 2. No tests performed
3.	DEVICES AND RESTRAINTS	Use the following **codes** for last 7 days: 0. Not used 1. Used less than daily 2. Used daily Bed rails a. Trunk restraint b. Limb restraint c. Chair prevents rising d.

END

QUARTERLY REVIEW FOR NURSING FACILITY RESIDENT ASSESSMENT AND CARE SCREENING (MDS)

(Sequence of questions on this Quarterly Review have been numbered to coincide with the Minimum Data Set)

Resident Name _____

IF COMATOSE, SKIP TO SECTION E

90	180	270

SECTION B. COGNITIVE PATTERNS

2.	MEMORY	(*Recall of what was learned or known*)				
		a. Short-term memory OK—seems/appears to recall after 5 minutes	a.			
		0. Memory OK 1. Memory problem				
		b. Long-term memory OK—seems/appears to recall long past	b.			
		0. Memory OK 1. Memory problem				
4.	COGNITIVE SKILLS FOR DAILY DECISION MAKING	(*Made decisions regarding tasks of daily life*) (**Code responses**) 0. Independent—decisions consistent/reasonable 1. Modified independence—some difficulty in new situations only 2. Moderately impaired—decisions poor; cues/supervision required 3. Severely impaired—never/rarely made decisions				

SECTION C. COMMUNICATION/HEARING PATTERNS

4.	A. MAKING SELF UNDERSTOOD	(*Express information content—however able*) 0. Understood 1. Usually understood—difficulty finding words or finishing thoughts 2. Sometimes understood—ability is limited to making concrete requests 3. Rarely/Never Understood			
5.	B. ABILITY TO UNDERSTAND OTHERS	(*Understanding verbal information content—however able*) 0. Understands 1. Usually understands—may miss some part/intent of message 2. Sometimes understands—responds adequately to simple, direct communication 3. Rarely/Never understands			

Key

◼ = Write in the appropriate numeric

▢ = Check (√) if response is applicable

SECTION E. PHYSICAL FUNCTIONING AND STRUCTURAL PROBLEMS

90	180	270

1.		ADL Self-performance—(**Code** for resident's **PERFORMANCE OVER ALL SHIFTS** *During Last 7 Days*—Not including setup)			
		0. **INDEPENDENT**—No help or oversight—OR—Help/oversight provided only 1 or 2 times during last 7 days			
		1. **SUPERVISION**—Oversight, encouragement, or cueing provided 3+ times during last 7 days—OR—Supervision plus physical assistance provided only 1 or 2 times during last 7 days			
		2. **LIMITED ASSISTANCE**—Resident highly involved in activity; received physical help in guided maneuvering of limbs or other nonweight bearing assistance 3+ times—OR—More help provided only 1 or 2 times during last 7 days			
		3. **EXTENSIVE ASSISTANCE**—While resident performed part of activity, over last 7-day period, help of following type(s) provided 3 or more times: — Weight-bearing support —Full staff performance during part (but not all) of last 7 days			
		4. **TOTAL DEPENDENCE**—Full staff performance of activity during entire 7 days			
b.	TRANSFER	How resident moves between surfaces—to/from: bed, chair, wheelchair, standing position (**EXCLUDE** to/from bath/toilet)			
c.	LOCOMOTION	How resident moves between locations in his/her room and adjacent corridor on same floor. If in wheelchair, self-sufficiency once in chair.			
d.	DRESSING	How resident puts on, fastens, and takes off all items of street clothing, including donning/removing prosthesis			
e.	EATING	How resident eats and drinks (regardless of skill)			
f.	TOILET USE	How resident uses the toilet room (or commode, bedpan, urinal); transfer on/off toilet, cleanses, changes pad, manages ostomy or catheter, adjusts clothes			
3a.	BATHING	How resident takes full-body bath/shower, sponge bath and transfers in/out of tub/shower (**EXCLUDE** washing of back and hair. **CODE FOR MOST DEPENDENT** in self-performance and support. Bathing self-performance codes appear below) 0. Independent—No help provided 1. Supervision—Oversight help only 2. Physical help limited to transfer only 3. Physical help in part of bathing activity 4. Total dependence			

(Continued on Reverse Side)

QUARTERLY REVIEW For Nursing Facility Resident Assessment and Care Screening (MDS)
(CONTINUED)
(Sequence of questions on this Quarterly Review have been numbered to coincide with the Minimum Data Set)

			90	180	270

SECTION F. CONTINENCE IN LAST 14 DAYS

1. Continence Self-Control Categories
(**Code** for resident's performance over all shifts)
   0. **CONTINENT**—Complete control
   1. **USUALLY CONTINENT**—Bladder, incontinent episodes once a week or less; bowel, less than weekly
   2. **OCCASIONALLY INCONTINENT**—Bladder, 2+ times a week but not daily; bowel, once a week
   3. **FREQUENTLY INCONTINENT**—Bladder, tended to be incontinent daily, but some control present (e.g., on day shift); bowel, 2-3 times a week
   4. **INCONTINENT**—Had inadequate control. Bladder, multiple daily episodes; bowel, all (or almost all) of the time

a.	BOWEL CONTINENCE	Control of bowel movement, with appliance or bowel continence programs, if employed			
b.	BLADDER CONTINENCE	Control of urinary bladder function (if dribbles, volume insufficient to soak through underpants), with appliances (e.g., foley) or continence programs, if employed			

IF COMATOSE, SKIP TO SECTION J

SECTION H. MOOD AND BEHAVIOR PATTERNS

2.	MOOD PERSISTENCE	Sad or anxious mood intrudes on daily life over **last 7 days**—not easily altered, doesn't "cheer up" 0. No 1. Yes			
3.	PROBLEM BEHAVIOR	(**Code for behavior** in last 7 days) 0. Behavior not exhibited in last 7 days 1. Behavior of this type occurred less than daily 2. Behavior of this type occurred daily or more frequently			

WANDERING (moved with no rational purpose, seemingly oblivious to needs or safety)	a.			
VERBALLY ABUSIVE (others were threatened, screamed at, cursed at)	b.			
PHYSICALLY ABUSIVE (others were hit, shoved, scratched, sexually abused)	c.			
SOCIALLY INAPPROPRIATE/DISRUPTIVE BEHAVIOR (made disrupting sounds, noisy, screams, self-abusive acts, sexual behavior or disrobing in public, smeared/threw food/feces, hoarding, rummaged through others' belongings)	d.			

			90	180	270

SECTION J. DISEASE DIAGNOSES

Include **ONLY THOSE DISEASES DIAGNOSED IN THE LAST 90 DAYS THAT HAVE A RELATIONSHIP** to current ADL status, cognitive status, behavior status, medical treatments, or risk of death.

2.	OTHER CURRENT DIAGNOSES AND ICD-9 CODES	a. _____ b. _____ c. _____ d. _____ e. _____ f.						

SECTION L. ORAL/NUTRITIONAL STATUS

2.	HEIGHT AND WEIGHT	**c.** Weight loss (i.e., 5% in **last 30 days**; or 10% in **last 180 days**) 0. No 1. Yes			

SECTION O. MEDICATION USE

4.	DAYS RECEIVED THE FOLLOWING MEDICATIONS	(**Record the number of days** during last 7 days; enter "0" if not used; enter "1" if long-acting medications used less than weekly)			
		Antipsychotics a.			
		Antianxiety/hypnotics b.			
		Antidepressants c.			

SECTION P. SPECIAL TREATMENT AND PROCEDURES

3.	DEVICES AND RESTRAINTS	Use the following **codes** for last 7 days: 0. Not used 1. Used less than daily 2. Used daily			
		Trunk restraint b.			
		Chair prevents rising d.			

(Continued on next page)

Adapted from and reprinted with permission from Briggs: Form 1820HH © Briggs Corporation, Des Moines, IA 50306 (800) 247-2343
Printed in U.S.A.

MDS Quarterly Review–Signature, Title and Date of Staff Completing the Assessment

NOTE: Indicate sections completed next to Signature and Title

90-Day Assessment-FIRST QUARTER
signature of RN
Assessment Coordinator _____

Others who Completed Part of the Assessment

Signature/Title   Date

_____

_____

_____

_____

_____

Date of Assessment:

Month   Day   Year

Review Indicates change necessary to plan of care:?

Yes   No _____

_____

_____

_____

_____

_____

_____

_____

_____

_____

90-Day Assessment-FIRST QUARTER
signature of RN
Assessment Coordinator _____

Others who Completed Part of the Assessment

Signature/Title   Date

_____

_____

_____

_____

_____

Date of Assessment:

Month   Day   Year

Review Indicates change necessary to plan of care?

Yes   No _____

_____

_____

_____

_____

_____

_____

_____

_____

_____

90-Day Assessment-FIRST QUARTER
signature of RN
Assessment Coordinator _____

Others who Completed Part of the Assessment

Signature/Title   Date

_____

_____

_____

_____

_____

Date of Assessment:

Month   Day   Year

Review Indicates change necessary to plan of care?

Yes   No _____

_____

_____

_____

_____

_____

_____

_____

_____

Adapted from and reprinted with permission from Briggs: Form 1820HH © Briggs Corporation, Des Moines, IA 50306 (800) 247-2343
Printed in U.S.A.

END

Activity Assessment

On a quarterly basis or upon a significant change, check the item(s) in each section that best describe the resident.	1st Date	2nd Date	3rd Date	4th Date	5th Date	6th Date	7th Date	8th Date
Date must include month/day/year→	/ /	/ /	/ /	/ /	/ /	/ /	/ /	/ /
PARTICIPATION IN ACTIVITIES:								
Participates in: all activities								
6 or more activities/week								
3 - 5 activities/week								
2 activities/week								
1 activity/week								
Unable to participate in group activities								
Chooses not to participate in group activities								
Participates in: independent activities of choice								
one-to-one programming								
one-to-one visits								
PARTICIPATION LEVEL IN ACTIVITIES:								
Attends activities independently								
Requires reminding to attend activities								
Requires assistance to attend activities								
Is an active participant								
Is a passive participant								
Participates: independently								
with assistance								
Behavior in activities is: appropriate								
inappropriate								
Responsive to one-to-one programming								
Unresponsive to one-to-one programming								
Responsive to one-to-one visits								
SOCIALIZATION PATTERNS:								
Prefers to be alone								
Prefers to be with people								
Makes friends easily								
Has difficulty in making friends								
Initiates conversations								

ASSESSED BY: INCLUDE SIGNATURE AND TITLE

1st		2nd		3rd		4th	
5th		6th		7th		8th	

NAME: Last   First   Middle | Attending Physician   Chart No.

Adapted from and reprinted with permission from Briggs: CFS 4-2HH © 1992 Briggs Corporation, Des Moines, IA 50306 (800) 247-2343

Printed in U.S.A.

ACTIVITY ASSESSMENT
❏ Continued on Reverse

Activity Assessment (Continued)

	1st	2nd	3rd	4th	5th	6th	7th	8th
SOCIALIZATION PATTERNS: (continued)								
Rarely initiates conversations								
Prefers to stay in room								
Prefers to be out of room								
Enjoys large groups								
Enjoys small groups								
Visits with family and friends								
Communicates verbally								
Communicates nonverbally								
Able to make needs known								
Unable to make needs known								
MOBILITY:								
Ambulates independently								
Ambulates with walker/cane/assist of others								
Wheelchair mobile								
Dependent on others for wheelchair transport								
Roombound								
VISION:								
Vision is adequate								
Vision is poor								
Wears glasses								
Blind								
HEARING:								
Hearing is adequate								
Hearing is poor								
Wears hearing aid								
Deaf								
MENTAL STATUS:								
Oriented to: person								
place								
time								
Disoriented X3								
Forgetful								
Alert								
Nonresponsive								
Adequate concentration level								
Short attention span								

Adapted from and reprinted with permission from Briggs: CFS 4-2HH © 1992 Briggs Corporation, Des Moines, IA 50306 (800) 247-2343

Printed in U.S.A.

ACTIVITY ASSESSMENT
❑ Continued on Next Page

Activity Assessment (Continued)

	1st	2nd	3rd	4th	5th	6th	7th	8th
PSYCHOSOCIAL NEEDS:								
Adjustment to placement								
Group interaction								
One-to-one interaction								
Intellectual stimulation								
Creativity								
Competition								
Spiritual growth								
Responsibility								
Independence								
Sensory stimulation								
ADAPTIVE EQUIPMENT:								
Magnifying glass								
Large print								
Talking books								
Book holders								
Built-in handles								
Head sets								
C-clamps								
Communication board								

FOR ADDITIONAL INFORMATION REFER TO ACTIVITY PLAN AND PROGRESS NOTES

NAME: Last   First   Middle   Attending Physician   Chart No.

Adapted from and reprinted with permission from Briggs: CFS 4-2HH © 1992 Briggs Corporation, Des Moines, IA 50306 (800) 247-2343

Printed in U.S.A.

ACTIVITY ASSESSMENT
END

Resident Assessment Protocol Trigger Legend

Residents Name _____

I.D. Number _____

_____ / _____ / _____

Date:

LEGEND

● Automatic Trigger—Go directly to RAP

▲ Potential Trigger—Go to RAP instructions for more detail

MDS PATTERN	MDS ITEM	CODE	Delirium (1)	Cognitive Loss/Dementia (2)	Visual Function (3)	Communication (4)	ADL Functional/Rehabilitation Potential (5)	Urinary Incontinence and Indwelling Catheter (6)	Psychosocial Well-Being (7)	Mood State (8)	Behavior Problems (9)	Activities (10)	Falls (11)	Nutritional Status (12)	Feeding Tubes (13)	Dehydration/Fluid Maintenance (14)	Dental Care (15)	Pressure Ulcers (16)	Psychotropic Drug Use (17)	Physical Restraints (18)
B. Cognitive Patterns	B2 a or b	1		▲																
	B3 a, b, c, d,	Fewer than 3 √		▲																
	B4	0, 1, 2				▲														
		1, 2, 3		▲																
	B5 a, b, c, d, e	any √	●																	
	B6	2	●													▲				
C. Communication	C4	2, 3				▲														
Hearing Patterns	C5	1, 2, 3		▲																
		2, 3				▲	▲													
	C6	2	●																	
D. Vision Patterns	D1	1, 2, 3			●															
	D2 a	√			●															
E. Physical Functioning/	E1 a, b, c, d, e, f	3, 4					▲													
Structural Problems	E3 a	3, 4					▲													
	E4 a, b, d, e, h, j	any √											▲							
	E7 a, b	any √					▲													
	E8	2														▲				
F. Continence	F1 b	2, 3, 4						▲												
	F3 b, c, d, f	any √						▲												
G. Psychosocial Well-Being	G2 a, b, c, d	any √							●											
	G3 b	√							●											
H. Mood/Behavior	H1 a, b, c, d, e, f, g	any √								●										
	H1 d	√														▲				
	H2	1								●										
	H3 a, b, c, or d	1, 2									●									
	H6	2	▲																	
	H7	2	●																	

(Bottom column numbers: 1 2 3 4 5 6 7 8 9 10 11 12 13 14 15 16 17 18)

The Trigger Legend is designed to organize those MDS elements that serve to identify Resident Assessment Protocols (RAPS) which need to be addressed in the Resident Care Plan.

INSTRUCTIONS:
1. Locate all items on the completed MDS form (or MDS Quarterly review) in which the response given indicates an automatic (●) or potential (▲) trigger. (Example: If the response to MDS item C6 is 2, circle the ● below the RAP #1, Delirium.)
2. Circle all RAPs that are "triggered" in step 1. (in the example given above you would circle Delirium.)
3. For all RAPs circled, proceed to corresponding RAP instructions.
4. Based on your review of the RAP instructions, proceed to the Resident Assessment Protocol Summary to document your care decisions

Adapted from and reprinted with permission from Briggs: Form 1829HH © 1992 Briggs Corporation, Des Moines, IA 50306 (800) 247-2343. ❑ Continued on Reverse Side

Printed in U.S.A.

Resident Assessment Protocol Trigger Legend (continued)

MDS PATTERN	MDS ITEM	CODE	Delirium (1)	Cognitive Loss/Dementia (2)	Visual Function (3)	Communication (4)	ADL Functional/Rehabilitation Potential (5)	Urinary Incontinence and Indwelling Catheter (6)	Psychosocial Well-Being (7)	Mood State (8)	Behavior Problems (9)	Activities (10)	Falls (11)	Nutritional Status (12)	Feeding Tubes (13)	Dehydration/Fluid Maintenance (14)	Dental Care (15)	Pressure Ulcers (16)	Psychotropic Drug Use (17)	Physical Restraints (18)
I. Activity Pursuit	I2	0, 2, 3										▲								
	I5	1										●								
J. Disease Diagnoses	J1 ee	√														▲				
	J2	260, 261, 262												●						
		263, 263.0, 263.1												●						
		263.2, 263.8, 263.9												●						
		276.5														▲				
		291.0, 292.81	●																	
		293.0, 293.1	●																	
K. Health Conditions	K1 b, c, f, h, n	any √														▲				
	K2 a, b	any √											●							
L. Oral/Nutritional	L1 c	√															●			
	L2 c	1												●		▲				
	L3 a, d, e	any √												●						
	L3 b	√														●				
	L3 c, e	√														▲				
	L4 a, b	any √														▲				
	L4 a, c, d, e	any √												●						
	L4 b	√													●					
M. Oral/Dental Status	M1 a, c, d, e	any √															●			
	M1 f	not √															●			
N. Skin Condition	N2	1, 2, 3, 4												●				●		
	N4 c, d, e, f, g	none √																▲		
O. Medication Use	O4 a, b, c	1-7									▲		▲						▲	
P. Treatment/Procedures	P3 b, c, or d	1, 2									▲									●

RESIDENT ASSESSMENT PROTOCOL TRIGGER LEGEND

END

Resident's Name:	Medical Record No:

Signature of RN Assessment Coordinator: _____

RESIDENT ASSESSMENT PROTOCOL SUMMARY

1. For each RAP area triggered, show whether you are proceeding with a care plan intervention.

2. Document problems, complications, and risk factors; the need for referral to appropriate health professionals; and the reasons for deciding to proceed or not to proceed to care planning. Documenting may appear anywhere the facility routinely keeps such information, such as problem sheets or nurse's progress notes.

3. Show location of this information.

RAP Problem Area	Care Planning Decision		Location of Information
	Proceed	Not Proceed	
DELIRIUM	☐	☐	
COGNITIVE LOSS/DEMENTIA	☐	☐	
VISUAL FUNCTION	☐	☐	
COMMUNICATION	☐	☐	
ADL FUNCTIONAL/ REHABILITATION POTENTIAL	☐	☐	
URINARY INCONTINENCE AND INDWELLING CATHETER	☐	☐	
PSYCHOSOCIAL WELL-BEING	☐	☐	
MOOD STATE	☐	☐	
BEHAVIOR PROBLEM	☐	☐	
ACTIVITIES	☐	☐	
FALLS	☐	☐	
NUTRITIONAL STATUS	☐	☐	
FEEDING TUBES	☐	☐	
DEHYDRATION/FLUID MAINTENANCE	☐	☐	
DENTAL CARE	☐	☐	
PRESSURE ULCERS	☐	☐	
PSYCHOTROPIC DRUG USE	☐	☐	
PHYSICAL RESTRAINTS	☐	☐	

Adapted from and reprinted with permission from Briggs: Form 1813HF © Briggs Corporation, Des Moines, IA 50306 (800) 247-2343

Printed in U.S.A.

END

Resident Care Plan

LONG-TERM GOAL	BY DATE
DISCHARGE PLAN OBJECTIVE	ESTIMATE DURATION OF STAY

#	PROBLEM		DATE IDENTIFIED
SHORT-TERM GOAL (MUST BE MEASURABLE)		BY DATE	
		BY DATE	
		BY DATE	

PLAN/APPROACH	RESP DISP	DATE REVIEWED	DATE RESOLVED	SIGNATURE

#	PROBLEM		DATE IDENTIFIED
SHORT-TERM GOAL (MUST BE MEASURABLE)		BY DATE	
		BY DATE	
		BY DATE	

PLAN/APPROACH	RESP DISP	DATE REVIEWED	DATE RESOLVED	SIGNATURE

RESIDENT NAME	HOSP#	PAGE 3

Adapted from and reprinted with permission from Briggs: Form 3277HH © 1 Briggs Corporation, Des Moines, IA 50306 (800) 247-2343
Printed in U.S.A.

❏ Continued on Next Page

Resident Care Plan (continued)

#	PROBLEM		DATE IDENTIFIED	
SHORT-TERM GOAL (MUST BE MEASURABLE)		**BY DATE**		
		BY DATE		
		BY DATE		

PLAN/APPROACH	RESP DISP	DATE REVIEWED	DATE RESOLVED	SIGNATURE

#	PROBLEM		DATE IDENTIFIED	
SHORT-TERM GOAL (MUST BE MEASURABLE)		**BY DATE**		
		BY DATE		
		BY DATE		

PLAN/APPROACH	RESP DISP	DATE REVIEWED	DATE RESOLVED	SIGNATURE

#	PROBLEM		DATE IDENTIFIED	
SHORT-TERM GOAL (MUST BE MEASURABLE)		**BY DATE**		
		BY DATE		
		BY DATE		

PLAN/APPROACH	RESP DISP	DATE REVIEWED	DATE RESOLVED	SIGNATURE

Adapted from and reprinted with permission from Briggs: Form 3277HH © 1 Briggs Corporation, Des Moines, IA 50306 (800) 247-2343

Printed in U.S.A.

END

Sample Progress Notes

(month/day/year)

Mrs. Johnson remains somewhat disoriented to place. She frequently gets confused when leaving the dining room and activity areas and is unable to locate her room. Mrs. Johnson will be involved in reality orientation five times a week to help her in adjusting to the new surroundings. All staff will be instructed on how best to assist Mrs. Johnson in finding her room. The activities director will post a picture of a familiar object on Mrs. Johnson's door to help her in identifying the right room.

_____ (Name, title)

(month/day/year)

Mr. Samuels is now walking to the activity room on a daily basis with the use of a quad cane. He is anxious to do things and talks openly about his frustrations following a recent stroke. Mr. Samuels was reassessed to determine activity interests and level of participation. Mr. Samuels will be encouraged to participate in daily therapeutic activities in woodworking, gardening, and ceramics. The activities director will adapt each project to accommodate his left-sided weakness and staff will be reminded to praise Mr. Samuels for his efforts at recovery.

_____ (Name, title)

(month/day/year)

Due to medical condition (resident is bedridden) Mrs. Barber is unable to participate in group activities. Mrs. Barber needs sensory stimulation. Since she previously enjoyed classical music, a tape player will be used as a bedside activity 15 minutes a day three times a week to provide some stimulation.

_____ (Name, title)

DAILY RECORD OF RESIDENT PARTICIPATION

MONTH _____

KEY	
+ = Religion	S = Service
C = Crafts	O = Community
R = Recreation	I = Individual

NAME	1	2	3	4	5	6	7	8	9	10	11	12	13	14	15	16	17	18	19	20	21	22	23	24	25	26	27	28	29	30	31

Adapted from and reprinted with permission from Briggs: Form 3342R © Briggs Corporation, Des Moines, IA 50306 (800) 247-2343
Printed in U.S.A.

Quality Assurance

Reviewed By: _____

Date: _____

	ACTIVITIES	YES	NO	COMMENTS
1.	The activities section on the MDS is completed within 14 days of admission or before the first care conference.			
2.	An activity assessment of resident needs, interests and potential is completed within 14 days of admission or before the first care conference.			
3.	Assessments are updated at least on an annual basis or as often as needed.			
4.	A physician order for activities including specific restrictions is available on the medical chart.			
5.	Interdisciplinary care plans reflect the activity plan approach.			
6.	Activity progress notes are written at least on a quarterly basis and are signed and dated.			
7.	Activity progress notes reflect the plan of approach as documented on the care plan.			
8.	Activity attendance records indicate that activities were provided as planned.			
9.	If a resident is unwilling or unable to participate in group activities, one-to-one activities are planned consistent with resident needs, interests, and level of functioning.			
10.	Responses to one-to-one activities are documented.			
11.	Photo release forms and permission slips for outside activities are signed by the resident or the responsible party upon admission.			

❏ Continued on Reverse Side

Quality Assurance (continued)

	ACTIVITIES	YES	NO	COMMENTS
12.	Lists of residents' birthdays, religious affiliations, and dietary restrictions are maintained for staff and volunteer use.			
13.	Scheduled activities are announced on a daily basis.			
14.	Reality orientation boards are posted on all floors and information is readable and up-to-date.			
15.	Monthly activity calendars are posted throughout the facility.			
16.	Each resident receives a copy of the monthly activity calendar.			
17.	The activity calendar reflects a variety of programs based on the proportion of residents with different levels of functioning abilities			
18.	The activity schedule includes physically, mentally, socially, emotionally, and spiritually stimulating programs.			
19.	Activities are scheduled at hours convenient to residents including mornings, afternoons, evenings and weekends.			
20.	Seasonal, holiday, and special events are part of the schedule.			
21.	Activities are scheduled in a variety of locations.			
22.	Independent one-to-one, small and large group activities are offered.			
23.	Outside activities are planned on a regular basis.			
24.	Activities are age-appropriate.			
25.	Activities are offered for all age groups.			

❏ Continued on next page

Quality Assurance (continued)

	ACTIVITIES	YES	NO	COMMENTS
26.	Programs are available for men and women.			
27.	Seasonal decorations are present and appropriate.			
28.	Residents' council meetings are scheduled on a regular basis			
29.	Minutes of the residents' council meetings are on file with documented follow-up on resident concerns.			
30.	The facility has a monthly resident-oriented newsletter.			
31.	Families are invited to participate in activities.			
32.	Volunteers are recruited to assist with activities.			
33.	An orientation program is available for volunteers.			
34.	Volunteers are assigned to a supervisor.			
35.	Volunteers receive ongoing training.			
36.	A volunteer recognition program is conducted each year.			
37.	A community resource file is maintained by the activities department.			
38.	The activities department has a budget and is responsible for maintaining proper records.			
39.	A file of resource materials is maintained.			
40.	Activity areas are neat and free of clutter.			
41.	Supplies and equipment are properly stored and maintained.			

❑ Continued on Reverse Side

Quality Assurance (continued)

	ACTIVITIES	YES	NO	COMMENTS
42.	Adaptive equipment (large-print books, card holders) is available.			
43.	Calendars and attendance records are maintained for at least one year.			
44.	The activities department has a list of department goals and plans.			
45.	The activities department has an up-to-date policy and procedure manual.			
46.	Current job descriptions for the activities staff on are on file.			
47.	The activities program is directed by a qualified person.			
48.	An orientation program is provided to newly hired activity personnel.			
49.	The activities staff is familiar with the organizational structure of the facility.			
50.	The activities department has a system for interdepartmental communications (i.e. requesting help, notification of resident changes, etc.).			
51.	The activities department has a copy of the federal and state regulations and understands the requirements.			
52.	The activities department participates in: • care conferences • staff meetings • in-service training • QA meetings and survey exits			
53.	Continuing education opportunities are made available to the activities staff.			

Other Books From Venture Publishing

Leisure Education: Program Materials for Persons with Developmental Disabilities
     by Kenneth F. Joswiak
Leisure Education Program Planning: A Systematic Approach
     by John Dattilo and William D. Murphy
Leisure in Your Life: An Exploration, Fourth Edition
     by Geoffrey Godbey
A Leisure of One's Own: A Feminist Perspective on Women's Leisure
     by Karla Henderson, M. Deborah Bialeschki, Susan M. Shaw and Valeria J. Freysinger
Leisure Services in Canada: An Introduction
     by Mark S. Searle and Russell E. Brayley
Marketing for Parks, Recreation, and Leisure
     by Ellen L. O'Sullivan
Outdoor Recreation Management: Theory and Application, Third Edition
     by Alan Jubenville and Ben Twight
Planning Parks for People
     by John Hultsman, Richard L. Cottrell and Wendy Zales Hultsman
Private and Commercial Recreation
     edited by Arlin Epperson
The Process of Recreation Programming Theory and Technique, Third Edition
     by Patricia Farrell and Herberta M. Lundegren
Protocols for Recreation Therapy
     edited by Jill Kelland, along with the Recreation Therapy Staff at Alberta Hospital—Edmonton
Quality Management: Applications for Therapeutic Recreation
     edited by Bob Riley
Recreation and Leisure: Issues in an Era of Change, Third Edition
     edited by Thomas Goodale and Peter A. Witt
Recreation Economic Decisions: Comparing Benefits and Costs
     by Richard G. Walsh
Recreation Programming and Activities for Older Adults
     by Jerold E. Elliott and Judith A. Sorg-Elliott
Reference Manual for Writing Rehabilitation Therapy Treatment Plans
     by Penny Hogberg and Mary Johnson
Research in Therapeutic Recreation: Concepts and Methods
     edited by Marjorie J. Malkin and Christine Z. Howe
Risk Management in Therapeutic Recreation: A Component of Quality Assurance
     by Judith Voelkl
A Social History of Leisure Since 1600
     by Gary Cross
The Sociology of Leisure
     by John R. Kelly and Geoffrey Godbey
A Study Guide for National Certification in Therapeutic Recreation
     by Gerald O'Morrow and Ron Reynolds
Therapeutic Recreation: Cases and Exercises
     by Barbara C. Wilhite and M. Jean Keller
Therapeutic Recreation Protocol for Treatment of Substance Addictions
     by Rozanne W. Faulkner
A Training Manual for Americans With Disabilities Act Compliance in Parks and Recreation Settings
     by Carol Stensrud
Understanding Leisure and Recreation: Mapping the Past, Charting the Future
     edited by Edgar L. Jackson and Thomas L. Burton

Venture Publishing, Inc.
1999 Cato Avenue
State College, PA 16801